Jackie Trent Being Me

Illustrations by
Steve Shooter
Kwa Zulu – Natal, S.A

Clink Street

London | New York

Published by Clink Street Publishing 2017

Copyright © 2017

First edition.

The author asserts the moral right under the Copyright, Designs and Patents Act 1988 to be identified as the author of this work.

All rights reserved. No part of this publication may be reproduced, stored in a retrieval system or transmitted, in any form or by any means without the prior consent of the author, nor be otherwise circulated in any form of binding or cover other than that with which it is published and without a similar condition being imposed on the subsequent purchaser.

*ISBN:
978-1-911525-95-0 paperback
978-1-911525-96-7 ebook*

Wasn't she married to TONY HATCH, the songwriter?

Didn't she write the lyrics for PETULA CLARK's hit songs?

PET CLARK: "...*they changed my life. They changed the whole course of my career.*"

(PET, speaking as a guest on the famous TV programme '*This Is Your Life – TONY HATCH and JACKIE TRENT*').

Didn't she co-write NEIGHBOURS, the Australian soap opera?

Didn't she count many of "showbiz royalty" as her friends?

Yes, all of that...and more.

Yet little – almost nothing – is known of the ups and downs and the sometimes bitter truth of her life.

Why? Because, behind her exterior and public face, Jackie Trent was a very private person; shy almost.

For the first time, this account, told in Jackie's own words, finally sets the record straight regarding her extraordinary life. From the early days as a girl growing up in wartime Britain; entertaining the troops and brushes with death overseas; her meeting with Tony Hatch, subsequent marriage and acrimonious split; her numerous successes; her glamorous life, through to the catalogue of people she met along the way, both the famous and the infamous.

All told with the candour and humour for which she was renowned.

'Keep True To The Dreams Of Thy Youth'

Freidrich von Schiller- German dramatist and Poet (1759-1805)

'Being Me'

There's an out-side and in-side that so few ever know
No-one sees the real me that I found long ago
It's all part of an image that I put on for show
Being Me ...

Jackie Trent – Singer/Singwriter/Actress

'You see...'

There are some people that come into your life,
who are special unique souls.
They are kissed by the Almighty above, as if they are angels.
Not only do they leave behind a body of work for generations to love &
enjoy, they leave a piece of themselves ...
in everyone that they touch.
That was my pal, Jackie.

With Love,
Julie Budd
1-2-17 NYC

Acknowledgments

We are pleased to acknowledge the help, guidance and encouragement given by so many people around the world, finally bringing Jackie's life story into print. Without your support, the task would have been impossible; without your love for Jackie there would have been no point...

Australia	Vickii Byram, Rod Collman, Peter Herman, Oliver and Stella McNerney, Mike Penberthy, Jan Stewart, Brendan Wills, Dennis Standfield (a genuine Tolpuddle Martyr!). With special thanks to Margo Thatcher in Sydney and Craig Ferguson in Melbourne
Canada	Patricia Eastwood
Caribbean, Saint Lucia	Eugenia Dickson and Nicholas John LLB
Cyprus	Sally Stratton
Greece	Ted Carfrae, record producer
Malta	David Agius
NZ	Rex McClenaghan
Philippines	Reg Cranage
South Africa, Kwa-ZuluNatal	Stephen Shooter, our gifted illustrations artist
Spain	John & June Curtis, Barry Stevenson, Richard Tomlinson
Tasmania	David Dart
Turkey, Fethiye	Ian Offler & Nigel Robertson

UK Alan Bailey, Mike Baker, Ronald Bourne, Brian Brett, Douglas Brock, Ray Callingham, Alan Cookman, Byron Davis, Roger Duffy, Ann and Bruce Haycock Neil Henson, Mandie Holland, Brian and June Morley, David Page, Ray Parkes, John Pye, Maureen Prest, Peter Robertson, Maija Savolainen, Angela Severn, Ann Vaughan nee Shaunessy, Keith Walley, Val Ward, Barry Watson, Tim Wedgwood, Mike and Christine Whittaker.

With special thanks to Martin Tideswell and Vanda Gibbons at the Stoke Sentinel newspaper and Peter Coates of Bet 365 and Stoke City Football Club.

USA Julie Budd, Donnie Ferraro, Muriel Geigert, Marc Juron, Geoff Lapin

With very special thanks to John Leahy, writer, and Owen Davies, textile artist extraordinaire. John and Owen are Jackie Trent devotees; their contribution to the completion of this book has proved invaluable.

And to Craig Dougan and Carolyn Wright at Conservatree Print & Design, Reading, Berkshire, UK. Our printers, and so much more...

Colin and Paul

OUR JACKIE.

For me, as an entertainer who started his career in the 1960's in Stoke-on-Trent doing the Working Men's Clubs, Jackie Trent was an inspiration. She had proven that one could make the move from the safety of hometown venues and go and ply one's trade further afield. Stoke-on-Trent was not exactly a hotbed of Show Business talent at that time. Before Jackie, the last person to take the same path was Gertie Gitana, best remembered now for her famous signature tune 'Nellie Dean.'

Gertie and Jackie shared something else…

In the early 1950's, Frederic Street in Hanley, Stoke-on-Trent was renamed Gitana Street in Gertie's honour. Gitana Street leads to the rear of what was the Theatre Royal in Hanley where, in 1951, an 11 year old Yvonne Burgess, soon to be Jackie Trent, won a talent competition that would change her life forever. Maybe Gertie was watching over Yvonne/Jackie that night…

There was a real sense of pride amongst entertainers in the city in that one of our own had gone off into the big world and been successful.

And how successful! Not only recording her own hit records, but also writing songs that would become standards in the music world. What greater accolade than having Frank Sinatra sing your lyrics! Although I never had the pleasure of working with Jackie, I enjoyed our time talking 'show business shop'.

I recall one evening her telling me about working with Sammy Davis Jnr and her friendship with Sammy's musical director George Rhodes and his wife…a long way from Stoke Labour Club!

Jackie was a star who never forgot her roots and her music will be her legacy.

Cheers Jackie! Thanks for the memories.

Glenn Fowler, Jackie and Pete Conway

I knew Jackie Trent for over 40 years. She was a lovely person and extremely talented, both as a singer and a songwriter.

Jackie wrote hits for other people, in particular Petula Clark, but her songs were also recorded and sung by such superstars as Sammy Davis Jnr and Frank Sinatra.

Jackie Trent will live forever in the songs that she composed.

Pete Murray – BBC Radio 2 Presenter

If memory serves me right, I first met Jackie in the 60's, when she was a guest on a BBC Radio show that I used to do, Parade of the Pops. Although I knew of Jackie Trent, I'd never met her until that moment.

And what a moment. She started to sing. These were live-to-air shows. I knew, we all knew, that we were hearing something special, a unique talent destined for great things. But nobody could have guessed where Jackie's talents as a singer and songwriter would take her.

My wife Annie said, "Oh Vince, that girl's just brilliant. I'd love to manage her. She really will go places." Female intuition, I guess.

Jackie certainly did go places.

She conquered the world with her voice, her music, her beauty and her ever-warm personality. Never a diva, she was everyone's friend, if they were worthy.

She came often to our place on the Thames. 'Sagamore Sundays' we called them: the river Thames, the boat, the wine, the BBQ, all of it, more of it!

So often I would slip off to bed exhausted, whilst Annie and Jackie talked long into the night, planning their new hit musical, sipping their favourite port and dreaming dreams. And songs she did write. Hit songs, number 1 songs, some four hundred songs in total, almost all with Tony Hatch, her husband and songwriting partner. Songs that were and still are sung and recorded by the biggest stars all around the world.

Over the years, Jackie and I made our own sweet music, singing duets. She also lived through the bitter-sweet music of life that can face us all at times. But she was ever strong, fronting up to the world, "All eyes, teeth and hair," as she was so fond of saying.

Jackie's story is one of courage and adventure, laughter and tears, mixing life with the famous and at times the infamous, as you are about to read in the pages ahead.

The world of Show Business has lost a brilliant shining star. I don't know who first wrote that, but it works for me. The lady and I never lived in each other's pockets, but she lives on in our minds, Annie and I.

They say she's dead and gone, but I don't have to believe that if I don't want to...

Vince Hill

This autobiography is dedicated to those who dream.
As a young girl I too dreamed of fame and fortune. I
lived the dream and made it all come true. Believe in
yourself, your ability and hard work

Jackie Trent

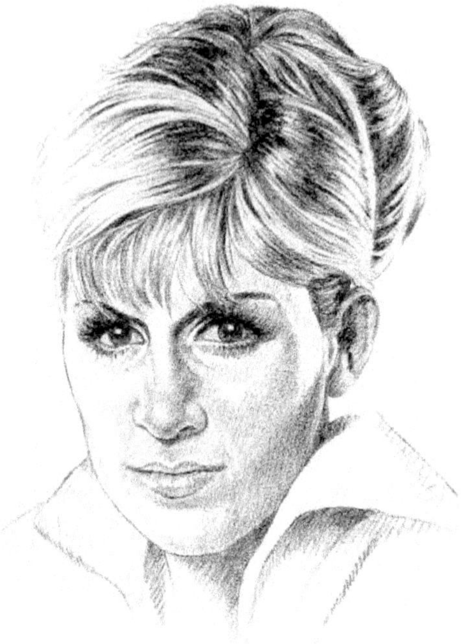

Chapter 1
The Beginning of it All

"This is it, Lil!"

Les and Lily Burgess crouched in terror as a German bomb screamed down from the sky onto them. Only the Anderson shelter in the garden could protect them now, as they huddled inside, clinging to their two young daughters.

It was Friday 1 September 1940 and a Heinkel He 111 of Luftwaffe Squadron KG55, en route to blitz Liverpool, decided to drop a bomb our way, in Chesterton. Our way? I was still curled up inside Mum at the time.

My elder sister Sheila later described an almighty explosion that shook the ground violently. Come daylight, they found a massive hole the bomb had ripped from the ground in Massey's field, just over the fence from our garden. The whole area was devastated with roofs ripped up and shattered glass everywhere. Our neighbour couldn't understand all the fuss. He was stone- deaf and slept through the whole night, God bless him.

Hello World

I emerged on 6 September 1940, five days after the bomb and just two days after my parents' wedding anniversary. And I couldn't even manage that quietly. When Dad first saw his new daughter

Being Me

at the nursing home, I was turning a nice shade of blue. At birth, the umbilical cord had twisted around my neck, leaving me with a breathing restriction. Dad apparently had to give me mouth- to- mouth resuscitation. I finally gave out a loud holler!

We lived in a closely knit community of small townships and villages, which included Audley, Barthomley, Bignall End, Halmer End and Chesterton, collectively Newcastle- under- Lyme. In December the Luftwaffe struck again, when a lone German raider suddenly appeared, dropping a stick of bombs on Chesterton. 14 people died and lots more were seriously injured. Six houses were completely flattened. The main street was strewn with shop window glass and sale goods. The Alexandra cinema on Heathcote Street took a hit. Just minutes earlier, the cinema had been filled with children enjoying the Saturday matinee films. Luckily the show had finished and the kids had all gone home. My parents, everyone, talked of that disaster for many years afterwards. Even the Duke of Kent visited Chesterton to show support.

The Alexandra, we all called it Maggie's, was the centre of our lives. Every Saturday morning we kids would stream in to watch the films, hissing and booing at the baddies on- screen. Maggie and Eric Shemilt ran the Alexandra. Eric clipped anyone caught misbehaving, with his torch. That wouldn't be allowed now, of course. In the early 1940s we kids could escape the harsh reality of war in the darkness of Maggie's.

Daily, my Dad faced another darkness, 2000 feet underground at Brymbo pit, working double shifts. Coal miners were retained from military service, hewing coal to keep the furnaces burning for the war effort. And every day, I remember seeing my Dad come home, his body and his work clothes covered in coal dust. Mum had to rub salt into his cuts and bruises over our Belfast sink. There were no pit showers. Every underground man came home covered in coal dust. The pavements outside every pit were covered in phlegm from men coughing their lungs up, Lord help them.

That was a miner's lot, nationwide. Better than the battlefields, though, I suppose.

Brymbo Colliery

Dad did serve in the Home Guard, "Bloody stupid. We're uniformed, but armed with sticks. What use are we if there's an invasion?" Dad had his own sporting guns though, and kept us fed with rabbit and wood pigeon to supplement food rationing.

From being a babe, I really don't know why I was singled out to be different. "Be careful to lift her pram off the pavement. Don't bump her over the kerbs." Mum's instructions to Babs and Sheila were very strict. Mum had five children in all. None of the others had that special treatment, as far as I know.

I remember American troops arriving in Staffordshire. They brought light relief to the area with their youthfulness and energy. In November 1944, troops of the American 345th Infantry Regiment, 87th Infantry Division, drove by our house on Talke Road in troop carriers, throwing Hershey bars and nylons to the local girls. "Look mum, real nylons!" shouted my sisters Barbara and Sheila, grabbing their share of goodies from the road. I stood in our doorway, marvelling at the excitement of it all.

Being Me

Years later I did a little research. On 17 October 1944 those young Americans had sailed from New York harbour on the still new *Queen Elizabeth* liner, racing unescorted across the Atlantic to the Clyde, then by train to Staffordshire. Within a few weeks of leaving Staffordshire, they would be on their way to the war front in the Saar, Germany, (years later, I would cross the Atlantic on one of RMS *Queen Elizabeth*'s last journeys across the Atlantic, as a guest of Frank Sinatra).

The *Queen* had almost been lost on her maiden voyage from Clydebank to Southampton in March 1940. As she sailed, Winston Churchill, at the last minute redirected her to New York, taking the surprised Southampton harbour pilot with her. On the morning of her planned arrival in Southampton, the Luftwaffe bombed the approach harbour. German spies were strongly suspected.

In wartime England, food rationing was severe. Our big treat was one egg a week and an apple or orange in our Christmas stocking was special. There were no bananas in the shops until the 1950s. In 1951, when I won a major talent competition, the bunch of grapes that came with my floral bouquet were the first grapes I'd ever seen.

One Christmas after the war, Dad was laid off work, injured, no work, no pay. He was a coalface worker, operating the massive coal rippers. A great lump of coal fell from the roofing, crushing his back. "It was that big I could hear men muttering, 'Les is a goner' from t'other side of the lump," I heard him tell Mum. His body seemed to be permanently black and blue from injuries down that damn pit. No worse a fate than other miners, of course. Brymbo Colliery, or Holditch, by its correct name, was once the main employer in Chesterton, employing some 1,500 men, injuring many. On 2 July 1937, the pit had claimed the lives of 30 men, with eight others injured. I often wondered how I would feel going down that hellhole daily to earn money to keep my family alive. I wanted my Dad out of there.

That Christmas, Uncle Don, a farmer, gave us a goose for our Christmas dinner. After one small serving each that cooked goose looked like a burnt out aircraft, "That bloody thing must have been running round his yard for years" said Dad, with a smile on his face.

My Christmas present was last year's doll, mended and redressed at the Doll's Hospital in Newcastle- under- Lyme. Yes, there really was such a place! I treasured that doll for years. It sat in pride of place on my bed, not to play with, just to look at.

As kids, a bus day trip to Rhyl in North Wales was our annual holiday. "Stay off the sand, you'll muck your clothes up." Our big treat was a toffee apple and a stick of rock. On the bus journey home, my little brother Les and I would sing with everyone joining in, then Les would go round with Dad's cap, giving the takings to the driver.

Oh yes, Little Les was born on my fifth birthday, "Your birthday present, Yvonne."

I would have preferred a dog. I'd been asking for a dog for ages. "No, puppies wee and poo and need feeding."

'So do babies,' I thought to myself.

I started tinkling on the ivories when I was four. I couldn't keep off the piano, but eldest sister Barbara was the one destined for musical fame. Each week my parents scraped together ten shillings for Barbara's piano lessons. Barb gave a few recitals and my parents had high hopes for her as a concert pianist. Then she met her future husband Bob, serving in the Fleet Air Arm nearby and that was that. I only ever saw Bob in uniform before they wed.

Dad was furious. He locked the piano lid, "No one will play this piano again!" Precious money had gone to waste.

Finally Dad relented. I had my first piano lesson with Mr. Rigby at Cross Heath. "I can't teach her piano, Mr Burgess," he reported. "She does it her way." I would listen to Mr Rigby play a tune once, then I'd play it back from memory, mostly ignoring the sheet music. I still do that, although I can read music. I would have to, for the top line melody. "But I *can* help develop her diaphragm for singing power."

So for eight weeks Mr Rigby coached me with books, masses of heavy books, not to read, but all piled up on my chest and even my head, while he coaxed ever louder sound from my diaphragm, between very deep breathing exercises. He had me sweating because I really pushed myself. And that's where the famous Trent voice power came from.

Remember that German bomb hole of 1 September 1940? On hot summer evenings, after heavy rainfall, that bomb hole gave us kids a pond to play in, until Dad's "Time for bed, Yvonne," rang out across the field a few times. His stern shout "Time up!" usually meant a smack coming my way.

Quite a few smacks came my way. I remember one time taking little Les along to the Saturday matinee at Maggie's. He kept jumping up and down, his cap perched on his head, being a nuisance.

"Stop it," I said. He wouldn't, so I gave him a swipe across the face.

"I've got a nose bleed!"

"Well, you can just sit and look at the film now."

Yes, I had lots of smacks from Dad.

I've always found depth in the power of words. I still do. As a child, I sometimes sat in Audley church graveyard, absorbing the powerful emotion of words etched into those worn headstones, words spoken from the heart, at a time of family grief. I never found that morbid, just emotional.

But most times I'd be singing around the house. Our house was filled with music. Writing and singing came easy to me. It felt so natural to just get up and sing. Odd really, because my private life is exactly that. I'm actually quite shy.

As a small child, my parents often had me standing on our dining table to sing for visiting relatives. I was keen on that, because I could stay up after 7 p.m. But I thought, *'If they ask me to sing Vera Lynn's 'My Son, My Son' again'*, a very popular song at the time, *'I'll scream.'* It seemed a bit ludicrous for an eight year old to be singing 'My Son, My Son'.

My first written work, age 8, was a poem about the courageous Captain Carlsen and the SS *Flying Enterprise*. I won a national competition for that. On 10 January 1952, despite heroic efforts to save her, the *Flying Enterprise* sank in heavy seas off Falmouth. National newspapers headlined the event, New York City gave Captain Carlsen a ticker tape parade and I won five guineas for my poem. (There was speculation at the time that the ship had been carrying zirconium, destined for use in the USS *Nautilus*, the USA's first nuclear submarine.)

Jackie Trent

Until his back injury, Dad was quite a sportsman. He was the regular fast bowler at Bignall End Cricket Club and at tennis, he often played doubles with Ethel Burgess, a distant cousin. The local Amateur Dramatics Society used the upper floor of the club building. One day I was introduced to Frank Jervis and Vic Burgess. We were not related. There were a lot of Burgesses living in the Bignall End/Audley area. I was shown the function room and stage upstairs, where the Unnamed Society put on shows.

"Your Dad says you sing?"

I climbed up onstage and belted out 'Music, Music, Music'.

I saw them all beaming from ear to ear, "How about becoming one of the Bignall End Babes?"

"Wow, I'd love to!"

The Unnamed Society rehearsed in the evenings, after work. That meant I could stay up late. No more bedtimes at 7 p.m.! But travelling there was another matter, two buses across town, then up Boon Hill, where most of us met up. Dad had told me stories of the Boon Hill Bear, so I warned the other girls. After that, we all agreed it was safest to run hell- for- leather to the top of the hill, to the safety of the Cricket Club. Well, the tale might just be true.

Our Christmas pantomimes with the Unnamed Society and the Bignall End Babes were the best, glorious costumes and make- up, and all of us singing and tap dancing together on the stage. The floor bounced so much, it's a wonder we didn't break it. By now I was completely hooked on performing and nothing was going to stop me.

"Yvonne, where did the chocolates come from?"

On Saturdays, I was bringing home boxes of chocolates and my parents were becoming worried. "It's OK," I said. "I win them at Talent Time contests at the pictures. But I've been told not to come so often, to give someone else a chance."

Chapter 2
A Small Taste of Things to Come

The summer of 1951 was one long sports day for me. At school, Mrs Sexton and her assistant Mrs Bedson encouraged me. I joined Newcastle Harriers Athletics Club and trained and swam with them every day. I was very fit, so when a physical challenge came along, I was there.

"Snowy and his friends are planning a bike ride to Buxton. He says it's too far for girls, so we can't come." Snowy was my friend Dorothy White's elder brother.

I found Snowy, "Don't think we couldn't do that."

"Go on then. We dare you."

"Right, we're going."

Off we went, Dorothy on her brand new cycle, me on my elderly Trent Tourist bike that Dad had renovated for me. Yes, Raleigh Industries of Nottingham really did make a Trent Tourist. The boys set off ahead of us girls on the tough ride up the southern edge of the Pennines, the low mountain ridge that splits northern England. It was a hot summer day but we girls finally made the 48 mile round trip. Snowy didn't. He ended up in hospital with heat exhaustion. I admit, I couldn't walk properly, or even sit down, for days afterwards. That's really "sitting on your blisters," as the Aussies say. But no matter, it felt good. Nothing tastes sweeter than success.

Being Me

September of 1951 found me starting at Broadmeadows Secondary Modern School, Chesterton. Modern in name, but old and Victorian in reality, with its high ceilings, tall, narrow windows and cold classrooms that soon echoed of me.

"Burgess, stop singing. Be quiet, let the other girls be heard." That was Mrs Baker, our music teacher. At choir practice my voice overpowered everyone, even then.

At school I made a name for myself for being energetic and outgoing. It was just me being me. I even defended other girls against the school bullies. Some of the teachers found me quite a challenge, so when just one single place became vacant at the local Orme Girls' High School, the teachers voted in favour of Dorothy White. We'd both passed the entrance examination but she won the place. I'd wanted that chance so much, and the sports facilities were fab, but it was not to be. I was thrown off the swings. Then the roundabout came along to scoop me up...

Jackie Trent

Henry Solly and the WMCIU

One evening Dad read out an ad from the *Evening Sentinel*, our local paper, "Now listen to this:"

'Carroll Levis and his Discoveries.

Auditions to be held at the Theatre Royal, Hanley'.

Today's equivalent would be *X- Factor* or *America's Got Talent*.

I knew of Carroll Levis, everyone knew of Carroll Levis in the 1950s. He was born in 1910 in Toronto and worked as a talent scout and radio broadcaster. One day, in a live broadcast from Edmonton, he invited an unknown singer from his audience to fill in a last minute gap in the programme. The idea proved so popular that a regular talent show was born. In 1935 Carroll Levis took his idea to the UK. I read somewhere that in its heyday in the 1930s, the *Carroll Levis and his Discoveries* show on BBC radio attracted a 20 million plus audience. That's success! Yet he would die in obscurity in 1968. It was reported that he left only a few hundred pounds from the several fortunes he had made along the way. In 1950, in the latter part of his career, Carroll Levis returned from Canada to the UK for what would be his final series of *Discoveries*, touring the UK. In 1951 the road show hit Stoke- on- Trent, Staffordshire.

Rejection

"You could do that," said Dad.

"What am I going to wear?" Is every woman born with those words in her head?

"Well, I could shorten your sister's wedding dress," said Mum. Sheila had recently married.

Mum's scissors went to work and soon the dress just covered my 11 year old knees.

My big problem was getting to the theatre as auditions would be in school time. I'd never missed school, ever, but I just had to do this. So the following week, instead of afternoon lessons with Mrs Baker, I climbed aboard the local Potteries Motor Traction bus, all dressed up in my sister's finery: mini wedding gown, high heeled shoes, suspenders, stockings and full make- up. My Sunday best coat more or less covered this extravaganza to tone things down on my two bus journeys across town to Hanley. (Writing these words now, I can hardly believe I did such a crazy thing.)

Arriving at the Theatre Royal, Hanley, my face dropped a mile when I saw the long queue of hopefuls already stood in line. *'I'll be here forever,'* I thought. Then someone came out and shouted, "Anyone with surname beginning with A, go in now."

I thought, *'That's better. I'm a Burgess, so B's next.'*

I didn't feel nervous at all as I finally entered the theatre, but I was awestruck at the grandeur of the décor inside.

'I Believe'

I sat in the front stalls with the other B's while the A's did their thing onstage. The organisers were sat somewhere behind us making notes, I suppose. We were called up in groups of six, to walk through the pass door, left of stage, into the wings. I thought, *'Hey, this really is what I want in my life!'*

It wasn't long before my group of six was called. I was third in line. "Next" was finally me. I clumped across the stage in Sheila's too large shoes and gave the totally bored pianist my music for 'I Believe', a rangy song which suited me perfectly. All week I'd been filling our house and my parents' ears with 'I Believe'.

"What tempo?"

I tapped out what I wanted, walked up to the riser mike at front of stage and sang. A loud "Thank you" suddenly stopped me dead, right in the middle of the song. And that was it. I walked offstage without even being asked my name. Not wanted! Years later that stage would be mine, closing the first half of a show headlined by Tommy Trinder, the famous comedian. But not for now...

I dragged myself back across town on the bus, bitterly disappointed, but determined to try again. "I'm going back again tomorrow, but this time in school uniform," I announced to Mum and Dad.

Determination

And that's exactly what I did. At school for morning lessons, then the 10 minute run back home for lunch, then two buses across town again to the Theatre Royal, this time in full school uniform, no make-up and no curlers in my hair, just bunches.

Another session of "A's and B's first" from the never ending queue stood outside the theatre, more waiting time in the front stalls, then the wings and "Next" all over again.

I handed the same music score to the still bored pianist but this time I took charge. I walked straight to front of stage and said, "Good afternoon, everyone. My name is Yvonne Burgess. I'm a singer." Then I turned to the pianist, gave him his intro, "Thank you," and went straight into my number, using all the body actions I could, without losing the fixed riser mike. This time I made it to the end of the song, with no interruptions, applause even, from other contestants waiting in the wings.

A male voice beyond the footlights called out, "Thank you, Yvonne. That's fine. Would you like to wait at the back of the stalls?" Just eight of us were finally selected. "Congratulations, you're through to the show. Be prepared to turn up for the whole of show week." An official invitation was to follow by post. And that was my first lesson in stage presentation, self taught. *'Make yourself known, otherwise you're invisible onstage.'* I'd planned that strategy as I lay in bed the night before. The lesson has stayed with me ever since.

Now I was eager to fly home as fast as the corporation buses would take me. The journey seemed to take forever, stopping at every pedestrian crossing, corner, even the pubs it seemed. I just *had* to get home to tell Mum and Dad the news! When I finally made it home, I burst through our front door, "Aaargh! I'm through. I'm through!" Hardly the TV melodrama of today's *X- Factor* machine, but good enough for me.

Next morning at school, I quietly handed in Mum's sick note, blaming my absence from school on sickness with my little brother, Les. I didn't tell a soul at school where I had really been. That day my head was near to bursting with thoughts of the talent show: school, lessons, friends, even home life, were just somewhere else.

The following Monday a letter addressed to 'Miss Yvonne Burgess' arrived in our letter box. Mum opened it while I was at school. She couldn't wait. When I arrived back from school, Mum handed me the grandest sheet of paper, headed 'Carroll Levis and his Discoveries' with a picture of the great man himself at the head:

Dear Miss Burgess,

You are formally invited to perform onstage at the Theatre Royal, Hanley, on the Tuesday of competition week. Note: Bring your music and costume. A dressing room will be provided. Please be at the theatre no later than 6.30 p.m. Good luck!

A Royal Command Performance invitation couldn't have thrilled me more at the time. And I would perform before Her Majesty years later.

Day and night I planned and rehearsed my performance. Believe me, the family, even the neighbours, became thoroughly fed up with 'I Believe.' My next crisis was how to escape school to be in time for the show. For that I had to face Miss Mills.

Miss Mills

Miss Mills was headmistress of Broadmeadows Secondary Modern School. I knew I would have to come clean and ask her help if I were to take part in the Carroll Levis Show. It was now or never. Next day at lunchtime, instead of running home to eat, I walked upstairs to the first floor school office. "Is it possible to see Miss Mills?" I asked Mrs Caddy, our kindly school secretary. We'd come to know each other quite well over recent months, mostly about my punishment order marks and detentions.

"What is it about?"

"Me."

"Sit down and I'll go and see Miss Mills," said Mrs Caddy to the 11 year old upstart.

A few minutes later I was stood in front of Miss Mills. "Sit down," said she. "What is the problem?"

Deep breath. "Miss Mills, I have a problem."

Now it was Miss Mills who looked concerned.

"Last week I had two afternoons off school covered by a sick note from my parents and that wasn't the truth because really I auditioned for the Carroll Levis Discoveries Show at the Theatre Royal and I got through for next week's competition and we have to be in the theatre by 6.30 which means I need the extra half hour and I need to leave school at 3.30 to get home and changed into costume. We don't have a car and I have to be in Hanley for 6.30. It may not happen every day, I might not make it through the first evening..." All in a gabbled rush. Once I'd started, I couldn't stop. I just ran out of wind at the end, waiting for the storm.

"That's very honourable of you, Yvonne, and I'm proud of you. So you have my permission. I will inform the staff."

I saw her eyes moisten. She even suggested I should leave at three o'clock, a whole half hour earlier still! Oh you beautiful, darling Miss Mills. Right then, she was bigger to me than Carroll Levis himself.

"Thank you! Thank you! I'm going to do my best."

"I know you will. You always do."

And with that I shot out of the school gates to the corner shop and bought a threepenny packet of Smiths crisps, the ones with the blue twist of salt inside. Mum had given me the three- penny piece that morning after I told her I had to face up to Miss Mills and I wouldn't have time to run home for lunch that day.

Running

I ran everywhere, the daily 10 minute run home at lunchtime because Mum couldn't afford the 1s 10d per week for school dinners. I was clocking up two miles a day running from home to school and school to home, rain or shine; then I'd run from home, the two miles to Newcastle- under- Lyme, to swim in the public baths, 50 laps, then a penny hair dry and a penny Bovril; from the baths to the Newcastle athletic ground to train in track, high jump and javelin four time a week, as athletics was my other passion besides singing; and the final sprint home.

After Miss Mills' blessing, the remainder of that afternoon at school was a complete blur. At four o'clock I dashed home, running hell- for- leather. I burst in through our front door which was suffering serious damage by now, "Miss Mills has given me time off for the Carroll Levis Show. She said she's proud of me!" I was so pumped up that I jumped up and down in the lounge then threw a high kick, smashing a fine glass lampshade hanging from the ceiling. I was an energetic child. More running exercise as Dad chased me across the fields, his leather belt in hand.

Next day, to top off a fab week, I was amazed to find that I'd come second in an English exam that I must have taken the previous, magical, afternoon. To this day, I can't remember a thing about that afternoon.

Austerity

This was 1951. The UK would suffer food rationing until midnight on 4 July 1954. Clothing came off rationing on 15 March 1949, but clothing materials were still scarce and costly. During the war, even turn ups on men's trousers were banned to save valuable material for the war effort. But I needed a stage dress for the competition. Mum managed to buy enough blue taffeta to make me a dress. She was really skilled with her handed down, paddle drive Singer sewing machine, the type with scrolled cast iron legs that now grace so many chic pubs and coffee bars as table legs. White ankle socks and my Clark's summer sandals would put the finishing touch to my very first stage costume. There was so much excitement running through our house that weekend.

Elation

The Tuesday came along. I'd had my hair in rags the night before (no heated rollers in 1951), so there were plenty of "She looks like Shirley Temple" cat calls thrown at me around school that day.

"Take no notice, Vonnie. They're just jealous."

"Thanks, Val. Can't wait to be at that theatre!"

I was let out at three o'clock, as promised, and ran home to prep myself. Then I gathered my new taffeta dress, my cosmetics, my music and my Dad and set off, catching two buses across town to Hanley, and destiny...

Late that afternoon I walked through my very first stage door, plain and simple as they always are, with bare corridors leading to back stage, not the glamour of front of house at all. Four of us were allocated a first floor dressing room to prepare for the show which was a stark, tacky and worn out box room with discoloured, peeling mirrors, empty lamp holders and a few pegs to hang our clothes. Yes, this was the theatre, folks! In all, we were six persons crammed into that dressing room, four acts, plus two fussing Mums. It was bedlam in there. While I was trying to apply block mascara in the right places, one girl was throwing herself around, practicing back bends and handstands in that crowded space. It was very messy. '*Keep calm, Yvonne, we've reached this far,*' said I to myself.

My Dad had taken one look inside that changing room then promptly excused himself to front of house to sit quietly in the stalls, waiting. The fourth member in that dressing room was a boy. He had to cope as best he could, poor lad. Suddenly, the dressing room tannoy crackled into life. A roll of drums, a fanfare, then, "Ladies and gentlemen, please welcome Mr. Carroll Levis and his Discoveries." And the show was on.

It seemed no time before "Yvonne Burgess, come down to stage right" came over the P.A. Someone appeared to guide me to the right spot and to make sure that I didn't run off in panic, which some actually did. And a few threw up in the wings from stage fright. Very moving. Finally Carroll Levis himself called me on stage which probably had my Dad bouncing in his seat. I strode out there to be greeted by his fabulously lovely assistant, Violet Pretty and The Man himself. "I want to introduce a lovely young girl," he said in a smarmy, Canadian accent I'd never heard before. "Her name is Eevonne Ber- Jesse."

"No, Mr. Levis, its Yvonne Burgess," Which raised a laugh from the local audience. (Stage presence, remember?)

"I hear you're a lovely little singer."

"Thank you, Mr. Levis."

"And what are you going to sing tonight?"

"'I Believe,' Mr. Levis."

And I certainly did, giving it full power. I had a ball onstage and loved every minute, and so did the audience. I was given a standing ovation and brought the house down. Yippee!

Maybe it was the sight of a kid stood larger than life on that big stage under the spotlight, in white ankle socks and sandals, maybe it was the blue taffeta dress and the two bows tied in my hair, maybe it was the big voice. Whatever, I was invited back again on Thursday night for the quarter finals, then again on Friday night for the semi finals, a standing ovation every time. 'I Believe' seemed to be gathering 'Believers' nightly.

Being Me

For the final on Saturday, I wore a new white taffeta dress Mum had made to complement the Clarks sandals, white ankle socks and two white bows. What a bobby dazzler! Mum, Dad, Miss Mills and her mum all turned up on the Big Night to see me do two numbers this time, 'Secret Love' and 'I Believe,' which had a final belting with more passion than the Bible Belt, believe me. The audience 'Believers' were certainly gathering. I was given the biggest standing ovation of the night. Then things went really crazy. Carroll Levis called me out onstage again and announced me the winner, Violet Pretty presented me with a bouquet of flowers, fruit and a box of chocolates, I had my picture taken with Carroll Levis for the *Sentinel* local paper and Dad announced, "We're going home in a taxi!"

Never before had I been in a taxi, the fare was a fortune for us. When we got home, Dad poured himself a (rare) vodka and lime, Mum had a cup of tea and I had a bottle of Tizer. Our first rich rewards and taste of success! Dom Perignon champagne would never taste better than my bottle of Tizer that night.

Chance

Of the 10 acts in the final, one was a semi- pro comedy duo who just happened to have a double booking problem. Backstage, after the competition, they approached Mum and me and asked if I would like to take over one of their bookings, Longport Working Men's Club. "It's worth twenty five bob."

"Yes!" shouted Mum. "And what's a working men's club? What does she have to do?"

"Get up and do two spots of two songs. We think she should do it. They'll love her."

"Right, she'll do it." Mum was on a real high by now. Not for the money, but for the moment in time for which I'd been working.

"OK. We'll phone the Entertainment Secretary of the club and tell him we're sending the best young talent the Potteries will ever have." (And no, I haven't made that up!).

But neither of us told Dad. We left him in peace and glory with his one glass of vodka and lime that night. Dad, typically of the time, firmly believed that women should not be seen in pubs or working men's clubs.

Frankie Laine

I had borrowed 'I Believe' from Francesco Paolo LoVecchio, a Sicilian who became Frankie Laine. He took that song to No 1 in the UK charts where it would remain for 18 weeks in 1953. I was to share two major similarities with Frankie Laine:

1. My voice could fill a theatre, without a mike, and like Frankie, my lung power developed through athletics and sport.
2. We both had criminal connections. The Kray Brothers, the infamous East End gangsters, became my fans, protecting me, a young girl alone in London and Frankie's father was Al Capone's barber.

Chapter 3
New name, New Beginnings

Mum finally found the courage to tell Dad, "Our Yvonne has taken her first booking, Longport WM." The WM was short for 'working men's club,' part of the national Working Men's Club and Institute Union (WMCIU). All were licensed premises.

"Indeed she will not!" I can still hear Dad saying that, very loudly.

"But we accepted the booking and we can't let them down."

Mum finally won the day.

I still recall that Saturday night, stood with my Dad looking up at the CIU lantern shining over the Longport club entrance door. We'd just arrived, fresh off the bus. Dad watched over me as I straightened my hair before the big moment. We opened the door to see a huge lounge filled with people, pints of beer and tobacco smoke. And the noise! Everyone seemed to be talking at once. As we walked in, I saw a long bar at one end, and a stage, *my* stage, in the far corner. This was Saturday Night Out in Longport, Staffordshire and everyone was smartly dressed with the men, mostly in suits, sporting trilbies or traditional flat caps. And the ladies, well, they looked dressed to kill, with fine hairdos. Their hair must have been in curlers all day.

Every table was occupied but one, a small table by the stage, with a card, 'Reserved for Artists.' *'Hey, that's me!'* So there we sat, Dad in his best trilby, holding a pint of mild and bitter, guarding my music case and me, busy looking over my glass of fizzy orange at the audience, who were all watching us. This certainly was not the Theatre Royal, Hanley.

The Entertainment Secretary came over and introduced himself. He was short, sharp and to the point. "Hello, Whyvonne. It's a pity the comedians were double booked, the silly buggers. Still, you're here and they've said you're good. You're a bit young" (he didn't know just how young!), "so let's hope they're bloody right." I thought Dad would choke on his beer, maybe even yank me off home, there and then. The Entertainment Secretary was still talking, "You'll be on at eight, two songs, and again at nine, two songs." The pianist looked 100 years old to me. Dad had another pint to calm himself down.

The evening's entertainment started with a juggler who wouldn't even be able to catch a cold. The pianist gave it his best with a shower of notes to match the juggler's flying missiles, but the audience took no notice of the action onstage whatsoever. The chatter of background noise grew ever louder. I was fascinated by it all. Later, someone told me the juggler was really a comedy act. I was that green. The juggler finally collected his debris from all over the stage as the Entertainment Secretary called out the numbers for a few games of bingo. The prize for a 'full house' was either ten shillings or £1. "Dad," I said, "I'm going to change in the dressing room now while this is going on."

"All right, Yvonne. I'll stay here."

Dressing room? It was just a storeroom stacked with boxes, with just enough floor space for me to step into another of Mum's creations, a pink taffeta job (a bit over the top) with black tulle frills, puffed sleeves and a big bow at the back, with matching knickers. More black tulle on the leg tops. Mum had really gone to town, big time, but I was up for it.

Someone said "You're on." I walked out in my finery and gave my music to the pianist. This was it. But where was my audience? Off to the toilets, that's where. I waited, patiently. The room settled down as members returned to their seats. And there I was for all to see, me on a professional stage for the first time in my life, waiting to be announced.

The Entertainment Secretary stepped up onstage to introduce me. He coughed into the microphone, tapped it a few times, then said, "Attention, ladies and gentlemen. The main turn has double booked themselves. I know you like them here, but never mind, they'll be back, when I decide to book them again that is. We've got a young singer here, wouldn't have booked her myself. She won the Carroll Levis Discoveries, so she must be OK. Will you welcome... Whyvonnie Burgess." Thanks a bundle. Couldn't even get my name right! Polite applause followed. I waited, then went straight into my first number, working the stage as the pianist warmed to me. Halfway through the song, I realised the audience had gone quiet. I finished the song, and the whole room was suddenly cheering me. Me! Oh Lordy! That minute, my Dad was easily the biggest man in the room and people started offering him pints of beer. And believe me, I'm shedding a few tears even now as I write this, remembering that moment. I finished the spot with my second number. The audience all stood, applauding me. Wow! I came off that stage with my knees shaking, I can tell you. Dad was grinning like a Cheshire cat, but I couldn't get near him. Harry Evans, Dad's workmate at Holditch Colliery, was shaking his hand. We were surrounded by people.

Before I knew it, I was back on stage again. My last song of the first spot had been Vera Lynn's, 'My Son, My Son'. So at nine o'clock, when the Entertainment Secretary stood onstage again to announce me, it was a very different story. "Yet again, Whyvonnie, the Potteries' Vera Lynn!" And I gave my audience another belting.

Dad and I came away that night with 25 shillings and some firm advice from the Entertainment Secretary, "Take her along to the open auditions next week. They're at Stafford. All the Entertainment Secretaries will be there to pick their acts for the next few months. You'd best take a diary but I'll have first pick." And he gave us two more bookings for Longport club before we left.

I met Dame Vera Lynn many years later in Chicago and told her of my Potteries title. She chuckled. And why not? Vera Welch started her own career just like me, singing in a working men's club, aged seven. And, just like her, I would entertain our troops abroad. Vera became known as "The Forces' Sweetheart". I too had my moments.

Being Me

Two weeks after Longport, Dad and I were on the bus to Stafford WMC and the open auditions. The club was the same set up as Longport, a bar, a stage and a large smoke filled lounge. I registered and was told, "You're number seven, two songs."

Stafford Club had a very nice grand piano. I went onstage and did my party piece, all eyes and teeth. "That went well, love," said Dad. There was a break, and we were suddenly surrounded by Entertainment Secretaries from all the North Staffs clubs. In no time, we had 30 bookings in my brand new diary. I was surprised and Dad was as pleased as punch. Someone gave us a booklet listing all the club details and addresses. On the bus back home we checked the bookings against the club addresses. "At this rate, we'll be travelling all weekend," Dad said. "Some Sundays you've a booking at lunchtime, then another club in the evening, miles away. I'd best collect a bus timetable for us." No more weekends with school friends for me.

My weeks were suddenly filled to bursting with school and after school sports training mid week, then Friday night bath and hair wash, with my head in rags over the whole weekend. My fee went up from 25 to 30 shillings. Then Dad insisted on two guineas, very posh. A few clubs said it was out of their budget, but they still booked me nonetheless. Some weekends I was earning six guineas, a lot of money, but most of that went into my dresses, shoes and music. The rest I gave to Mum to help with housekeeping.

Pianists became a problem. They were used to playing in the standard key, from the standard printed sheet music of the day. Dad found a local pianist who could rewrite popular music in my key.

Sometimes I accompanied myself. I became pretty good at it. I practiced piano a couple of hours after school when I could. Sometimes a pianist would struggle with my music, "I can't play this." So I would say, "OK, I'll play myself." Sometimes I did piano and voice with a little tap routine thrown in. Eat your heart out, Jerry Lee Lewis!

One evening, a dreadful thing happened. I gave my music to the club pianist and went off to change. Five minutes later the poor man was dead, I was told from a heart attack. They laid him out in the corridor outside the dressing room, covered with a coat, while the Entertainment Secretary went onstage to cancel the performance as I closed down the grand piano.

Hello, Jackie Tremayne

I was 14 years old. For almost three years I'd suffered the Whyvonne, Whyvonnie and Eurvonne introductions onstage. I was always happy with my own name and I had no pretentions to be anyone else, but business is business. I had to raise the game.

I'd seen a John Tremayne starring in a TV series, '*Tremayne. That's got a nice ring to it.*' I was almost a Madeleine but Jackie seemed snappier, so I settled for Jackie Tremayne for a while. Dad was fond of French names. I still have a newspaper cutting from 1954, 'Porthill Girl in B.B.C. Radio's *What Makes a Star*,' with a glam photograph of me I'd signed 'Yours, Jackie Tremayne.' I was billed as a 17 year old. No one ever questioned my age.

Staffordshire Big Bands

As my fame spread, the local big bands wanted me, so I mixed working the clubs with the big band dance nights. I handled bookings from my 'office', the post office red public phone box at The Hollows, off Gainsborough Road, Chesterton, near where we lived. It was a good walk away, but I always ran. I ran everywhere. I always carried a little plastic make up bag of cotton wool soaked in Dettol to swab the phone handset clean. My voice was my life and I wanted no germs around me. My whole life has been mostly on the road, sometimes taking me into very strange places, so Dettol has been my safeguard, (as I recall, Petula Clark used TCP as *her* safeguard.) Three pennies in the slot, press button A, then speak with the bandleaders or Entertainment Secretaries to agree a list of booking dates. I would 'phone the band leaders at work as all the musicians had day jobs.

A special moment was when Ken Griffiths turned up at my home. "Yvonne, would you be interested in doing a few gigs with the band? How much do the clubs pay? I'll match it." Wow! Most of the top local musicians were members of the Ken Griffiths Band, and he was asking me to work with them! Ken would stand up front onstage, conducting and smiling away as the band belted it out.

I also worked with Reg Bassett. Reg ran a bus company, but the Reg Bassett Big Band was his passion. And the Norman Jones Band of course, resident in the Grand Ballroom at Trentham Gardens. (The Bank of England took over that ballroom during the war and the Beatles took it over in the 1960s when fans flocked to see them.) And let me tell you, standing up there onstage fronting a big band, mike in hand, is very special indeed. Only a performer onstage can know the intoxicating breathless sensation of front line brass driving a number, the couples dancing, the singer belting it out, even the band itself! There's no better feeling, not in my life.

Our musical arrangements all came from London. They were known in the trade as 'Jimmy Lallys.' Jimmy, in London, scored arrangements for bands across the UK. Singers all used the same scores. My personal scores were written by Peter Chell, a local musician. I took those to London when I headed south in 1956.

Chapter 4
The 'A' and 'B' Sides of Life

Just like vinyl records, there's always a flipside to life. On the A side I was now Jackie Tremayne at weekends, and schoolgirl Yvonne Burgess on the B side midweek. I was a hit with the local big bands, working men's and British Legion clubs, most probably entertaining my school friends' parents at weekends, me all glammed up and looking in my 20s. Then it was back to school midweek, and the B side of life. From age 11, every weekend I swapped school uniform for mum's homemade ballroom gowns, often made from war surplus parachute silk. Britain was full of war surplus.

Childhood was over. I could feel a growing resentment in school at my weekend fame. Each Monday morning I made the transformation from singing star to schoolgirl, removing the make up and dressing down to school uniform. Yes, on Monday mornings maybe there were still traces of mascara on my face. It was a bugger to get off and my head was running at a million miles an hour. And would anyone in my position really want to put out that fire? Certainly not me!

Some Monday mornings, my best friend Val Ward had to read out my name at morning assembly. Val was a school prefect, and prefects had to read out the list of those up for 'order marks' punishment in front of the whole school. Broadmeadows school assembly hall became my 'other stage' in life at the time.

Being Me

One time, out of jealousy I suppose, a few girls ganged together, covered me in ink, then locked me in a steel cupboard. Mrs Baker, our class teacher, ignored my pleas to be let out. In class she even hit me on the head with the classroom board ruler a few times. We had a problem, she and I.

"You look like a coal miner," she said one day, seeing traces of stage mascara on my face. By then I'd had enough, "Well, I am a miner's daughter," I said.

"And you'll never get far as a singer. You're just a crooner," said she.

Even when I won the School Music Prize singing an aria from Handel's *Messiah*, there was no praise from Mrs. Baker. "You're nothing but a crooner and you won't get far."

By this time I was resolved on leaving school, so I had nothing to lose, "One of these days I'll play the Royal Albert Hall and I'll send you tickets."

The first time I played the Royal Albert Hall, I sent tickets to Mrs Baker. She didn't attend, but headmistress Miss Mills came along with her mother and cheered me. Mrs. Baker was our music and English teacher. She was employed by the county to educate us, not to humiliate me and beat me up. These days it just wouldn't happen. But she wasn't beating my resolve, no way.

The final straw at school was someone scrawling a strange four letter swear word across my exercise book. The teacher saw it and sent me to immediate detention to face Miss Mills.

"What's the meaning of this, Yvonne?" she asked as she held up my exercise book.

"What, Miss?"

"This," she repeated, showing the offending f— word scrawled across my pink exercise book in black ink.

"But I didn't do it."

"Well, the teachers are agreed that you will be suspended as school sports team captain and you're not allowed to go to school camp next week."

"But that's not fair. I didn't do it and that's not my writing. It's childish. Why would I do that on my own book? And anyway, tell me what it means, because I don't know."

Miss Mills would not tell me the meaning and dismissed me. I ran and ran home across the fields, crying all the way. I burst through our front door to pour out my heart to Mum and Dad. I was heartbroken. Next morning, both my parents walked up to school for a meeting with Miss Mills. They told me they'd left her in no doubt that I was an honest person.

"She's an honest girl and certainly wouldn't lie," said Mum. Dad agreed.

"And it's not fair she should be penalised. My Yvonne's captain of the sports team and was looking forward to school camp."

"This is a serious matter and the teachers have made a decision," said Miss Mills.

"Well, tell me what the word means, because I don't know," said Mum.

My parents came away none the wiser. No one ever swore in our house.

On reflection, years later, I can only see that kindly Miss Mills was facing a teacher rebellion and had to take the weaker course, despite the obvious facts that the handwriting was not mine. I'd simply become a threat to school normality. After that I refused to go back to school until the following week, when almost everyone was away at the South Staffordshire Sports Championship, which we would have won with me in the team. We lost. And I never did learn the meaning of the f— word until I was working in London, and that's the honest truth. But there were plenty of good times at school...

The school concerts

I had an idea to entertain the school. "Miss Mills, I'd like to put on a school concert at end of year. Some of the girls and the school choir are for it. Will you give permission?"

"Yes, Yvonne, I will. I'll tell the teachers to help."

I wrote something for the school notice board, 'Anyone who'd like to join in?'

Our shows went down very well. My school pals Ann Shaughnessy ("Nessie"), Audrey Jones and Val and June Ward had

Being Me

a ball as main characters, along with me of course. One year we presented *Musical Memories*. Nessie was Al Jolson, in authentic costume bought by her parents from a theatrical shop. I was a ballerina, tripping along behind her. Inevitably I tripped over, sending us sprawling, which brought massive cheers from our audience. Another year we were Cossack dancers. The production ended as a comedy act, but didn't start that way. We'd practised in the school playground, but never in wellies (rubber Wellington boots). Lordy, we tripped and fell about the stage, with wellies flying everywhere. Happy days!

Boys

Sure, boys were cat calling and whistling at us across the street. Maybe my whistling straight back at them, very loudly, cooled their ardour. There was one boy, a prefect at the boy's school next to ours, I thought was nice. We never spoke, but one day I sent him a letter via Nessie which just said, 'I like you.' Next break in lessons, a note came back from him, 'I like you too.' Oh, excitement! But we never spoke or even wrote again. That was my one attempt at courting.

Taking a dip

One sunny day Nessie and I dressed up nicely and took a bus trip to Trentham Gardens, looking the bee's knees in our pretty dresses and frilly petticoats.

"Let's take a rowing boat out on the lake!"

"Ooh la la! Pity we don't have parasols."

All went swimmingly until, "Vonnie, let me have a go at rowing."

The boat was small. We were not. As we moved to change ends, the boat tipped us nicely into the middle of the lake. We both emerged from that dodgy water, spitting and giggling. "Aargh! Now look what you've done!" we spluttered at each other. Slowly, we waded towards the shore, giggling our way through the bulrushes and water lilies. Onshore, we stood a while, teeming water, picking bits of debris from our now not so fine dresses. Time to go home, we stood giggling at the bus stop, still leaking water.

A bus finally came along, "You're not coming on my bus," said the conductress and rang the bell to drive on, leaving us behind. That happened twice. A third one finally let us on. We stepped inside but, "That's as far as you go into my bus. I'll have to clean all this up when you get off, you two. And you smell awful!" We sat on a bench seat, just inside the bus, dripping water everywhere. In Newcastle town, we dared not get on another bus. We walked the remaining four miles home, feeling pretty miserable.

Seven days a week I was busy. My weekends were filled, working the clubs and dance halls. Mid week I was in school, in the evening working to expand my song repertoire at home. While school friends were reading *Girls' Own* and *School Friend,* I had my head into *Melody Maker* and *New Musical Express.* Tom Hinks, our local newsagent, ordered them for me specially. I read those music trade mags from cover to cover, soaking up every precious word like blotting paper.

Athletics Champion

My old cycling friend Dorothy White, she of Orme Girls' High School, popped up in my life again at the Inter Schools Sports Championship of 1953. I was still training four days a week in swimming and athletics, so I was really fit. I entered three events in the competition: javelin, relay and high jump. I won at javelin and I was in the winning relay team. Two down! Only the high jump now, to make it three in a row. Dorothy White was level pegging with me to win. We had one final jump each. The rail was reset at 4ft 9 inches and Dorothy went first. "Good luck," I shouted, just before she set off. Oh dear, Dorothy just failed to clear the rail. I gave it everything with a mighty scissor jump and cleared the rail. Oh glory! Then, bang! Stars in my eyes as Mrs White clouted me around the head with her handbag, several times.,"You distracted her!" she shouted. There were witnesses to the handbagging, but no one helped me out. Mrs White was a mite peeved at me winning, perhaps. One all, Dorothy. High school for you, high jump for me.

I desperately wanted to finish school at the end of summer term in 1955. London was calling. "I'm sorry, Yvonne," said Miss Mills, "but your birthday is one week late for that. You'll have to stay on until at least Christmas. But I'll make you head girl if you do." Miss Mills *really* wanted me to stay on at school. I declined.

Brymbo's beauty queen

One final local glory awaited. In the summer of 1955, Dad brought home a leaflet from the pit. "Yvonne, I brought this from the pit to show you. What do you think?"

It read: *"North Staffordshire Collieries Beauty Queen Pageant. Open to all miners' daughters. Minimum 16 years of age."*

"I can't enter this, I'm not 16."

"Well, you look it."

"I can't enter a beauty queen competition."

"You'd be representing Holditch Colliery." Dad worked there.

"Well, if you think it's OK, I'll have a go at it." Dad filled in the application form. I found out, much later, that he declared I was 17.

The following month Dad took me along, all dressed up, to Burslem Town Hall for the local heat of the competition. He showed his lamp number, all underground miners had lamp numbers. It was a simple safety procedure to know who was underground at any one time "This is my daughter, Yvonne."

"Yes, we have her on our list. Which pit is your Dad at, Yvonne?"

"Holditch. He's a face worker and I'm proud to represent Holditch Colliery."

"And what do you want to do in life, Yvonne? "

"I'm a singer and I'm going to be an international star."

"Good for you, Yvonne!"

Jackie Trent

'Crikey, that's going it!' said my inner self. But I really was that focused and determined to make a singing career for myself.

The contestants lined up across the stage, in front of the local mining community. We were asked to walk around 'fluttering our wings.' I 'flutter' very well. Three of us were selected to go through to the final, to be held at Stafford Town Hall.

A few weeks later, Mum and Auntie Dolly Plum, sister Sheila's mother- in- law, went along with me by bus to Stafford. This time there was a catwalk for us all to strut our stuff. There was a good turnout of miners' families from all over North Staffs there to welcome us, supporting their local beauty of course. We were asked the same questions as before. I gave the same answers. Once again we were invited to 'flutter,' but more grandly, the audience cheering us as we paraded along the catwalk. There was a break while the judges conferred, selecting six of us for the final walk down. I was still in with a chance. More applause from the audience, all cheering loudly for their home contestant. Finally, we six were lined up onstage, facing the audience. The Maids of Honour were announced: "Miss Ankers and Mrs Joan Smith." And then, "The North Staffordshire Collieries Queen for 1955, representing Holditch Colliery" *'what!'* - "is Miss Yvonne Burgess!" *'Oh, my goodness me!'* "The crowning of our Queen will take place at Tamworth Miners' Week Festival."

Two weeks later we were in Tamworth, looking down from the Town Hall balcony at the large crowd gathered below. The Lord Mayor and Hugh Gaitskell, Chancellor of the Exchequer no less, crowned me North Staffordshire Coal Queen 1955 and the crowd gave a mighty cheer. We three were then paraded through the town on a horse drawn dray decked out with flowers and bunting, me wearing my crown, my ladies in waiting with their coronets and all of us wearing brilliant blue sashes with "Coal Queen" in gold lettering. What a day! I was definitely Queen of the moment, waving to the crowd. We spent the afternoon in Tamworth Park, surrounded by admirers and photographers, all of us having a great time. No one knew I was only 14.

Fifty four years later John Abberley wrote in the *Sentinel*, in the 'Memory' column, 'of 16 year old Yvonne Burgess singing for 100 guests at the Crown and Anchor Hotel, Longton,' to celebrate my becoming Coal Queen.

Back home at Brymbo pit, everyone was as pleased as punch that one of theirs had won the beauty pageant, "Bring her along to the pit, Les. We're all proud of her." They stood me in front of the winding gear with several pit officials, stuck a miner's helmet on me and took photos of us all. I managed a few cheeky grins. Winston Rowley, under manager at Wolstanton, presented me with a crockery set and a silver framed letter of congratulation. Yet more pictures were taken.

"Right, now we'll take you down the pit."

There really wasn't any option, so I just said, "Yes, OK." I was a miner's daughter and wasn't about to back out.

"We'll take you down gently."

And they did, but it was still scary, and a long way down. There were two mine shafts at Brymbo, both around 2000 feet deep. I was taken by train along the underground roadway. It seemed forever. I was terrified, but didn't say so. Finally I was brought back to the surface, and daylight!

I'm pleased I went down that pit. As said before, on 2 July 1937, just three years before I was born, 30 men lost their lives and a further eight were injured down Brymbo pit. My Dad could easily have been one of them. I'd thought of them all as the cage took me down one of those two mineshafts they'd all used, 18 years before. To this day, 72 bodies, men and boys, lie below Ravens Lane and Bignall End, from a disaster at Audley Colliery on 14 January 1895. Every day across much of the UK so many men went down those pits, risking their lives to earn a living, providing for their families. After my underground experience, I made a secret promise to myself to help Dad escape the pit.

On a brighter note, I remember a few precious nights out with Dad, who might take me along to a boxing match now and then. I wasn't over keen on the boxing, but Dad always bought me a bag of crisps and an orange. I sucked the orange through a hole in the skin, squeezing until it was dry of juice, while he watched the match through the smoke filled air.

Other times, we kids were allowed to take the short bus ride to Audley for Wakes Week. Mum's sister, Auntie Vera, lived nearby in Wilbraham's Walk, by Audley Church. Wakes Week in Audley was special, a week of fairground rides and amusements on land at the bottom of the village. One year there was drama, "You'd better come quick. Little Les is hanging on the Jungle Speedway by his feet!" That was Cousin Jean.

And there he was, screaming for his life, his feet hooked to the roundabout, his little body swinging horizontally as the ride spun him around and around in a giant circle. People were keeping well clear of this flying missile. The whole scene was complete bedlam as fascinated spectators were screaming along with him. "What are we going to do?" I asked the two ride operators.

"Well, if we speed it up he's likely to shoot off sideways, and if we slow it down, he'll bang his head something terrible along the ground as his body falls." Eventually they slowed the ride down gradually and caught hold of him. Treasure! I got a smack from Aunty Vera and another from Dad when he heard about it. "You should have watched over him better."

Chapter 5
1955 - On Track to London

Autumn 1955 and my final term at school.
Time seemed to drag by. *New Musical Express*, *Melody Maker* and *The Stage* magazines were bursting with the latest musical news: Bill Haley and 'Rock Around the Clock'; Alan Freed produced the first rock and roll concert; Pat Boone first appeared on Dot Records, and 45's outsold standard 78's for the first time. New stars were hitting the headlines almost daily: Elvis Presley, Johnny Cash, Chuck Berry, Patsy Cline, Eddie Cochrane, Little Richard. Everything was happening and I wasn't there!

Val and I left school at Christmas 1955. We both took jobs in town. I talked myself into a telephonist's job with a firm of solicitors. Talking my way in was easy after working with people at the clubs. The telephone switchboard proved another matter altogether. I was a complete disaster. After two weeks I resigned, before they sacked me. We had a few laughs though. The firm even apologised for letting me go.

I tried day work again at Ristes Wires & Cables, as a typist. I never was a typist and noise from the factory floor caused me constant nose bleeds. I bled all over my typewriter. What a bloody mess. I quickly sacked myself before they did. At least I was honest about it!

Being Me

'Get your act together, girl,' I told myself.' *'You only know music and singing.'*

London here I come!

My fast- track to stardom focused on the rail track from Stoke to London. I needed a new name, but wanted to keep my local identity. I didn't exactly see Jackie Tremayne hailing from Stoke- on- Trent. *'Trent! That's what I'll become: Jackie Trent!'* Now I was ready.

On track to London

One damp, winter day in early 1956 saw me standing on the platform at Stoke- on- Trent railway station, my massive suitcase and my handbag crammed to bursting. My parents were seeing me off, to whatever...

I had no agent, no contacts and no work, just absolute belief in myself. Yes, I had my eldest sister Barbara's address in Chelmsford as a temporary home; that was the one condition Dad set me, letting me go to London, all alone. But that was it, just 15 year old me against the world.

The train hissed and clanked to a halt at my platform. "Just be careful and look after yourself," were Dad's final words as he lifted my suitcase into the second class carriage. Minutes later I was on my way, leaning out of the carriage window, shouting "Goodbye!" and waving like a lunatic to my parents as the train steamed out of Stoke station, my hair blowing wildly with soot from the loco. Suddenly they were gone. That memory still frightens me a little. I really don't know where I found the guts to go. I just did it.

I was probably five hours sitting on that train as it slowly steamed southwards, stopping everywhere. The passing countryside kept me company as I sat, watching it slip by, my head whirling with the possibilities that lay ahead in London. Right then, travelling from one life to another, I felt trapped in a time capsule, a British Railways second class compartment capsule. There were no connecting corridors in those days for second class passengers and no toilet, no refreshments.

'Well, we've done it now, Jackie.'

Of course! I had my old self to keep me company.

'Yes. I just hope we find the right breaks, Yvonne!'

London 1956

Euston Station, London. People were pouring off trains, everyone in a hurry. 'Here we go,' I thought, hauling my heavy suitcase off the train onto the platform.

"Can I help you?"

"Mais oui, Monsieur. Merci."

'You little tart! Where did that come from, Jackie?'

'I don't know, Yvonne, but it's fun!'

"Have you just arrived in London?"

"Oui, monsieur, I 'ave. My brozzere is meeting me."

My Good Samaritan carried my heavy suitcase down the steps to the nearby underground station. Naughty me, I walked alongside him, twittering in supposed French/English. Thank goodness, he obviously spoke no French. (Two years later I would bump into Keith Goodwin again at the 142 Club, around the corner from Denmark Street, in the area we called Tin Pan Alley. He was a writer for the *New Musical Express*. "You bugger," he said. "I was convinced you were French!")

From London, two more trains to reach my final destination, Chelmsford, my 'near London' base, staying with Bob and Barbara. We had a lovely afternoon together, me on their garden swing while Bob tape recorded Bar and I singing together. Yet somehow I felt remote to it all, as though I'd already crossed a bridge in life. At last I was in London, as near as damn it, and I couldn't wait to be out there. *'Oh world, wait for me!*

I held off looking for work for a couple of days while I unpacked my gear and sorted out my music and professional gowns. Then it was time to hit the town. I caught the train to Liverpool Street station and went in search of Archer Street.

The Windmill Theatre
Archer Street was known as a fixers' street. Fixers booked acts for shows around the country and they were to be found on Archer Street. Right away, I saw a billboard on the pavement across the road, outside the Windmill Theatre, 'Auditions held daily. Enquire at Stage Door.'

I made a beeline for the stage door, "Good morning. My name is Jackie Trent, I'm a singer and I'd like to audition."

"OK. Turn up here tomorrow, 11 a.m. prompt. We hold auditions for two hours only, before the show opens."

There was little point in travelling back to Chelmsford, so I called my sister. "Hi Bar, its Jackie, I have an audition early tomorrow morning, so I'll stay over at the YWCA tonight." Except that I didn't. Always short of money, I saved the price of a double trip to Chelmsford by sleeping overnight in the ladies' waiting room at Liverpool Street station. I had a snack of toast and a cup of tea in a local café before bedding down. I had the waiting room to myself. In those days ladies' waiting-rooms at major railway stations were comfortable and quite safe, and I would be saving precious pennies towards buying my next stage dress. My overlarge handbag held cosmetics, rag rollers, my ablutions kit, even sheet music for auditions. Independence was always me...

Next morning, bright and early, I prepped myself for the audition. At the Windmill Theatre, I was told after I auditioned, "That's fine. Now you understand, you have to do a cameo nude appearance onstage. One week per month, no exceptions. We cover you in chiffon and you stand perfectly still, so nobody out there really sees anything. So we'll need to see you nude."

My sheltered upbringing was really challenged. Lordy, dare I do that? Oh, what the hell! So I stripped. They nodded approval. I quickly donned my clothes again, then signed the contract.

'Blimey, Jackie, it's a good job Dad will never find out.'

'I can't believe I did that, Yvonne, but it is the Windmill and I'm in!'

The world famous Windmill Theatre on Great Windmill Street started life as the Palais de Luxe. In 1932 Laura Henderson, the eccentric new owner, employed Vivian van Damm as manager. He devised the *Revudeville Nude Tableaux Vivants* show of singers, dancers and showgirls, a format that ran until 1964. There were six shows a day, from 2.30 p.m. to 11 p.m., which made things pretty busy backstage. It was a compact theatre with a deep set stage and dressing rooms stacked at several floor levels, all accessed by stairs, very crowded stairs, with a constant flow of showgirls in high heels passing up and down. Nothing stopped at the Windmill, even in wartime. 'We never close' was their motto. During the Blitz, beds were set up for the performers under stage level.

I was given two or three short mornings of rehearsals. I proved popular with the clients (fully clothed!) and looked forward to making my mark at the Windmill. The bad news was transport and the long journey home to Chelmsford each night after work. I had to face the Tube, a train and a bus, then walk the last mile home, all late at night. I stuck it for a few days, then rented a room near the theatre where

Being Me

I could sleep overnight. All sorted, and a great future with great pay, until *that* phone call. "Yvonne, I'm coming down to London to make sure you're OK." That was my Dad calling from Stoke.

As luck would have it, Dad's visit would coincide with my 'chiffon' week. He was certain to explode and take me home as soon as he saw the revue style performances at the Windmill. I could just picture his face, watching a tableau of nude girls surrounding the nude star (me) dressed in chiffon and forbidden to move a muscle or even blink! My Dad would see red, no question. Panic set in.

"I'm sorry Mr Van Damm, but I have to hand in my notice. My Dad's coming to visit and I know what he will say."

"Well, Jackie, you've a very bright future here. You are very popular and the clients like you. You'll be leaving a good job. I'll be really sorry to see you go."

"I'm sorry, too, Mr Van Damm. I don't want to leave, but I must."

I moved back into my sister's house and 'rested,' as they say in showbiz.

A knock-out

Dad came down to join us at Barbara's. I never mentioned The Windmill. When he left, I headed off back to Archer Street, looking for work again. I went into the Musicians Club, ordered a fizzy orange drink and mingled, looking for useful contacts. Some fool made contact all right. He grabbed my breast, so I chucked my orangeade straight in his face. He punched me and knocked me out cold. I fell to the floor. Good start. Welcome to London.

I came round, pulled myself up and tried to clear my head, "Are you OK, kid? What happened," said a friendly voice.

"I was looking for work. I'm a singer and I've just arrived in London."

Someone else nearby chipped in, "I heard there's a job going at the Two Puddings pub."

"Where's that?"

"East Stratford."

I looked up the number in the phone directory and called them right away.

The Two Puddings Pub

"Hello, my name's Jackie Trent. I believe you're looking for a singer?" And I told them about me. A rich Cockney voice invited me to "come on over an' bring ya music for us. By the time ya get 'ere, we'll be closed, so just ring tha bell on tha door", all said in an accent so strong I could hardly understand what he said. I threw myself on the Tube to Stratford East. Walking down Stratford High Street, I found the pub and rang the doorbell. The door opened, "Hello, I'm Jackie. I rang you earlier."

"Kem upstairs, darlin', we jest made a cuppa tea."

I followed the landlord upstairs and met his wife, "So what've ya bin doin', darlin'? Wot experience 'ave ya got?"

Over tea and biscuits I told them about my life in the Potteries.

"So let's 'ear ya sing, darlin'."

"OK. Let me get on the piano, switch on the mike and I'll sing." Lord knows what I sang, but the landlord said," Great. Wot a powerful voice ya got. Tha job's yours if ya wan' it." God bless him.

"Yes, I do want it. How much are you paying?" We agreed terms, there and then. "Where ya livin', darlin'?"

"At my sister's in Chelmsford."

"Well, we carn 'ave that, can we? For one fing, you'll not be able to travel easy, that time o' night, an' for anover fing, it ain't safe, a young woman travellin' late at night. Wouldn't let me own dawta do it if I 'ad one. Look, we got a room 'ere you're most welcome to 'ave."

"That's very kind."

"Caan ya cook?"

"Yes, I learned to cook at school." I told them of Mum's pneumonia and me having to cook, wash and iron for the whole family when I was 11.

"Right, mi gal, ya start Fwiday." That settled, we went back upstairs, had another cup of tea, and chatted about the pub and its customers. "What kind of music do they like?"

"Everythin'."

So I would give them lots of Cole Porter, Sammy Cahn and pop songs of the day. The kindly landlord and his wife showed me my bedroom. I wish I could remember their names, they were so kind to me. "Why doncha move in on Fursday t'unpack an' settle in. Then ya carn take a ganda at tha punters."

Being Me

My head was spinning all the way back to Chelmsford, finding work so quickly. I started planning what I would sing. Bob and Bar were so happy for me, until they found I would be working and living in a pub. "They're really nice people," I said, "and I'll be quite all right."

I moved in on the Thursday, as agreed, "Why doncha kem dahn inta tha bar an' meet a few of aah rega- lars"

I went down, all dressed up. They were a nice, hearty crowd. "Kem on 'en, Jackie. Give us a song."

I stepped up on the stage and took over from a group already up there. The pianist introduced me, "This is our new resident singer, Miss Jackie Trent!" And away I went, belting out a couple of numbers. I was flying, and the crowd gave me a great reception. I was in again.

Life was good at the Two Puddings. The punters were all well turned out and obviously had a few bob. They were market traders, car salesmen, bookies and local businessmen, all with their ladies. I worked four nights a week, living full time with the licensees. They had no children and they treated me like a daughter. They were really kind to me.

Then Dad turned up to check on me. He watched me perform, then spoke with the landlord, "I don't like all the bad language here. There's too much swearing. It's a bad influence on my daughter."

"Ya silly old baastard. Vere's nuffin' meant by it."

"Right, I'm taking her home. She's not staying here."

"She's old enuff ta make up 'er own mind, ain't she?"

"No she's not. She's only sixteen."

The following day, Dad made me leave those lovely people. "Let's go home."

"No," I said, "let's go to Barbara's. You can see your grandchildren."

I was determined to stay put in London.

Incidentally, at the Two Puddings I finally found the meaning of the f— word that someone had written across my school exercise book. Even then I didn't really understand it.

Chapter 6
1956 - 'Sheiking' It All About, Singing For The Troops

I started singing in nightclubs too. By early 1956 I was established as a minor star, working the West End nightclubs. Sunday was my only day off. Things were looking good, but I didn't want Dad interfering again. Besides, I was restless for adventure. Someone said, "Try the Grade Organisation," so I looked them up in *Stage* magazine.

A day or so later I just walked into their rather grand foyer, feeling brazen I must admit. "I'm Jackie Trent, I'm a singer. I've read your ad in *Stage* magazine. Could I audition for you?" The receptionist directed me upstairs, where I met Bernie Lee, Grades' main booking agent. Bernie interviewed me there and then. He must have liked me, because he said, "Turn up at Radio Luxembourg's studios for audition next Tuesday."

Radio Luxembourg
Wow! Radio Luxembourg was the "in" radio station for young people. It played popular music, for which the listening public craved. After the war, the newly liberated public wanted popular music but granny BBC said "No." It had a monopoly on broadcasting rights over British soil, since the 1920's can you believe, and was against providing

Being Me

popular music to listeners. Radio Luxembourg filled the breach, reaching millions of listeners every day. It skirted round the Beeb's UK broadcasting monopoly by transmitting from the Principality of Luxembourg, but Luxy's shows were actually recorded in dear old London Town, just off Park Lane, in Hertford Street, which is where I turned up at 3 p.m. that following Tuesday. "Good morning, I'm Jackie Trent. I'm here to audition." The receptionist was expecting me and escorted me to a nearby studio where I came face to face with the formidable Lew and Leslie Grade together with Nat Berlin, collectively the most powerful theatrical agents in London. I knew I was facing Mr Big. And did they play the part, those three sombre men in Homburg hats and black overcoats, all staring at me. I was bloody frightened!

Syd Boatman sat at a piano nearby, "Ready when you are, kid." I sang to these great men who could make or break an artiste. I performed for them as I would onstage, flinging myself around but without a mike. I finished my song and waited for the verdict. All three impresarios burst out talking, all at the same time, "She's great! What the hell can we do with a 16 year old on the road?" They liked me!

Then they all came up with CSE, "It'll be a good grounding for you, Jackie." Combined Services Entertainment provided artistes travelling the world to entertain British troops in still occupied countries. Remember, the war had ended just 10 years before.

Jackie, why are you doing this? We've got it made already on the London nightclub circuit.'

'Yvonne, I really want to do this. It sounds exciting!'

I was under age to work abroad so my parents had to give written approval. "Yvonne, are you really sure you want to do this?" said Dad, pen poised in hand over the various legal papers (it took a few years for my parents to call me Jackie). They did sign the papers, though.

Armed with my new Government permits, I turned up at Mill Hill Military Inoculation Centre where I met the rest of the cast: singer Bobby Britton of the Ted Heath band, Syd Boatman, the pianist from my Luxy audition, and a comedian whose name I cannot remember. Sorry, Mr Comedian. The four of us sat in line, waiting to be prodded with needles, "You go first, Jackie. Best to get it over." They all agreed. I didn't. (I've disliked hypodermic needles since childhood, after contracting scarlet fever and suffering the daily injections. Each day the poor district nurse had to catch hold of me, then Mum would hold me down as the needle went in. My bum was a pin cushion.) *'Thanks a bundle, lads.'*

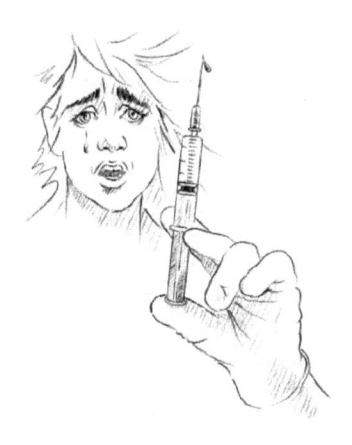

The hypodermic syringe truly looked enormous. I broke into a hysterical laugh at the very thought of it about to stab into me! Five injections later, exit stage left and out to the boys. "Just you wait till you see the needle," I said, "It's bloody enormous. And the pain!" Bobby Britton promptly turned grey and fainted, never to live it down for the whole tour. The following day I felt really ill. I was bed bound for two days.

Four days later, I joined the others at Hendon RAF Centre, first stop Aden. It seemed a lifetime away, at the bottom end of the Persian Gulf. We were led out to an RAF plane, me drawing a few catcalls from the squaddies already on board. We had reserved seats up front. The plane was full. The first big prop engine kicked off and through the window I could see loads of black smoke belching out. I thought, "That was loud!" With all four engines fired up, the vibration running through the plane was monstrous. "How will we ever take off in this heap?"

Being Me

This was my first experience of flying. Cabin noise eased after take- off and we settled down for the run to Aden. There were basic toilets at the back of the plane but no air conditioning, so the cabin temperature rose steadily as we flew further and further south east into the Med. Our first refueling stop was Malta. We all escaped the plane to grab some fresh air, a cup of tea and sandwiches. It was nice to see blue sky. Three hours later we were airborne again, refueling in Cyprus and then on to Aden, the longest leg. Overall, the journey took 24 hours. It seemed to last forever. We landed in Aden at 8am in the morning, walking into the unknown.

The "unknown" soon materialised, a typecast Army Regimental Sergeant Major in tropical white shorts, shirt, socks, shoes, even his bristling moustache looked white, with a polished silver topped pace stick under his arm. He escorted us to our hotel, my first big hotel ever. It looked very grand to me, and said, "No warkin' about outside the 'otel. You will kaindly stay inside the grounds, an' your pint of lime cordial an' two salt tablets are obligatoree, mornin' an' night. No exceptions, you unnerstand?" Yes, sir!

The guys were dying for a long, cold beer so they headed for the bar. I followed, "Great, there's orange pop," my favourite tipple.

I drank my orange then went to find my room. My suitcase was already there. I showered - oh yes! I had my own hotel bathroom for the first time in my life. I suddenly felt very grown up. Me in a foreign hot land with my shampoo, talc and precious bar of Pears soap spread around me. I had a quick nap, then I was out the door, eager to explore the hotel, wearing my now suitcase crushed new cotton dress. The incredible humidity soon shook out the packing creases.

I wandered into the bar to find my three Musketeers. Yes, they were still there. "Hi Jackie, you look good. Have a drink!" I was soon surrounded by lots of curious RAF personnel. After all, I was the only female in the place until later when a few nurses came in from the Brit hospital. Then it was dinner time, 6 p.m. on the dot, with "regulation lime juice and tablets" already laid out in front of each placing. I downed the lot in one go, or no dinner! I can't remember what we ate. It could have been a scabby dog for all we cared. We were starving. The hotel catered for Brit tastes, so bangers and mash were part of the fare. After dinner, I had one more fizzy orange in the bar, then left the boys and hit the hay. I had a great night's sleep, even with the ceiling fan spinning and creaking away above me.

We were up for brekkie at 8 a.m., the lads looking a bit bleary after too many beers. More lime juice and salt tablets, then food. After breakfast the vision in white turned up again, "You all 'ave officer status an' will act accordin'lee. You, madam, may wear shorts only in the garden. Smart aa- ttire in the dinin' room at all times an' be prompt at meal times."

Oh dear, we thought, he's going to cramp our style. We were professional entertainers, not on a parade ground. They'd have us marching next. So Bobby made it quite clear to the RSM that we didn't want to be ordered around and that we were here to simply entertain the troops. Of course, we'd yet to actually work out a show. We'd simply been bundled onto a plane in UK, then dropped in the desert. We were expected to sort ourselves out. Somewhere in the hotel we found a piano. We rehearsed a few songs and sketches, including a few numbers for the squaddies to join in, 'Always involve the audience.' At last we were all happy and ready to rock and roll.

Showtime

The first show was critical. It had to work. Our theatre was a large room, with simple stage and lighting that was just passable. I've always believed, 'If they can't see you, they can't hear you.' The battered piano was hopelessly out of tune. I can still picture poor Syd hammering away on it as we ran through our routine. That joanna would have done Winifred Atwell proud.

The audience loved us, standing ovation! After that the RSM visibly softened his attitude towards us. But when we asked if the piano could be tuned, you would have thought we'd asked for an audience with God. "*It was good enuff for Miss Atwell!*" We were amused. Winnie always played what we called 'the jangle piano', deliberately de-tuned. She had many hits with that style, bless her. "If I'd known, I could have brought my own tuning tool," said Syd. In truth, the piano needed an axe through it, but somehow it was retuned.

We really enjoyed the second show, especially our Brit section throwing in all the wartime and Cockney songs. The troops sang along, beaming ear to ear, with lots of applause and seat-banging. "We'll see you again," then smartly off stage left, well satisfied with ourselves. In no time we were back at the hotel bar, me happily with my orange pop. We were due to fly up the Gulf to our next gig, but I started feeling unwell. A medic brushed antibiotic powder under my upper arm, around where I'd had my smallpox jab. It had become infected. After that I didn't look exactly glam, with an elastic bandage around my upper arm, but hey ho! The show must go on.

We had a very early morning call at 2 a.m. Our plane, a DC3, was waiting on the desert strip for our bumpy ride to Doha. Our seats were just rope netting affairs that swung madly as the DC3 tossed in turbulence from the rising desert heat. We were flying at just 10,000 feet. Then, disaster. "Folks, the landing gear's playing up. We may have to crash land. Brace yourselves!" That was the captain, shouting back to us from the open cockpit. Bobby Britton had an anxious moment. All I could see below us was sand, miles of it, with no hopeful sound coming from the undercarriage.

'Jackie, why are we here?'
'It'll be all right, Vonnie... I think!'

We all stayed silent as the plane dropped towards the desert. Last minute, we heard the creak and groan of the undercarriage. We landed normally, to the sound of two RAF Hooray Henry flyboys laughing away up front. Apparently they practiced this routine on everyone. Bobby was a little late exiting the plane behind us, scrambling for a change of clothing.

The Sheikh
We were driven to a camp in the middle of nowhere only to find 250 young National Servicemen living under canvas in the desert, all waiting to be entertained. This was to be an open air show, with a big tarpaulin hung over one area as our stage, a very small stage with a piano that Syd said was in better nick than the one in Aden. It was just 9 a.m. but the temperature was already 100°F. The squaddies were all seated, wearing just shorts and hats. But why was the front row empty? Then the answer turned up in the shape of the local sheikh, complete with armed bodyguards, all bristling with guns and bandoliers of ammo. Real Lawrence of Arabia stuff. Great, we all thought. We were here for the troops, not the locals. Worse still, I was told to cover myself up. My arms, legs and chest quickly disappeared under swathes of bandaging. "I feel like a damned mummy and it's boiling hot in here." The others thought it very funny. I wasn't the least bit amused.

Being Me

Mum had made me the lovely dress I was wearing, from parachute silk she'd bought on the local market. I'd looked great in it but now I'd become one of the walking wounded. After my first song, I burst out laughing and apologised to the audience, "Sorry, guys, I had a bit of an accident. And they were worried about me getting sunburn." That raised a laugh. But inside, I was fuming, *'I'm not here just to entertain this front row.'* I found it offensive. And, I was told, the sheikh had been Cambridge educated, spending most of his time in London. I bet women he met in London weren't bandaged up. The front row locals left during the show, disappearing in a cloud of sand. So I made a big deal of removing the bandages onstage, with Syd playing 'The Stripper' as each bandage came off, to loud cheers from the squaddies as the cast helped untwine me. We really threw ourselves into the final number, a Blighty medley, both cast and audience. The squaddies did their own sand dance, giving us a standing ovation.

An officer came over; we thought to congratulate us, but no. "You're invited to the sheikh's palace for lunch, all of you, but you must cover up again, Miss Trent."

"That's very kind, but I'm not having those bandages on me again."

"Miss Trent, this is a great honour. Out here, women are never invited to eat with the men. You must cover up." I finally accepted a single sheet of cloth to hang around my shoulders, then off we went in Army jeeps, into the desert. Half an hour later, as we mounted a final sand dune, there it was, an encampment of Bedouin tents, some beige, but mostly black, surrounding a massive black tent. "That's where the sheikh hangs out," we agreed (when he's not in London). In the sheikh's tent we sat on carpets spread over the sand, and were served endless cups of black tea. "Don't speak to the sheikh," I was told. "It's not protocol." Why just me? Servants brought out large platters of couscous, but one plate had an ominous, very large sheep's eye set right in the middle of the couscous. It really seemed to be staring at me. A servant laid my food before me, and there it was, that damn sheep's eye again, looking at me from close quarters. Someone was playing games here. "I'm really not hungry and I don't feel well," said I to the British officer sat beside me.

"But you must eat, Miss Trent, or his lordship will be offended."

My Musketeers were looking at me, "Oh my God. What's she going to do now?"

I picked up the beastly thing, this raw, glazed horror, and swallowed it whole. I tried hard not to retch and managed to keep it down, smiling sweetly. My lot applauded, which gave me even more satisfaction. After that I excused myself and asked to be taken back to the camp. Back at base, I made myself retch up the eye, then had bangers and mash in the Naafi and, for the first time in my life, a real beer shandy. It was heaven on earth.

The guys eventually returned, downing several beers each and having a laugh at me. "Just think of it, Jack, you'll be able to see out of your backside, now." We were told we were staying overnight. I was installed in a small compound, the map store, surrounded by barbed wire, with an Army issue 2ft 6in camp bed. How could I sleep in this stifling heat? I called for the NCO, "I can't sleep here, it's far too hot. And I can't move with all this barbed wire around me. And how can I possibly talk to the troops?"

"Madam, the barbed wire is there to stop the buggers gettin' in! They 'aven't seen a woman in six months. They're livin' on bromide." (I later found out what bromide was for.) But he relented and escorted me to the mess, the biggest tent, where I spent the night with the other cast members and a few of the officers.

Our plane arrived at first light, back to Aden. But now I was suffering chills and an ominous dark red line was spreading up and down my arm from the smallpox jab. I was in a bad way. My tour of the Gulf was at an end and so, nearly, was I.

Laid up

Back in Aden, I was smartly admitted into the military hospital and laid out in bed, under mosquito netting. I was put on a drip, with constant injections. It was all a bit of a blur. I felt as if I'd been hit by a ten ton truck. The medics told me I was suffering from septicaemia, blood poisoning. Back home, some suit was sent to my parents' home to say, "Expect the worst." We had no phone at home; very few people did in the 1950's, so I couldn't speak with them. They must have had a very worrying time.

My doctor, a tall gangly man, moved around at snail's pace but obviously knew his job. After three weeks bed-bound, I was able to stand again. My snail doctor proved to be one Roger Bannister, the first man to run a four minute mile (on 6 May 1954). Dr Bannister was on National Service in Aden. At the time, I felt that he'd saved my life.

In 1961 Spike Milligan arrived in Aden on the SS *Arcadia*, which ran aground on a sandbank. In a letter to Harry Secombe, Spike described the passengers going overboard to help push the ship free, before breakfast. Spike saw Aden as a hot, sticky coaling station. I wasn't over impressed either. And it wasn't uncommon to see *'Go Home Tommy'* signs hanging out of windows.

After recovery, I had a choice, "You can return to the UK, or rejoin the show. They're now in Cyprus."

"OK. Where's my gear?"

"Oh, it's in Cyprus. Your compatriots took it all with them. I'm sure it's safe."

No choice. "I'll take Cyprus, thank you."

I was flown there almost right away. The gang were so glad to see me back, and I was glad to be back, "We've been busking our way up the Gulf, Sharjah, Mazera, Salalah and Bahrain, you name it. God awful places. We filled in the act with some blue jokes, but we missed our singer. Let's have a beer!" I had orange pop. The lads treated me with kid gloves. I still hadn't fully recovered to working pitch, but the warm company and the laughter spurred me on. I was back onstage. I had a couple of checkups at the medical centre, it takes a long time for one's system to recover, "And beware of penicillin in the future, it weakens your immune system." They'd pumped a lot of penicillin into me in Aden. (In the 1990s I was to be very ill, and almost died, from being given penicillin.)

Cyprus and EOKA: dicing with death

So we were back on the road, in beautiful Cyprus, living in the best of style at the Ledra Palace hotel in Nicosia. Then we were issued with combat gear. Hello, what's happening here?

'Get real, Jackie, this is bandit country.'

'Yes, Yvonne, I know that. Isn't it why we're here, to support our troops?'

Jackie Trent

By May 1956, when we hit Cyprus, British troops were heavily engaged, fighting EOKA, the Greek Cypriot organisation which was determined to win political union for Cyprus with mainland Greece, against Turkish wishes. But British troops and their families, and seconded UK policemen, were the main target of deadly attack. Hostilities started on 1 April 1955 with the bombing of government buildings in Larnaca, Limassol and Nicosia. On 26 November Field Marshall Lord Harding, Governor of Cyprus, declared a State of Emergency, with the death penalty for miscreants. He narrowly escaped death himself, from a bomb placed under his bed.

One time, we were issued with extra combat gear, for an armed escort convoy that would take us high up into the Troodos Mountains to entertain troops, probably the Para's, engaged in mountain guerrilla warfare against EOKA. As we assembled, two young squaddies from the convoy enjoyed the chance to chat up the young blonde singer. They were finishing their tour of duty and would be back in Blighty pretty soon, they said. I watched as their armed Land Rover led our convoy out of town. We drove into the hills. Suddenly there was an almighty explosion at the head of our convoy. We stopped briefly, then drove on, past the mutilated bodies of those same two young squaddies and their now wrecked vehicle, blown up and tossed aside by a landmine. I wept for those young men. Unwittingly, they'd given their lives, doing their duty, just to keep us safe.

OK, we carried on. We still did the show, but we were all in a state of shock for a long time afterwards. From that moment onwards we felt under siege. The four of us developed a special bond to cope with the stress. We stayed close together and spoke in whispers. After all, we were living on the frontline of a war zone. Yes, we feared for our lives.

The final crunch came at the Ledra Palace hotel itself, our HQ. We'd just returned from a show and were stepping off our bus when a shout came, "Mills bomb! Run inside the hotel *now* and lie down flat on the floor!" We just made it inside before a loud explosion rocked the building, shattering all the windows. We stayed absolutely glued to the floor until given the all clear. When we did dare to rise, we saw that our bus had been blown to bits. We headed for the bar, legs crumbling. Whiskies all round, me too. I still remember that gold liquid burning my throat as it went down, my first whisky. What a dramatic way to discover whisky. It tasted awful but did the trick, bringing some colour back to four very grey faces. I became as daft as a brush. This was my first experience of neat alcohol.

'I need this whisky too, Jackie. You really do get us into some daft situations.'

'Yes, Vonnie, I'd better be more careful after we escape this lot. It's not a lot of fun!'

The guys had refills while I was still sipping my first. We said little to each other. The very thought of being part of that mangled wreck outside hit us all very badly. There was just one week of the tour to go but it felt like a lifetime. We were in a seriously dangerous situation and everyone was a target. I always wondered if someone in the hotel was an EOKA informer. The hotel had our schedules, times of leaving and arrival at the hotel, destination of the day etc., From now on, even leaving the hotel was an act of courage for us. 'The show must go on' would never mean more than it did, that final week in Cyprus 1956.

Mad dogs and Englishmen

In one performance in military barracks in Nicosia, I included Noel Coward's song 'Mad About The Boy' in my act. I was a serious fan of his work and I had his mannerisms down to a T. After the show, we were invited to the Officers' Mess for a drink. The C.O. came up to me and said, "Someone would like to meet you."

"I'd like to compliment you on a fine rendition of my song, young lady." Goodness, the man himself! No one had told me that Noel Coward had been in my audience that evening.

I found him to be an utterly charming man, "I see a great future for you, Jackie."

"Thank you, Noel. That's very kind."

The following Sunday, our day off, we were all invited to tea at his home in Kyrenia, a very proper English tea, with tiny egg and cucumber sandwiches, no crusts.

"I know quite a few of your compositions, Noel," I said. He replied, "I'm surprised that someone so young could be so interested in my music."

"You only learn from the best," I hoped this flattered his ego, but I meant it.

We spent quite a while talking, about the stage, theatre, entertainment and about writing music. It was a great privilege to have spent time with the great Noel Coward.

On the other hand, some British officers could be quite priggish and over superior. Lita Rosa, a famous Liverpudlian singer, preceded me on this tour. She told me a tale, "An officer came up to me after one performance. He looked me up and down, then said, in a very condescending manner, "And what do you do for a day job, my dear?"

"I was so insulted. I told him 'I'm a Tampax tester'."

I had a taste of that. One night, after a performance in Nicosia, we all went into the Officers' Mess. A very senior officer calmly walked up to me, "You'll be sleeping with me tonight." I dismissed the superior bastard with a few simple words.

The tour came to an end. We flew back into Hendon RAF Centre and went our own ways. I took the bus back home to Stoke. I burst in through our back door to surprise Mum and Dad, "I'm home!" Mum nearly dropped whatever she was holding at the time. Dad was home too. They were delighted, and shocked, to see me back, safe and well. Like most of the UK, we had no phone, remember? In truth I was still recovering from septicaemia, so I took a break from work to rest up.

Chapter 7
'I Do Like To Be Beside The Seaside'

Eventually, I gave Bernie Lee a call at the Grade Organisation in Regents Street, "Hi Bernie, is there anything going? I'm ready for work again." We agreed on a package of London nightclubs, with a few provincial one week theatre shows. I said my goodbyes to Mum and Dad and caught the train back to London.

In one of the London clubs I worked, the Gargoyle, I befriended Alan Kane, the bandleader. "Jackie, we're booked for the summer season at Butlin's, Skegness. You're a great singer, would you like to come along and sing with the band?"

I travelled to Skegness by train. The line stopped there, but the wind didn't. Skegness, on the Lincolnshire east coast was famous, or infamous, for its constant strong wind. The town's famous advertising poster was a cartoon of a seaman, arms outstretched, being almost blown off his feet in the wind with the caption, "Skegness is so bracing!"

I found some digs within walking distance of the holiday camp. Alan Kane's pianist and his wife were staying at the same guest house. Then the bad news, the pianist's wife was favoured with the standard ballads that I wanted to sing, and I had to pump out the pop songs of the day. Not really me.

'Jackie, why don't we just pack it in and head back to London? That woman can't sing.'

'Yes, I know Vonnie, but we'll stick it out. I told Alan I would.'

Vic Flick, already a top guitarist, was working in the rock and roll ballroom at Butlin's Holiday Camp that year. We sat for hours together on the endless sands at Skegness, knitting a sweater. Yes, both of us. Why on earth would we do that? For something to do is the simple answer. When it was finished, that sweater was big enough for three people. Vic, a tall, shy guy, would be a regular session musician on my recordings a few years later. He was a great musician. He went on to join the John Barry Seven and played the *Juke Box Jury* riff. His guitar playing became world famous when he was lead guitarist on the James Bond theme, first heard in *Dr No* in the 1962 theme tune: dum- dee- dum- dum dum, dum- dee- dum- dum- dum.

Back at the B & B, sleep was not easy. The pianist and his not so good singer/wife were having wild sex in their room, next to mine.

"Vic, is he trying to kill her?"

"No, Jackie. Welcome to the world."

The summer season came to an end, so I headed back to London and the nightclub scene. "I can rent you a room at our house, if you'd like, Jackie?"

So for a while, I rented a room in Alan Kane's family home in Acton. The Kane's were a very staid Jewish family and maintained the Jewish tradition of locking up the house from 6 p.m. Friday until 6 a.m. Saturday. If I forgot my door key on Friday, I'd find myself locked out for the night. Of course, my work always finished late. More than once, I sat outside on the doorstep at Alan Kane's home until someone rose the following morning and let me in. Eventually I gave up and found a bedsit in Cricklewood, the Irish area of London. Money was tight, so one day I put an ad in the local newspaper:

> *'Flat sharing.*
> *Accommodation for 2 honest girls.'*

Honest! They worked in the day, I worked at night. One night I came home, tired after a hectic show, to find they'd cleaned me out, even my spare underwear. Thank goodness my stage gear was safe at the club I was working.
'Never again!'
'Oh really, Jackie. Let's get it right sometime?'
'Yes, Vonnie, I know.'

Chapter 8
Stateside in Germany with USAFE

After a year working the London club scene, I was becoming restless. Surprise, surprise! I missed being on the road, travelling abroad. The memories of danger and working in Cyprus under the threat of EOKA terrorists, were fading. I wanted more adventure.

'Here we go again. Life's good in London and UK. Why push it, Jackie?'
'Because I have to, Yvonne. That's me.'

Trains and boats – but no planes
Bryon and Alan Blackburn had a rolling contract to supply entertainment shows for the US Air Force in Europe, USAFE. "Jackie, we know you were a hit with the Brit troops and CSE. How would you like to work for USAFE in Germany?"

I'd never been to Germany. Bryon was London based and his brother Alan was based at their Wiesbaden office. They offered me a contract entertaining US air force personnel in Ramstein, the biggest air force base in West Germany. The nearest I'd consciously been to an American was in 1944, when those GIs passed our house in convoy, throwing Hershie bars and nylons to my elder sisters, on their way to war in France and Germany.

Germany sounded fun so I signed on the dotted line. "Here are your tickets," said Bryon, "They'll take you all the way." They were tickets for trains and boats, but no planes.

So one damp autumn morning in 1956 I was off again with my trademark big handbag, lugging my massive suitcase, first to London, then to Harwich, by bus and train and finally a bus trip across Harwich to catch the overnight ferry to the Hook of Holland. I was booked into a two berth cabin. The upper berth was already taken by a girl who spoke no English. She just lay there, constantly scratching herself. No sleep for me that night with the potential plague above and the rolling sea below.

Day two: Holland and starving. I faced the longest stretch of the journey, the Hook to Frankfurt. My emergency supply of apples and sandwiches were long gone. I needed food, so I charmed a ticket office clerk into changing a few pound notes for Deutsch Marks. A cup of coffee, a sandwich and some water for the journey made me feel a whole lot better. My mind wandered as the train crossed Germany. I gazed at the passing scenery, a kaleidoscope of colour, with the tall minarets of grand schlosses towering over the shimmering Rhine valley with its seemingly never ending floating trains of barges. But I also saw another Germany, one of shattered buildings, large areas laid flat by Allied bombing just over a decade ago.

'It's certainly different from that first grimy train journey from Stoke to London that we took in 1955, I'll give you that, Jackie.'

Jackie Trent

'We'll have a great time, Yvonne. We'll do OK.'

I carried two personal aids to foreign travel, my little language phrasebook and the universal blonde female smile, which made all the difference. It always does.

We pulled into Frankfurt, a huge bustling station, but alas no gallant reporter from *New Musical Express* to carry my bags this time. A few trägers, bittes and a little you know what flashing of the eyes found me assistance onto the small, local train service to the Rhone port of Mainz, then across to the city of Wiesbaden. At last, after two days of constant travel by bus, ship and train with little food or sleep, I arrived at the Hotel Weiss Ross (White Horse) in Wiesbaden. This was to be my home base in Germany for several years to come. I was completely exhausted.

The chaperone

"Where have you been? Look, sorry about this, but I'm your chaperone. I was supposed to travel with you, but I managed a flight out, three days ago."

I was looking at a woman in her late 20s. This was Joan, one of the dancers in our troupe, the person charged with escorting me across Europe as I was still under age to work abroad.

'How did she manage that, Jackie? You're the star of the show and we've just roughed it.'

'Yes, Yvonne. It's bit of a bugger, but smile sweetly for now.'

Joan handed me a massive room key.

"Well that's great, isn't it?" I said. "Anyway, I'm Jackie, and I'm starving."

"We eat across the road. The hotel proprietor doesn't allow us to eat in here."

Food. The very mention of food had me dashing to my room for a good wash and some clean clothes, then back downstairs and across to the bierstube. One steaming bowl of oxtail soup and a plate of chips later, I was crashed out in bed, snuggled under my very first duvet, my head floating on huge pillows. But the bed kept moving. It took a long while before the motion of 48 hours of constant travel would leave my head in peace.

Early next morning there was a knock on the door. "There's a meeting in an hour for rehearsals and costume fitting."

"I could do with a cuppa first!"

Morning rehearsal went well. Afterwards, a couple of the pros took me along to a little shop to buy my Performer's Survival Kit, a little heating gizmo to boil water in a mug, and a can opener, the secret to economy eating in hotel rooms. I used that gizmo to heat water in the chamber pot, boiling cans of baked beans, soups, meatballs and tinned frankfurters. And I had fresh tea every morning.

"Put your valuables in the wardrobe, lock the door and take the key with you," I was told. So the gizmo and my stash of forbidden tinned food lived in my wardrobe. We were on minimal allowances and every pfennig counted. Once a week we had a major spree at the bierstube, chips, egg and a frankfurter for me, with a big time bowl of oxtail soup to start. The best!

I grew up fast in those first three weeks at Wiesbaden. The pros gave me an education I'd never forget and they looked after me like a baby. Professionally I still *was* a baby. It made me realise what a sheltered life I'd led in my own comfort zone in the Potteries. Sure, I'd done the CSE tours, but that was a regimented system of where to go and what to do. "Take your salt tablets, drink your lime juice and plenty of water." Here I was on my own. USAFE and the American way of life was a whole different ball game.

USAF Ramstein

We moved over to the air base at Ramstein, for a three month engagement. Professional and first class, that's what hit me when I first saw the facilities. There were three entertainment clubs:

The Enlisted Men's (EM) Club, large but basic;

The NCOs' Club, large and full in your face spectacular, with a revolving stage and illuminated dancing water, even;

The Officers' Club was something different again, exclusive and elegant, with silver service, the full works.

At weekends we provided a small floor show for officers with singer (me) and comedian. We made a perfect combination. We won lots of applause and invitations to tables, "Gee, your accent is real cute!" The atmosphere in that club was like being in the best golf club in the US with a 100 year waiting list. These guys ran the Strategic Air Command in Germany. Our on base accommodation was fab, more like the Hilton than living quarters, with two girls to a suite. My roommate Joan, my chaperone, was very easy going and a great dancer, but ancient, I thought, at 29. We got on really well and did most things together, including the shopping for all the girls. Armed with our long shopping list, Joan and I would take the bus to Ramstein to pick up the necessaries. The chemist gave us some odd looks as we placed our bulk order for sanitary wear, toothpaste, shampoo, razor blades and nail polish. One day we stopped at a little bar by the bus stop. Joan had a beer, me a coffee. The bar owner offered us a harmless clear liquid, "Good for the damen."

"What is it?"

"Schnapps. Try, very warming."

Down it went, and promptly took my breath away! Joan had another. I declined. My head was already spinning and I giggled all the way back to base. Put that in your diaries, girls. Don't take gifts from strangers.

I also took back to the base too many mind pictures of despondent, frail looking people sat quietly in that bar, eyes staring at the floor, all with the tell- tale mark of the concentration camps stamped on their left wrists. Such people were a common sight on the streets of Germany. I thought, "Why would such cruelly victimised people remain in Germany?" Then I realised that they *were* Germans who happened to be German Jews. Germany was their homeland.

Master Sergeant Tellerico

The last week before our big opening was chaotic. The revolving stage jammed and the "dancing water" suddenly had a mind of its own, bursting into life and drenching us all. Better now and not on opening night. Soggy ostrich feathers don't give a girl her best look. And this week was when we were first confronted by Master Sergeant Tellerico, the club custodian, who summoned us all to the auditorium. "You've all been seen fraternising with soldiers of a different colour," he said. "You are white. Stick with your own kind."

None of us had ever encountered racial prejudice, and really didn't understand. "If it happens again you will be sent back to the UK, contract null and void."

Suddenly a female voice piped up, "We've signed a contract to perform, not to be told who we should or shouldn't talk to. In England we speak to whoever we like. It's the British way and we won't live with dictatorship." With that, the spunky lady clicked her heels smartly and gave Tellerico a Nazi salute. "We are entertainers, not soldiers. OK?"

There was a deadly silence. Thirty seconds later we all plucked up courage with a few "Hear, hears". All very British, you know.

Tellerico backed down that time. And who was our hero? Not me this time, but Joan, my quiet room mate and chaperone. She later admitted being terrified of the consequences, but just couldn't stop once she'd started. Tellerico was a complete bullshitter and a bully, especially with black GIs. No one seemed to like this 5ft 6in little Hitler. I added S.O.B. to my vocabulary, son of a bitch. Yvonne whispered '*S.O.B.*' to me a few times. It made me feel grown up as I sipped my first Coke, another new taste. The bartender asked, "Would you like a little sweetener in that?"

"No, thank you. I don't take sugar."

That brought some strange looks, then a polite, "Yes, ma'am." How was I to know the guys all had shots of Bacardi in their Coke?

The Show was a terrific success and Tellerico was lapping it up. The show was his baby, so precious that he would sit watching us all eat, regulating our diet to keep off those extra pounds. In this American paradise of food we were all eating for England. I stuck with the fab salads on offer. I had to be strict with myself because my bustettes had started to sprout and my body was taking on a whole new shape. Wardrobe finally took out the bust pads from my dresses. I was certainly drawing attention up front.

I befriend the C.O.

One evening, after the show, I was invited to an officer's table. Would I like to go out to dinner and bring a friend? I graciously accepted, but explained we had only Mondays off.

"No problem, I'll have my driver pick you up at seven."

I told Joan the Courageous that our date was old (to me) but a very nice person, an officer and a gentleman. Joan agreed to go with me. What to wear? Conservative, but glam? "What rank is he?" Joan asked.

"I'm not sure, but the officer who brought me to his table said, 'The C.O. would like you to join his table'."

"Bloody hell, Trent. You've hit the bull's eye. He runs the whole shebang!"

On the appointed night, Joan opened our door and just stood there, looking at this drop dead gorgeous Major stood in our hall, all 6ft 3in of him, with his Brad Pitt face. Joan's eyes stayed glazed all evening. I don't blame her.

The C.O. was charming and funny, completely different from what I had expected. He behaved like an adoring father. I'm sure we laughed all night. "Is there anything you all need on base?" he asked.

"Cards for the P/X would be great. They've got everything and it would save our bus trips into Ramstein." We concluded a wonderful evening. Joan was still gaga when we got back and talked in her sleep all night. She did that when she was happy. Next morning she received flowers and I had a large envelope delivered, with a "Thank you for a lovely evening" card inside, "PS, let's do it again - soon?" You betcha! Definitely an officer and a gentleman. Eat your heart out, Richard Gere. In that large envelope the C.O. had sent a magic P/X card for every one of us. The cast were exultant as I handed them out like sweeties. "She was brilliant, you know. He didn't stand a chance. He hung onto her every word." That was Joan, telling the cast of my evening with the C.O. But how the hell would she have known? Her eyes never left the Major's face all evening.

The C.O. and I shared many more Monday evenings at dinner. I started reading the Base newspaper like crazy to match his conversation. I do like to hold my own. We both spoke freely, on a whole range of subjects, including his wife and family back home. I read a letter from his wife, saying of me, "She sounds a darling girl." I saw photographs of his handsome family. Very wisely, the C.O. had left his family back home to avoid disrupting their life, away from the inevitable jealousy that was rife amongst the kids on base.

Being Me

This was one hands on C.O. He knew everything and everyone and flew for several hours each week to keep up his hours. He'd flown out of Pearl Harbour after the disastrous Japanese air strike, he'd converted from props to jets, and certainly earned his stripes. What a wonderful man. Our evenings were filled with tales of his adventures. He never stepped out of line with me. In fact, he often said I felt like the daughter he never had. I was the same age as his son in football college back home, but he never knew that. I never did tell him how young I was.

Up, up and away
One night in the Officers' Club I asked about the jet trainers, "They seem very visible. They're out there every day."

"Yes, ma'am, they surely are. Would you like to go up in one?"

Gulp! "Well yes, that would be lovely. Could it be on a Monday, when we don't have a show? I'll have time to recover!"

The following Monday I was kitted up in a flight suit and helmet and driven out onto the strip, towards a line of matt grey, T- shaped planes. "They're fuel tanks on the end of the wings, ma'am. That's what makes the T. Climb up the ladder. You'll be in the front seat, the pilot sits behind. The world is about to be yours…"

I squeezed into the tiny cockpit. I was shown how to activate the ejector seat. Over the intercom I giggled to the pilot, "Does this plane have wing mirrors?"

"Boy, you Brits sure do have a sense of humour."

Then we took off. Wham! Geezuz H. Christ! The thing launched itself into space, pinning me to the back of my seat, the G- Force compressing my ribs way, way back. We tagged behind two other planes, with more following behind. Over the intercom came, "Now we're gonna do a loop. You'll feel pressure on your chest. If you feel queasy, just close your eyes." The plane slammed into a near vertical climb. Oh my God! Everything went blue. At the top of the climb, everything went quiet for a moment, then we were plummeting back to earth. Everything went green, including my face. At that moment I was really glad I'd not had breakfast.

"OK. Now we're gonna finish off with a roll." It was a victory roll, like a corkscrew. It felt like being in a food mixer.

The next thing I heard over the intercom was from the tower, "Clear to land."

Back on the deck, the ground crew really had a job getting me out of the cockpit. My legs felt like jelly. Somehow they got me back to the Officers' Mess. I sat there, sort of sitting in treacle, sipping coffee. Nothing of me seemed to work for a while. "Thank you, boys," I managed to blurt out before staggering back to my quarters and my bed.

One day Val Merrill, our band leader, and I sought out Master Sgt Tellerico, "We want to lay on a show for the enlisted men. We're prepared to give up our day off, they all deserve a show." EMs were excluded from our shows, so we performed purely for officers and NCOs.

"OK, maybe you could do a Monday show." Tellerico knew full well that the C.O. entertained me to dinner on Mondays and thought I'd back down on the idea.

"Great," I said. "Joan and I will be there." Tellorico's face turned purple.

That Monday night we played to a packed house of enlisted men and got a standing ovation. The whole evening was amazing. Can you imagine 1400 boots stamping? We repeated the finale eight times. Those guys deserved their moment and we enjoyed it as much as they did.

Ella Fitzgerald and Count Basie
Tellorico had one more stroke to pull, the biggest so far in my professional life. "Val, I know Mondays are your day off, but next Monday I got some black acts. I want you to follow them and be top of the bill."

The Val Merrill Band were all good musicians. Val himself would front up with patter and song, wearing a battered fur coat and straw boater. The "black acts" turned out to be none other than Ella Fitzgerald with the Lou Levy Quartet, and the Count Basie Orchestra, the best in the world, as far as we were concerned. Val and the band flatly refused to play. They had a set to and Tellorico was suddenly faced with no band through the week. No band, no show. The boys stuck to their guns, "Fire us if you like," Val said. "Count Basie is number one in the world, so don't make fools of us. We will not follow him. Take it or leave it."

Tellorico grudgingly allowed us seats at the back of the Basie/Fitzgerald show. I went in early to have a Coke at the bar and watch the sound check. What happened next was beyond my wildest dreams. Ella and the Count came to the bar before the sound check. Me being me, I walked over to them, "Excuse me, Miss Fitzgerald, Mr Basie. My name is Jackie Trent and I'm with the show here. I sing. Please, it would be such an honour to shake your hand."

They both smiled and invited me to sit front of stage. My legs shook with excitement as they ran through rehearsals. The band played full force and Joe Williams, Basie's incredible singer, went into a chorus of "Every Day I Have The Blues". This giant of a man and his incredible voice vibrated through my whole body. Then Ella followed with the pure sweetness of her perfect voice. I sat there in floods of tears. I didn't know what to do with myself. (I just wept again, recalling the moment.)

Ella smiled down at me and gave me her hanky. Me, Jackie Trent, a Potteries girl, taking a hanky from the world's greatest jazz singer! The concert was incredible, an evening I will never forget. Afterwards, I went outside to the coach to see Ella, Basie and the band on their way. Ella hugged me and said, "Good luck, Jackie." Wow, she even remembered my name! A very treasured moment in my life.

We met again, many years later in Holland. Two dozen of us sat on bean bags as Ella did an impromptu show for television. I reminded her of Ramstein, "Ella, you were so wonderful." "Well," she said, "you've done so well for yourself, with the wonderful songs you've written."

The downfall of Master Sergeant Tellorico

We decided to play our trump card: me. I was nominated to whisper in the C.O.'s ear. We had so many grievances with Tellerico that I wrote a list, a long list, and found a space at dinner to reel off the whole lot to the C.O. I was a little nervous and gabbled lots, but I managed it. The C.O. listened carefully, but his expression never changed. We spent the remainder of the evening as normal, in pleasant conversation.

The following week Master Sgt Tellorico changed his attitude towards us. Then he disappeared altogether. "Where's Tellerico?" we asked.

"He's been transferred elsewhere."

That pleased a lot of people, not just us; the teams of local German girls who depended on employment at the base cleaning the clubs (Tellerico enjoyed firing them, just for asking to go to the toilet) and the bartenders, mostly black, put on a charge for no good reason, and more. He had it coming.

Next dinner date I said a quiet "Thank you" to the C.O.

"It's been on the cards for quite some time," was all he said.

Our last month at Ramstein was really happy. The cast had become a close knit team and the new Master Sgt often invited Joan and me to his home where we played with his kids in the garden. Two of the girls had found romance on base, as had Joan with her Major.

I spent my last night packing, carefully wrapping two dresses I'd bought in the P/X. I treasured those dresses for years afterwards. Then Joan and I had a final glass of wine together - and a little cry.

Next day was our send off carnival. What a turn out from the base to see us off, with much hugging and goodbyes all round, people carrying balloons, some of the muso's spilling from the bar last minute in high spirits to board a bus full of balloons, which the muso's popped as we drove along.

First stop was Frankfurt airport to drop off the muso's and most of the cast for their flight home to family and friends. Next off the bus were two girls staying on in Wiesbaden. They'd rehearsed a new double dancing/singing act. I helped out with their vocals and the muso's wrote some charts for them. The girls even made their own hand beaded costumes. They were set up really well. Now we were just three, a very quiet, lonely threesome after all the excitement. We pulled up at the White Horse hotel, right back where I'd started, three months before. This time I had my own bathroom. I was independent, armed with my gizmo, tea bags and little pots of milk, my jug, mug and spoon.

We three finished the day at the bierstube with oxtail soup, schnitzel and fries and a bottle of Riesling. I hadn't drunk wine before. It tasted like pop to me so I only had one glass. The other girls finished it. Then we had coffee and schnapps, slowly drowning our sorrows after the excitement of the day. Yes, I was tiddly by then and giggled myself to sleep. At least I didn't have to walk down the hall to find a loo.

Next day we met someone from the Blackburn's who said, "Jackie, we've fixed two weekend shows for you in Frankfurt. You'll have Tim Gorman as comedian. The girls will open and you close. You've got good muso's so you'll be fine, and there's a VW bus to get you all around between gigs."

The VW transporter

The bus was an old VW Transporter. Imagine the scene, six of us, plus driver, squashed inside a Very Worn vanette thing with all our personal gear and full drum kit. Our double bass player had his own private moment in the back straddling his bass. He refused to risk his precious instrument on the roof rack. We girls were squashed around our comedy act, Tim Dorman. And it was freezing cold. We were in the middle of a German winter, in a van with almost non existent heating.

Tim's comedy act involved a supposed bottle of gin, with frequent toasts to "Guzzlers Gin", his speech becoming more slurred by the minute. At the end he collapsed onstage. Tim always brought the house down. No wonder, he wasn't acting. The liquid really was gin with just a little added water. He really ended up smashed every night! What a character he was.

The club we played in Frankfurt was a large US Services facility, but without the finesse of Ramstein. It was known as the Snake Pit and the audience was strictly segregated, whites to the right and blacks to the left. That really hit me between the eyes when I first walked onstage. I found it chilling, so I purposely included a couple of bluesy jazz numbers in my act, which pulled in the "blacks to the left", who became really vocal, "Yeah! Go girl!" I felt like Ella right then. My other songs were more commercial, à la Doris Day, which also went down well. I could sense antagonism out there, so I developed a patter to keep the whole audience along with me, "Where do you guys all come from? Anyone from New York? Or Chicago, Kentucky, Detroit, California, Texas?" It always raised a cheer. Sometimes the atmosphere boiled over, erupting into a free for all fight, hence the name Snake Pit. But never when I was onstage.

That night, we met up with other acts staying at our hotel. "So how did you get on in that god awful place?" they asked.

"Fine. They gave us return bookings already."

"What! The Snake Pit?" Oh yes!

I introduced some chat between my eight songs. It felt good and went down well. The girls did four songs themselves. Tim and his gin were a knock out. We were a winning cast and could handle the so called tough audiences. Time for a serious talk with management.

Chapter 9
Home Again - I Walk the Line

Home again

So far, I'd travelled the road the hard way. I was the star turn, but I was being sold cheap on the comforts of life. The American air bases, the American way of life and especially the fatherly C.O. at Ramstein had all raised my self- esteem. Time to stand up for myself.

I met up with the Blackburns' man, "I'm owed a break," I said. "I'm going to Manchester, so book me back in two weeks' time. I travelled here by boat and train, all alone with no chaperone even though she was part of the contract. Also it's illegal to transport a minor unattended. That's an Equity matter."

"OK, Jackie. We'll arrange your flight tickets." Easy as that!

'Why, oh why, didn't you stand up for yourself sooner, Jackie?'
'Better late than never, Yvonne. But no more crap from now on.'
Really?

I left a suitcase at the White Horse hotel, booked the same room for my return, then took a flight home in a Vickers Viscount with tons of legroom and a big window to view the sky. No suitcase dragging and no more DC3 troop carriers for me.

"Would you like a glass of wine, madam, red or white?"

"White, thank you." Me being grown up and all. Hey! This didn't taste like pop. Next I ordered a lemonade.

77

We landed at Schiphol airport in Holland to pick up passengers and refuel, then on to Manchester. Not the Manchester airport of today, more a few metal sheds and Nissen huts. I walked carefully down the narrow, fold out steps from the plane in my new high heels. I was on home ground again, dressed to kill, and it felt good. Passport Control and Customs were just a formality. A short walk through the airport building, then onto the street outside. I negotiated a good price for a taxi ride to the Potteries. There were no motorways in the UK then, but there was little traffic either as few Brits owned cars in the 1950s. I sat back in my seat to enjoy the drive home.

'Oh Lordy, Mum and Dad! I forgot to let them know I was coming.'
'Well it'll be more of a surprise, Jackie. After all, we're famous now.'

Family life

It was dark when the taxi pulled up outside our house at 5.30 p.m. Any car pulling up outside our house would be unusual. People didn't own cars. I saw the drawn curtains move, then the front door flew open. I almost fell out of the taxi to greet my parents. Mum was beside herself, laughing and crying, with lots of hugs and holding of hands. "You look so beautiful," said she, looking at the transformation in her daughter, now dolled up in a smart suit, hairdo, stockings and high heels.

One more special moment was to come. Dad would be knocking off at the pit any time now to arrive home "buggered up" as he always put it. When Mum had calmed down I stood in the front hall, waiting. The door opened, Mum started crying and Dad said, "What the hell's the matter?" Then I appeared. Dad just stood and cried so much, I thought he would collapse. We all held each other for a moment. And then, "Lily, I'm starving!" We all decided that fish and chips were in order. "I'll fetch the chips," said Dad. Oh no! I wasn't missing the chance to flash myself around in my new role. "No, I'll go and Mally can come with me." Off we went down the street, my little sister firing questions at me on the way. I did my Joan Collins thing as we walked into our local chippie, "Four cod, chips and peas, please, large ones." You could have almost heard a pin drop.

"Is it Yvonne?"

"Yes, but you can call me Jackie now."

Yvonne: *'You little bugger!'*

If it were possible, I do believe the chip shop proprietor's jaw might have hit the floor at that moment. "When did you arrive?" he asked.

"I flew in today, from Germany."

Yvonne: *'You little bitch!'*

Word went around so fast that people were standing outside their houses as we walked back up the street with our fish and chips, wrapped in newspaper. Someone must have phoned the *Sentinel*, probably the chippy, because a reporter and photographer appeared outside the house as we sat eating our food.

"Tell them I'm resting from the trip, and could they return tomorrow morning at eleven?"

Which gave Mum and I time to dust the house, put out the best china and send young Les off to buy a couple of packets of biscuits. I cut some of Dad's garden blooms and greenery. We opened the piano, then the scene was set. No longer 'The Potteries' Vera Lynn' but 'Jackie Trent, international artiste.' My own identity at last.

"So, Yvonne, what is it like to be back home?"

"My stage name is Jackie Trent and the Trent comes from a city I'm proud of."

Eventually the reporter gave up and it was "Jackie Trent" thereafter. It took a while longer for family and friends to adapt. If someone called me Yvonne, I had to ignore them until they grasped the point. This was business and this was my new life.

But family life at home was still the same. Tea at 6 p.m. then wash the pots while Mum put Les and Mally to bed, bed myself at 9 p.m., sharing with Mally, then awake again at 6 a.m. Life still had to fit around Dad's long shifts at the pit and Mum's hard work in the house.

Something had to be done to relieve the monotony. Mally and I decided to "ghostout" little Les. When everyone was asleep, we crept along the corridor with towels draped over our heads and made low moaning noises as we scraped on his door with our fingernails, trying desperately not to laugh. Then we beat a fast retreat along the corridor to lie in bed pretending to be innocent and asleep. Along the corridor, we could hear Les going it in our parents' bedroom, "They're coming for me. I'm frightened." "Go back to bed, son. Everything's OK." Right, give it five minutes, then back again. This time we made even louder noises and jumped on Les with a wet towel before running back to bed. "Now then," said Dad as he tipped our mattress, crashing us both onto the floor, game over. Mum had to change Leslie's bed sheets as he'd had a little accident.

At breakfast it was agreed that I could go to bed later in the evening. I decided to call at my old school and visit Miss Mills. She was wonderful and even called an assembly of the whole school after lunch, "Now girls, one of our ex- pupils has come along to prove you can make something of yourselves if you try. Let me introduce Jackie Trent."

"Jackie Trent". That surprised me, her saying that. I stood, dressed in all my finery, and gave a short summary of my escapades. It was nice to come back and say "Thank you" to Miss Mills for giving me that chance to compete in the Carroll Levis and His Discoveries show, just six short years before.

Stardom promotes the oddest behaviour. People would knock on our door and ask to look at me as if I was a zoo exhibit. They never said anything, not even hello. They just stood and stared, then walked out without a thank you or anything. Really odd.

One of my old friends said her brother wanted to give me a spin on his motorbike, "That's great, I'd like that," I said. I had a smart white leather trouser suit for horse riding in Wiesbaden. The young man duly pulled up outside our door and greeted me, all kitted out in my white leathers, "Hi, Yvonne. You look great." Then Dad appeared, frowning heavily.

"Please, Dad. Just let me go round the block. I've ridden horses."

"I don't care what you've ridden. You're not going on that!"

The lad scurried off without another word. (Many years later, in 2001, a motorcycle would 'get me to the court on time', beating London traffic to deliver me to the High Court in time to win a little financial justice against Tony Hatch.)

On the road again
Two weeks later I flew back to Germany and my friend, the VW Transporter. The Blackburn's put on a series of tours for me, singing at all the major USAF military bases in West Germany. I spent the next two years working in Germany and the UK, with trips to Bahrain

and the Trucial States, now the United Arab Emirates, to entertain British troops. I still have tattered and torn 1958 visas authorising me to visit Bahrain, the Trucial States and Kenya. I kept up a busy life, darting in and out of the UK to sing in places near and far, even US air bases in UK. There seemed to be a group of us doing the rounds, entertaining the troops; singers, dancers and comedians.

Margo Thatcher became a special friend. She and her partner Toni had a wonderful acrobatic and dance act. Margo was an accomplished ballet dancer and ice skater and we were often on the same bill together. We were a really mixed bag.

Sometimes I'd cross paths with Diana Dors, she of the blonde Marilyn Monroe looks and large breasts. Once, as we travelled together on the train to Newcastle-on-Tyne, I said, "I'm working the Dolce Vita club, Di. Where are you this week?" "Well, that's my week gone. You look good and you can sing. They only come to look at my tits." Di and I were great mates.

I walk the line

I always came home to Stoke whenever I could. One day I caught the London to Stoke train. The combination of exhaustion and the swaying motion of the train soon had me nodding off. I woke at 2 a.m. all alone in a now deserted train, in Crewe railway sidings, Cheshire. Stoke station was further down the line. I had slept through the stop there.

'Now what have we done, Jackie?'

'I can see the lights of Crewe station. We'll walk back down the line, Vonnie.'

I dragged my battered suitcase over the railway sleepers all the way back down the line to the distant lights of Crewe station. I was in total darkness. At that time of night the station was deserted, so I sat on a wood slatted bench until the 5 a.m. train took me back down the line to Stoke. At home, Mum and Dad were going hairless with worry. They'd stayed up all night waiting for me.

I recalled that moment when Tony Hatch and I wrote "Play It Again", a fun thing we recorded as a duet. I wrote:

Sing me a song of the years that are gone
Postcards of Scunthorpe and Crewe - what a view.

A humorous 'view' of harsh industrialisation, of course.

Chapter 10
Kit-Kat, Cabbages and the Champagne Ballet - 1959

Wishful thinking

One day I read an ad in *Stage* magazine, "The Fabulous 'Jet-Set' Kit-Kat Club, Beirut. Sophisticated Acts Wanted." In the 1950s Beirut was the place to be seen and the Kit Kat Club was top dollar, the playground of the rich and famous. I liked the sound of that. The booking agent's address was in nearby Sheffield, too good to be true.

I was staying with Mum and Dad at the time, so a coach trip to Sheffield was easy. Off I went, armed with my professional photos and my CV. The husband and wife agent's 'office' turned out to be a terraced house, just a two up and two down. I was a bit underwhelmed with that after working with London agents and their fine offices. They offered me a plate of chips, (French fries) and a cup of tea while we discussed business. I offered my CV as I looked around for the piano. No piano. Some audition this would be. "OK," I said, "I'd better sing for you."

That took them by surprise, but I stood up and belted out 'Happy Days and Lonely Nights.' They offered me the job there and then. The pay and conditions seemed about right, so I said "OK."

"The dancers are auditioning in Manchester right now, eight of them plus you singing."

I laughed all the way on my bus back to Stoke as I recalled flinging myself around that woman's kitchen while she was still frying chips.

Mum and Dad were really concerned when I described the days' events. "The agent sounds very unprofessional!"

"Come on, there are agents all over the county, not just London." Wishful thinking...

A few days later my contract arrived, along with the info for rehearsals, travel arrangements to Beirut and accommodation. Everything looked fine, even the contract, which seemed identical to the one Dad had signed for me when I'd worked in Germany under age, the standard Equity contract.

I met the dance troupe at rehearsals in Manchester. They were a mixed lot from Liverpool, Leeds, Oldham, Rotherham and Manchester. All very northern girls, they accused me of speaking "posh".

Our digs were basic but clean, with a small lounge/diner and a hall of fame lined with autographed photos of the "star" acts that'd stayed there. The landlady was full of gossip about her previous lodgers, "See him? He was a right bugger!" She really had us laughing. The food was a mass of cholesterol, a fatty cooked breakfast and a massive evening tea of bangers and mash, boiled ham, bacon, eggs, beans and chips, all cooked in lard. Some of the girls asked for grapefruit and cereal at breakfast. Our landlady looked at them as if they had three heads. For sweet there was steamed pudding, tinned peaches and custard, with stacks of bread and margarine and pots of stewed tea. Our slim figures would soon be sacks of potatoes! We took a vote and decided "no puddings".

Then one morning the booking agent turned up at our digs, "Right girls, you're on your way. Here's the travel tickets."

A few days later we set out on our adventure. We dragged our masses of luggage off the bus outside Manchester's London Road railway station. We couldn't afford taxis. We were all so excited as our train headed south. When the train stopped briefly at Stoke station I wondered what my parents might be doing. We still had no telephone at home. London and more suitcase dragging, down the steps to the Underground. Finally we boarded the train for Dover. As we travelled further south, tiredness and hunger set in and excitement turned to boredom. We slept as best we could, draping ourselves across the second class carriage seats.

'Jackie, why are we doing this? A few weeks ago you were top billing at nightclubs in London.'

'It's OK, Vonnie. We're off on a great adventure to the best nightclub in the world!'

'Ha!'

Once on the Channel ferry we crashed, and slept as best we could. And so it went on. In Calais, we found the train to Paris, changing trains there for Austria, Turin and then Genoa and our ship. After 48 hours of constant travel, little food and almost no sleep, we were exhausted. But hey! We were about to start our lovely Mediterranean cruise to Beirut!

The ship looked white and wonderful from a distance; up close she was a rust bucket, and a not very big rust bucket at that. We were allocated three tiny four berth cabins. I had my own cabin, but opted to share. That gave us a spare bunk in each cabin for our gear. At dinner we were served soggy pasta and fish, a whole fish, un- gutted, its eyes staring at us, daring anyone to eat it. Not so good.

At sea, we exercised and rehearsed on deck, ignoring the leering seamen as best we could, whilst other seamen constantly trailed fishing lines off the stern. "There's tonight's dinner." Our tiny cabins were baking hot and airless, so we snoozed on deck when we could.

Our first port of call was Alexandria, in Egypt. We were so relieved to step off that ship for a while. "Who'll join me for a ride

Being Me

through town?" I asked. I'd seen a line of Arabas stood nearby. "I'll go," said Marlene, so I haggled with the first driver for a good price, then off we went in our horse- drawn carriage. Alexandria was shabby yet beautiful, as much Mediterranean as Arab. So many street names were French, Greek and Italian. The streets were crowded with roadside beggars, all pleading for money. There were just so many beggars. And wherever we stopped, men gave us cabbages.

Just why, I never figured out, but we were both bonny looking girls. We arrived back at the rust bucket, our carriage filled with cabbages

Stark reality

Our next port of call was Cyprus. I said to the captain, "I worked in Cyprus in 1956, entertaining the troops. It'll be nice to call in there again. Will we have time to look around?"

"Certainly you will. Cyprus is our last port of call. You disembark there."

"No, we're going to Beirut, to the Kit- Kat Club."

"No. Cyprus is the last port of call."

We called a meeting on deck, all of us with plenty to say. We needed a spokesman. Four of the girls were in their 20s, I was just 18. But, "Jackie, you do it. You speak for us. You've worked abroad before."

In Famagusta harbour we looked down from the ship onto the quay for some ray of hope, anything. But all we saw was a sleazy looking man leaning on a stretched pink Cadillac, with a small truck nearby. I had bad premonitions.

Yes, Mr Sleaze was there to collect us. "What's happening?" I asked.

"I'll explain later," he said, "but there's been a change of venue. You will be working at a club in Famagusta." So much for the Kit-Kat Club and its rich and famous clientele.

We were driven into Famagusta, all of us staying icily silent. The pink Caddie pulled up outside a hotel. At least, that's what he called it, an anonymous looking 3-storey building, hidden up a narrow side street. Nervously we stepped inside, into a virtual Kasbah. It was ominously dark inside, with dark carpets hung on all the walls and floor. The whole place smelled bloody awful. We threw open the creaking window shutters to let in some daylight. Suddenly the front entrance doors burst open and in poured half a dozen Redcaps, (British Military Police) all armed, "What the hell are you girls doing here?"

"We really don't know. We were headed for Beirut to do a show and ended up here!" That was me speaking up, of course.

"Oh, you girls are Brits, then! Do you realise this place was closed down a couple of weeks ago? It's been a brothel for years, involved in white slave traffic." That was Sergeant Reg Cranage, whom we later christened our Dashing White Sergeant. "I suggest you come down to Headquarters in the morning and we'll try to sort a few things out for you. In the meantime, keep the front door locked and don't switch on the porch light. It's red and you'll have half the bloody town knocking at the door."

Saved by the military police

God bless the British Army. Our six Musketeers then drove us to the Army mess in their land rovers and fed us bangers, mash and beans. Absolute bliss.

Next morning, one of the Redcaps turned up again. He drove three of us to British military HQ, where we were greeted with a smart salute and a lot of "'Ello darlin's!" Word had gone round the base, "Nine Brit girls just arrived." We'd all scrubbed up, looking good.

"Lucky buggers!" one called out. "Where did you find them?" But they were all great lads.

Being Me

We were presented to the Major, who was very sympathetic. "We'll do what we can, but we only have so much jurisdiction. However, you are staying in a place of ill repute, so we can certainly keep an eye on you all. I suggest you register with the British Consul right away and state your case."

"Well, sir, right at this moment we don't know where we stand, but we will register," said I.

"Right! How about a spot of lunch at the mess first, ladies?"

Over lunch, the Major brought us up to speed with the terrorist situation. EOKA was still very active, by all accounts. "Now look, girls, everything's OK but you should know that EOKA are killing people. Just be careful."

"How careful, Major? I was here in '56, working for Combined Services. We were nearly blown up twice!"

"So far this year we've had thousands of Turkish youths rioting on the streets. Seven of them were killed and about twelve soldiers were injured. Then we had a spate of bombing, about fifty bombs in two months. British military and police personnel are being killed."

"Oh my goodness! Is it safe for us to stay in Cyprus?"

"In short yes, provided you exercise caution. And you'll have my MPs to watch over you, of course, so eat up!"

We ate our fill. One of the lads kitted us up with lots of tea bags and milk from the kitchen, then drove us back to our "hotel" with the goodies. We told everyone what we'd learned from the Major about EOKA. "We'll be OK. The Army are watching over us." With British Army support we were all feeling more light-hearted, so we found a local café to celebrate. "Just bring us what you all eat," we chorused at the owner. He produced lots of small local dishes and two bottles of Retsina, then mugs of thick coffee and freezing cold Ouzo. We almost crawled back to our ex-brothel, daft as brushes, with a good day behind us.

Cold reality set in next morning. Our cash was dwindling and there was no sign of the sleazy Caddie man who had brought us here.

Jackie, why did you bring us here? We were doing all right in London with the top clubs and lots of wealthy fans.'

'I just wanted to travel, Yvonne.'

'Travel's one thing, Jackie, Shanks's pony is another. And to end up here? You do get us into some scrapes.'

'We'll get there, Yvonne. We'll get there.'

"How are we going to manage? I'm almost out of money," one girl said.

"So am I," chorused several others.

I had some money saved, "I can pool what I have, but I hold the pot. We live on basics and count every penny we spend. There's one thing, we'll never run out of tea bags, thanks to the Army." God bless the British Army. We had food parcels of goodies and HP sauce delivered to the door (I love HP sauce to this day).

"I cook, you clean up," I said. "OK?" All agreed. We shopped at the local fruit and veg market and cooked at home with a small splurge now and then, eating out at the local café, all very cheap. I was chief cook, making meat and potato pie, just like I made when Mum and Dad were at the pictures on Friday nights. I alternated the diet with cheap, tasty salads.

After five days, Mr. Sleaze turned up. Two of us dealt with him downstairs while the others listened from their bedrooms. I gave him both barrels, "What the hell is going on? This is an ex-brothel and the Military Police are on to you. We need money, today, and we are starving. Come back in an hour with the money and explain yourself." To make sure he'd got the message, I added, "We'll report you to the police and the British Consulate. We know the reputation of this place and you're obviously involved." The man melted out of the place but was back 45 minutes later and gave us £250. "Big deal," I said. "We need twice that. And what exactly are we doing here?"

Nervously, he said, "The Kit-Kat Club was cancelled."

"I don't believe you. Tell the truth."

"Well, this wasn't my doing. It's those people in Sheffield. I'm having real problems because of them. It was their idea to fool you, to bring British girls to Cyprus. You were always coming here, never Beirut."

"Well, that's fine and dandy," was all I could say, really. I had enough cash saved to fly home and escape this crap, but I felt protective towards the other girls. They couldn't really put on a show without me. I decided to stick it out. We all looked at each other, cursed him and the Sheffield people, but realised we would have to make the best of it. After some bartering we finally agreed terms to put on a show.

"That's great, girls," he said. "Why don't you dress up and join me for drinks and dinner tonight at the club where you'll be working?"

Taxis picked us up that evening and drove us across town, all of us dressed to the nines.

The Champagne Ballet

After the brothel, the club was a pleasant surprise, stylish décor and silver service waiters with white gloves. The Greek owner hailed from Athens. He "ouzo'ed" charm. "I am so happy that you beautiful girls are joining us," he said.

Just before dinner, he handed me an envelope. In the loo I opened it and counted out another £250 cash. "OK girls. We've got the cushion of some more money now. Let's enjoy the evening." Looking around, we could see that the club was upmarket. Over dinner, we settled to the idea of working there for the time being. Our thoughts turned to the show we had planned. The calm before the storm...

Our costumes had been sent ahead, to Cyprus, of course, but were not what we expected. "They expect us to be bloody topless," shouted one of the girls as she pulled a dress out of the trunk. The idea of flying tits on stage was too much for us. Some of the girls had serious bosoms. "We are not working topless," was the general reaction, but the management stuck to their guns, "These are the costumes and that's that."

The thought of singing a serious ballad with my frontage showing did nothing for me, "If I didn't strip for Van Damm at the Windmill Theatre," I said, "I'm certainly not working topless here." Another girl pow- wow. We went back to the Major.

"Right," he said, "any of that and we'll close the place down for indecency. Please warn the Club that my men will be on the premises for the opening show."

The club relented and gave us some lace to cover the bra area. That gave us some semblance of decency, but we went further and hand stitched sequins in the critical areas, christening ourselves, "The Ballet with the Flashing Boobs". We were actually advertised in town as "The Champagne Ballet". Opening night came and the place was full. A German ballet troupe went on before us, wearing little leather shorts with braces, puff- sleeved blouses and hats with feathers. To us they looked like a Bavarian oompah band, all very proper. The compère sang a few songs in Greek and English in between telling jokes, well, I think they were jokes because I heard a few people laugh. It was all Greek to us. Some dance music followed. I peeked into the club room from backstage and saw feathered hats and tight leather shorted bottoms circulating the dance floor with the clients, the German ballet members, of course. And worse, they were the only females I could see. No doubt, we would have to do the same.

'Good God, Jackie, will this nightmare never end?'

'Let's not tell the girls just yet, Yvonne. Best get one show under our belts, first.'

We'd rehearsed in the club that afternoon, a big routine for the dancers, with some high kicking. Space on the dance floor was too small really. As one girl, end of the line, said, "I'm going to kick some silly bugger's head in," which had us laughing. We told the manager, who moved the tables further back.

Now it was our turn onstage. On we went, all eyes, teeth and sparkling boobs, four girls in red dresses, four in white, with me in sapphire blue. We were flying the flag for the UK. Masses of applause followed, even as we walked back to our dressing room and took a break. The manager showed his face around the door. "Some of the clients would like you to join them for a drink." Alarm bells rang in our heads, "Here we go." But it wasn't so bad. We were given supper and drinks and the company was good, although I'm sure some of the guys couldn't understand a word of what the two Liverpool scouser girls were saying. They spoke a language of their own.

Back at "Les Girls", our new name for the bordello, we went over events of the day. "Sitting with the clients wasn't a one off," I said. "I can see it will be a regular thing, but I'll find out the pros and cons tomorrow." I lay in bed and recalled the Carroll Levis Show and the lesson I learned as a child on that stage, *'Take charge and stay on top of the situation.'* As I slipped into sleep my final thought was, *'Why me? Why am I stuck with sorting everything out?'*

Next day I confronted the manager, who said, "Yes, you must sit with the clients, but we will pay you commission on the food and drink they buy." The club charged an arm and a leg for food and drink, so I agreed.

"OK, we sit with them and dance, but that's it, no funny business."

He smirked. "Whatever you do outside these premises is your choice." I nearly hit him. It felt as though we were being sold in a meat market. We could do with the extra cash, although none of us would be comfortable playing hostess. I decided right then to build up an emergency fund with any spare money we earned, just in case. And I found a little old man with glasses, a lawyer from Athens, to sit with each night in the club while he read *The Times*. I was safe.

One down…

Sunday was beach day. We were in sunny Cyprus, so the beach and swimming in the warm sea was part of our lives. Two of the girls couldn't swim. We laughed at them, floating in their rubber rings. One of the girls, pale skinned, slept all day on the beach. By evening she was lobster coloured, covered in blisters, vomiting and shivering. I found a doctor who spoke English. He examined her there on the beach and said, "This girl is seriously ill. She must go to hospital right now." An ambulance took her away. At the hospital we tracked her down, cocooned in silver foil to hold in the heat, with just her swollen face showing. We were warned that she had an irregular heartbeat and was being treated to avert a heart attack. She would be out of action for some while and needed help. We called in our Musketeers. The Army were sympathetic, and said that when she was fit to travel they might be able to get her on an RAF flight back to England. "But don't count on it. Report this to the British Consulate," was the Major's advice.

Two down…

Monday was a national holiday. Come Tuesday, in we trouped to the consulate. "I will need all of your passports, ladies," was the verdict after we'd explained our situation. Half an hour later came another setback, "One of you, Marlene, has a problem. She is a minor and will not be allowed to work." Now we were down to six dancers.

At that time UK citizens less than 18 years of age needed a government license to work abroad. I knew that from my first visit to Germany when I was 17. Marlene obviously knew too, from the way she behaved, (When I read up on the law, I realised we could have sent the Sheffield "agent" to jail for up to two years for "procuring a minor under false pretences". Marlene herself faced up to three months in prison if the Consulate chose to follow the rules.) She became hysterical, "How am I going to get back to England?"

"The Consulate will pay your airfare, to be reimbursed by your family," the official said.

"I don't see how. My parents are separated and there are two younger children at home."

We couldn't just leave her, even though Marlene had brought it on herself. But first things first, the show had to go on. Back at the club we explained the reduced numbers and said, "Give us a chance. We'll just spread ourselves a little further across the dance floor." The manager was not too happy but said "OK." Our dressing room was very quiet that evening, probably because we were worrying if we would have a job next day. We stormed on stage and gave it everything. All went well, in fact the manager released us from hostess duties that night, well pleased with our performance.

Back at Les Girls, the Marlene factor struck again. We'd left her a blubbering mess and came back to find her sat like a zombie in a corner. We'd had enough. We were shattered and in no mood for soft talk. One of the girls snapped, "Pull yourself together. And you've not even asked us how the show went tonight. I'm going to bed." We all went to bed. It might sound cruel, but we really had had enough. A short while later a small voice called out, "I'm sorry. Goodnight." What we hadn't realised was that, while we were working, the silly girl had switched on the red light outside the building and we were a bordello once again. There were furtive tappings and knockings on the doors and windows all night.

Next day two of us (yes, me again) went to the hospital to find the mummy wrapped in gauze with pads over her eyes. She was full of antibiotics and sedated against the pain. We said "Hi!" but there was no response. The doctor suggested we leave her a few days to recover but to stay in contact, just in case. And all for the sake of a suntan to show off back home. Our luck had to change, and quickly.

I've always believed that something will jump up in your custard. Later that week, back in hostess mode, we found that stroke of good luck. We were sat with a nice crowd and, in conversation, told them of our plight with Marlene. One said, "Hey, I'm a PR man for Middle Eastern Airways and I might be able to pull a freebie flight to get her home. We could use it as publicity for the airline." And so he did, arranging for a local reporter to interview Marlene for the publicity deal. But what appeared in the UK press was a complete distortion of the truth:

"Devastated young girl left alone at night in a brothel. British singer and dancers left stranded and penniless, forced to be club hostesses, performing topless to raise money to return home. Middle Eastern Airways repatriating poor Marlene."

This all went down the wire to London, where a feature article appeared in the press, "Jackie Trent stranded" with a picture of me singing. A complete pack of lies, and after we'd found her a free ticket to go home too. So we sent her to Coventry, not one of us would speak to her. I told her to go and pick up her own passport from the Consulate. We had nothing to do with her from that moment. In fact, we all went out to lunch on the day of her departure, to avoid seeing her off. After she'd gone, we found that Marlene had raided our emergency pot for her share of the money. A while later I had a letter from Marlene, asking if she had been paid up to date. She wasn't working and was short of money. She'd done just one shoot as a model - topless.

The saga ran on. A *News of The World* reporter appeared at our door in Famagusta, looking for some juicy titbits for a smutty article. He came armed with his notepads and a generous expense account. He left the island with his money all spent and an empty notepad. We'd charmed him beyond belief and enjoyed some fab meals at his expense, but gave him zilch in information.

After Marlene left, we cheered ourselves up, raiding the emergency pot for money to transform our 'home'. We haggled in the market to buy wonderful lacy curtain panels, then bought lots of flowers for the rooms, and finally a new pearl light bulb to replace the

"Frying Tonight" bordello red light. Les Girls went up the star ratings with sunlight flooding through the open shutters of our home at last.

Life settled down and our show ran smoothly at the club. We changed our routine, but not the costumes, which just held together, with sequins still in place in the strategic places. We really did resemble one of those glitter balls one sees spinning in ballrooms.

Aristotle Onassis
One sparkly night the club manager was unusually attentive to us, "Have a great show, girls. Anything I can get for you, just let me know."

"That's not normal. He's over the top. What's he up to?" was the general run of conversation between us in the dressing room. We soon found out what he was up to.

After the show, we were invited to a large table of men all wearing impressive silk suits, flashing rings and chunks of gold, à la "I'm very rich and I'm going to flaunt it." Ominously, six silver champagne buckets were set around their table, loaded with Dom Perignon. Up to then the only champagne in my life had been a sweet fizzy liquid I was given at a family wedding. I hated the stuff. I knew that Dom Perignon was supposedly "the best of the best", but maybe the intentions of those offering it were not the best of the best. Whatever, they were obviously spending serious money and the club manager was a happy bunny. We sat with them, but the decorative pot plants and ferns set around the tables drank well that night. I kept emptying my glass into the pots.

"Jackie; that is your name? You are most beautiful and your singing is wonderful. I would like to know you better," said the young head honcho sat at my side. "Not likely," I thought. "You make my skin crawl." I went to the ladies' room and found the manager waiting for me when I came out. "Jackie, the man sitting next to you has invited you all to his yacht for the rest of the evening." I'd a fair idea of what "rest" the man had in mind. It was already 1.30 a.m. and "w-rest-ling" someone's advances seemed more likely. Time to call out the troops. I managed to catch the attention of two other girls who excused themselves and followed me to the loo again. "We've got a problem here." I repeated the manager's message, more an order than a request, inviting us to the yacht. "I know what I think. If you want to go, it's your decision. I certainly don't want to be put in a position where if I don't play patty- cake I'll be swimming back to shore. And I can swim, some of you can't. You'd better pass this round the others. I'm going to throw a wobbly and go home."

The manager caught me again as we left the loo but I spoke first. "There's no way I'm going on board that yacht."

"Do you realise who this man is next to you?"

"No, and I don't care."

"Look, he's a very, very important man, Aristotle Onassis."

"I wouldn't know him from a bar of soap."

"But Ari will not pay the bill if you don't comply with his request."

By now the manager was really becoming hot under the collar. I could see him sweating, "I will fire you all if you don't comply."

Both barrels once again, "Look you, we are not hookers and you will not put us into a compromising position."

Over the years, I've thought about that meeting with Onassis and the impression he made. When Jackie Kennedy married him in 1968 I just could not believe it. OK, he was a very rich man, with all the trappings and big boy toys but, as I said, he made my skin crawl.

We all did a runner. Next day, the oompah band performers looked decidedly jaded. Lord knows where they hung out the night before.

Looking up

The next after performance meeting was far more pleasant. I was invited to a table of nice people and spent a congenial evening with them all. "We wanted to tell you how much we enjoyed the show. How much longer will you be here?" "That's all in the air, really. Our contract was to work in Beirut at the Kit- Kat Club." I filled them in with the details. The two doing the talking were English, "We are in Famagusta for a few days' break, away from our hotel in Nicosia, the Acropol. Do you know it? Anyway, we really would like you to join us there to put on your own show. We've had shows there, now and then, but not as good as yours." Oh, you beauty!

Two of the girls were due to fly back to the UK to work a summer season anyway, and the RAF was geared up to fly our walking wounded girl back to the UK when she was sufficiently recovered. So we were ready for a change, the more upmarket the better. The hotel owners gave me their card and we agreed to meet up next day at their hotel in Famagusta to discuss terms.

Back at Les Girls, the five of us talked into the night, discussing costumes, music, routines and the thought of no more sitting with the clients. Heaven. We were buzzing with excitement at the prospect of a new adventure, "You do the biz, Jackie. You've come up trumps before. Whatever you agree to is OK with us." They went to bed but I stayed up, busily making notes, ready for that meeting: contracts, salary, accommodation and so many other things, just to be in control for that meeting tomorrow, or, by now, later today. At last I fell asleep for the few remaining hours before daylight, my hair already full of rollers.

Next day I dipped into the emergency pot, called a taxi and set off in a nice fresh cotton dress, my best high heels, lippie, mascara, a nice topping of suntan and the famous big handbag full of notes from the night before. I was full of the joys of spring, brimming with confidence on behalf of our troupe. I strutted into the hotel feeling like a million dollars. I was greeted with nice compliments, "You look lovely." I said "Thank you," rather shyly, and meant it. So many people gain the impression that I am big, bold and brash. It's been said many times. I'm actually quite shy, the noise is a front. I've also been labelled as "a northern girl". What the hell is a "northern" girl? Anyone north of Watford? I have always been really offended by this remark, which is also inaccurate. I'm a Midlands girl and proud of it, as I would be if I had been born further north.

The lunchtime meeting proved very pleasant. We discussed the fine detail, one show per night, with Sundays off. We would have rooms at the hotel, with food, laundry and a decent salary too. There was even the prospect of me working a second show in an exclusive club in the basement of the hotel, the Key Club. "It's a bolt hole for execs and Brit officers to relax, or sometimes cause havoc, depending on the celebratory mood. The fly boys from the RAF Black Hunter squadron let loose sometimes." (They were later followed by the Red Arrows.) "It literally is entry for personal key holders only. Right now the club's closed for renovation. If you're interested, you can take a look at the place. We want to put in live music, subtle, but classy."

We discussed the musicians I would need. "Well, I play piano. If you put the word out, I would need a drummer, bass player and guitarist. Obviously, it would be a separate contract. Yes, I'd like to take it on." "Hey, there's loads of professional musicians on National Service here. They should be just right," said the owner, his eyes really lighting up. This was a job from heaven. Me with the girls in the garden area, then me again in the Key Club. We were all invited to the hotel on our next day off to look around, "I'll send transport for you and you can all stay overnight to get a feel for the place." "That would be very nice" said I. And that was that.

Back at Les Girls there was great excitement, "We even have our own en- suite bathrooms!" The following Sunday morning, the four of us were collected in a new VW minibus and driven across the island to the Acropol Hotel. We weren't disappointed. The foyer was a big open lounge, full of people chatting and enjoying drinks and snacks in a friendly, open atmosphere. It was what we'd now call a boutique hotel, offering very personal service, stylish public rooms and swish bedrooms, all with balconies overlooking the gardens and mature trees. In this warm, dry climate, the gardens would be our stage. As dusk fell, we could see that the gardens were a very attractive and well lit natural stage.

"Jackie, come and look at what will be the Key Club. We've one or two ideas for the place and we'd like your opinion too." Immediately, I could see the potential for the new club. It would be magical. "We need to change the colours and the lighting, then I can fill the place for you!" There's confidence!

Jackie, we ended up in Cyprus again because of your big ideas, remember?'

'Yes, Vonnie, I know. But this time it's a dead cert, and I'm in control.'

Overall, we spent a very pleasant Sunday at the Acropol and were treated like royalty. It really was almost too good to be true.

On Monday, back at Les Girls, we were hardly able to contain ourselves with excitement. Should we give notice or just walk out? "Jackie, you give notice for us" was the final choice. We half expected to be dismissed immediately, but no. I wondered afterwards if the owner was secretly glad to be rid of us, so he could go back to his "big booby" show. We gave two weeks' notice to help the club find their next main act to replace us.

The Acropol owners gave us a generous advance on our first wages to buy new costumes for the show. We chose one piece swimsuits, matching fabric for wrap skirts and high heel shoes in gold, very glam. Almost every day I used a public phone outside our local bar to stay in touch with the Acropol, back to my street corner office and Dettol again. Meanwhile, we four were busy making new costumes and copying all the music at the club, just in case there was a problem. Those final two weeks just flew by.

Famagusta forgotten

It was a sad moment, time to part with the three girls going home to Blighty. We'd been through so much together. I hauled out the now large emergency pot, "Let's go blow this, girls." We chose our favourite bar for a final lunch together and really pushed the boat out. The bar owner knew we were leaving, so he joined in, passing round the cold ouzo very generously. By the end of the meal we were quite tiddly.

Next day, we four never made it to see the other girls off. A glorious hangover saw to that. Besides, we were due onstage that night, then moving over to the Acropol next day. Some of the Royal Military Police turned up at the show, those who had helped us so long ago when we were desperate. "We'll miss you, girls," they said. "It won't be the same without you." We bought them all drinks and thanked them time and again for their help. Quite a few tears were shed all round.

At Les Girls, just as we were leaving, we put the red light- bulb back in the outside wall lamp and switched on: "Frying tonight!" Next stop Nicosia, and maybe an easier life. We didn't even look back as we were driven from Les Girls. There was too much ahead of us, especially for me.

The Acropol was heaven after Les Girls and the nightclub. At last we could relax a little. We rehearsed in the hotel gardens. Then suddenly we were one week from opening the main show, with just three weeks before the builders would be finished in the Key Club. Invitations had already been sent out for the grand opening. There was no turning back.

The main show opened to a blaze of colour, with diners sat at tables under the trees in the beautiful, illuminated gardens of the Acropol, under a starlit sky. Music floated through the air from a Greek band, specially brought in from Athens. Our speciality act went down well. But my mind was already racing ahead to the Key Club below, now nearing completion.

The Club was ahead of its time, offering members a discreet atmosphere. I'd worked the best London black tie clubs, but this was different. At times, the Black Hunter Squadron let loose and partied. These crack pilots often left the club the worse for wear, yet still flew sorties at dawn across the island, as low as 500 feet from the ground. "How do you do it?" I asked one of them.

"Pure oxygen, my dear. It blows away all the offending nasties and leaves one clear headed."

I admired them. They were a great group of guys, full of life and wicked entertainment.

I found my musicians for the Jackie Trent Quartet from the armed forces: Pete Shelley (navy) on drums and Ronny Minns (air force) on guitar. There was also a double- bass player (army). Sorry mate, I forget your name but I did enjoy visiting your family in Sandbanks, Dorset, where you wrote off your Citroen Pallas! I was lucky. They were all professional musicians on National Service and made a great combo. Somehow we even found an Ajax hand- cranked vibraphone, a real oldie, for me to play, alternating with piano. I would crank it up through the guitar solos. I enjoyed playing that vibraphone, though I never played one again after I left Cyprus.

Diving and driving

Sundays were special, a reason to be alive. Every Sunday I was collected by jeep to join the Royal Navy diving group at Five Mile beach, Kyrenia. The other girls weren't beach types. Five Mile beach is a most beautiful spot, with its warm, clear blue sea. We had great days on the beach. The freshly caught fish, cooked on hot coals, were some of the best I've ever tasted. It was a perfect time in my life, with good company and plenty of laughs. I was just one of the lads.

"Come on, Jackie, you're a strong swimmer, you'll enjoy diving."

"You'll probably drown me, lads."

The Royal Navy kitted me out with massive flippers and strapped a very large oxygen tank to my back. Lordy, it weighed a ton! Then I had to waddle into the sea at snail's pace. Reaching the water was a bit of a drama. I was queen bee at that. Underwater for the first time, I was soon coughing and spluttering, my guts full of seawater. After a few lessons on using the aqualung regulators and clearing the mask of water, "Spit it out, Jackie", I was OK. And the warm sea was gorgeous. "Right, what's next?"

Jack, our navy dive master, handed me a spear gun. I promptly speared him, pinning him to the seabed by his flipper, "Bloody hell, Jackie, you'll kill us all. You shoot at fish, not me," he said. In my excitement, I'd released the safety catch. They took the spear gun away from me. After that, I really enjoyed diving and the underwater world.

Diving one day, I stepped on something nasty, the back of a large stingray! Jack noticed its wings moving and its tail starting to swing. It was not happy. He calmly signalled me to rise slowly to the surface, covering me all the way with his spear gun until I was clear of the stingray's tail. I surfaced with my eyes popping like organ stops. Back on the beach, I had a severe case of the shakes, thinking, *'What might have happened?'*

I heard that, years later, Jack perished in Maltese waters, struck by a speedboat while competing in a Forces diving competition. He was a great man. I have just one battered photo, taken at Five Mile beach in Cyprus, to remember him by. I also drove a sports car for the first time, in Cyprus. Sergeant Peter Herrett sat me behind the wheel of his Triumph TR3. I promptly knocked down a stop sign!

Fond farewells
The Jackie Trent Quartet - Sylvia, Gloria, Muriel and I, had a ball at the Key Club, a straight eight month run of hilarious entertainment. Then National Service came to an end for the boys. We'd become a really tight knit unit, so I thought, 'Time to move on myself, back to the limelight in Europe.'

'About time, Jackie. You've been away too long.'

'You're right, Yvonne. But I would have missed the adventure!'

I said my goodbyes for the moment to Pete and Ronnie, said my sad farewells to the Acropol and flew back to the UK alone. The three dancers had left months before to pursue new careers. I'd already written to the Blackburns in Germany and to Bernie Lee in London. Answers soon came back, "We've plenty of work for you, Jackie." I'd disappeared off the showbiz map and it was time to re- establish myself. I flew back to Germany to work at US bases for USAFE, and in London of course.

Chapter 11
Radio Luxembourg, London and The Kray Brothers

Radio Luxembourg

I was invited along to Radio Luxembourg's London studio, which is where I first met Alan Bailey. Alan loved Radio Luxembourg so much that he wrote a book about the station:

'*208: It Was Great,*' which quickly sold out.

In the book Alan recalls:

[It was] 1956 when Her Majesty's Government called me up for National Service in the Royal Corps of Signals. My service was spent in Germany in which time I spent most evenings listening to Radio Luxembourg. I was so enthused that on demob in 1958, I applied to that radio station for a position in their studios.

In 1959 at Radio Luxembourg I was a recording engineer and was designated to record The Bert Weedon Show, organised by Bob Brown who was an ex member of singing group, The Stargazers. He was also Head of Production for Radio Luxembourg at that time. He had previously heard an attractive young girl who he thought would make a good guest singer for the programme. The name of that singer was Jackie Trent. They were happy and enjoyable sessions and it gave me the chance to record her first ever broadcast (which I still have).

Being Me

I had great fun, dropping in to the Radio Luxembourg studios, making those recordings for the Bert Weedon Show and it was nice to be back in the mainstream of London life.

The Jack of Clubs and the Kray Brothers

Jack Isow owned the Jack of Clubs, set under Isows Kosher Restaurant & Deli on Brewer Street. He was one very shrewd Jewish businessman. Theatrical agents, music publishers, businessmen, mostly Jewish, and artists from theatre- land were the club's clients. After all, the club was right in the heart of theatre- land. Tuesday nights were publicans and underworld night. Money no object and the atmosphere was fabulous as the publicans escaped their pubs that night.

The characters frequenting the club were larger than life, especially the infamous Kray brothers. They were strong fans of mine. The Krays knew I was alone in London and they put out word on the streets, 'Don't touch her'. They sometimes sent a car to deliver me to the night club door and they also showered me with teddy bears! With their protection, I was safe in London.

The Kray Brothers

I didn't know at the time but, in the 1960's, Ron and Reggie Kray ruled the London underworld. They terrorised, intimidated and extorted their way to the top, using levels of violence that are shocking to this day. Human bodies were torn apart. Reggie Kray reportedly pushed his knife through Jack McVitie's face, below the eye, stabbed him repeatedly in the chest and stomach, finally pinning him to the floor with the same knife, driven through McVitie's throat. Blood everywhere...

In 1964 the Daily Mirror ran an article accusing Ronnie Kray of a homosexual relationship with Lord Boothby, the Conservative peer, who was openly bisexual.

Satirically, Boothby was known as 'The Palladium,' for his 'twice nightly' sexual appetite. Ronnie Kray was reportedly offered money to assassinate the Fascist leader, Colin Jordan. Their 'Firm' once held discussions for a contract to free Moise Tshombe, the Congo despot imprisoned in Algiers. Ronnie Kray was eventually certified insane and in 1969 both were imprisoned for life, for murder. It took a tenacious Nottingham police detective, Leonard 'Nipper' Read, to finally bring them to justice. Naively, I knew them as fans…

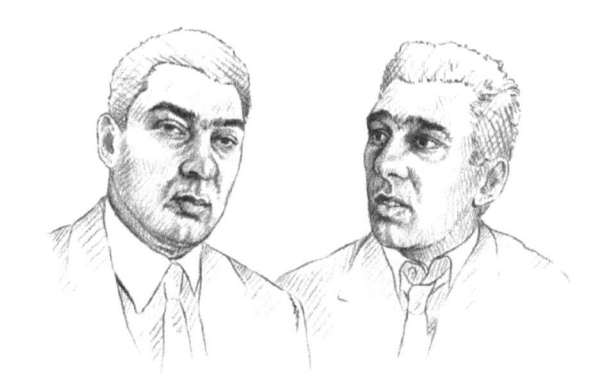

One night the maître d' drew me aside, "Jackie, Ron and Reggie would like you to join them at their table after your show."

"Fine, I'll be there."

"Hi Jackie, you look luvly, as usual. Great show!"

"Thanks, Reggie. And thanks for all the teddy bears. I'm running out of shelf space. I can hardly get in the room!"

There were two other people sat with the Krays. "Jackie, d' ya know Mick and Sue Donovan? They keep the Pride uv the Isle in Millwall an' they wan a word wiv you."

"Hi Jackie. Tha boys said you were great, an' you were. Would you consider workin' wiv us at the Pride? It's a great place, great atmosphere, an' tha punter's ud luv ya. What'cha fink?"

"Sounds great."

"Where you livin' right nar, Ja- ackie?"

"Just existing really. I've got a room in a place I really don't like."

"Well we got great accoma'dation, lotsa livin' space. We'd glaadly offa ya yur own room, be one a tha family, like. We just got the two boys ar- selves, Brian an' Tony.

Yoo'd be most welcome. By the way, ya don' mind dogs, do ya?"
"I love dogs. I always wanted a dog but I got a little brother instead!"
That raised a laugh. "OK. When shall I visit?"

Pride of the Isle
The following Sunday, the Donovans had someone collect me from my lodgings and drive me across to the East End. It seemed a long way. We passed through Chinatown. The streets were lined with Chinese restaurants and laundries and vividly coloured Chinese dragons and bunting seemed to hang everywhere. This was the original Chinatown in the UK, I was told.

"Mornin' Ja- ackie. Welcum ta tha Pride." I was greeted by Mick and Sue, their two sons and a bloody big German shepherd dog which leaped up to greet me, almost knocking me over.

"Ere's ya room Jackie. We 'ope you'll be comfy 'ere." I was. I became a member of their family right away.

The Pride of the Isle had a big lounge with a long bar at one end and a fine grand piano onstage at the other end, much like the Two Puddings in Stratford East. The resident musicians were all top notch. The punters were much the same too, an easy going, well dressed crowd of businessmen and 'dodgy business' men with their wives and girlfriends, all well- dressed too and free spending.

The Krays soon called in to see how I was doing. "Lookin' good, Ja- ackie. Your very pop- ular wiv tha punters, we 'ear"

"Thanks for the intro, boys. It's a happy place. Mick and Sue treat me like family. I'll sing the next number for you both."

"That's great, Ja- ackie."

The Pride had live music Wednesday to Saturday. No pubs had a licence for Sundays. The muso's were top rate, and we pulled in a good crowd every night. Mick and Sue were always inviting people upstairs, after hours, to party. They had a big lounge and loved entertaining. Sue Donovan and I became great friends, "Kem on, Ja-ackie, let's go da- arn East Lane market faw a cuppla pair a shoos. Ah'll treat ya!"

We had a laugh together. Great times, with genuine people. Yes, they were tough on the outside, just to survive in their world, I suppose. Mick Donovan 'went down' for eight years, for shooting someone. But all of them were alright by me.

Chapter 12
Ramadan and Romance in Turkey

Turkey and Ramadan

"Jackie, do you fancy working in Turkey? We can organise a tour of the US bases there."

"Why not? Said I.

I was back in Germany working for USAFE. I collected my tickets from Alan Blackburn in Wiesbaden for a Pan Am night flight from Frankfurt to Istanbul, where I spent two nights. For ten centuries known as Byzantium, the devastated city was rebuilt by Constantine the Great, remaining under Roman influence for a further 16 centuries. I so enjoyed exploring its beauty and the historic buildings that remained. Istanbul was still undeveloped and unspoilt in 1960.

109

Being Me

I flew onward to Ankara by Turk Havo Yollari, Turkish Airlines. As I remember, they were all prop planes at the time. Can you believe, I saw people cooking food in the centre aisle? I stepped off the plane straight into Ramadan, the Islamic month of fasting, with no daytime eating, drinking, smoking (or engaging in sex). But I was starving. I needed food. USAF transport delivered me to the Ankara Palace Hotel. I met up with my muso's for the tour, including Mike, my pianist. "When do we eat?" I asked.

"After six. Welcome to Turkey, Jackie." Next day we were taken to the US airbase for rehearsals. At least we could enjoy the food and unlimited hospitality of the base. We put together a show, ate our fill, and returned to the Ankara Palace Hotel for the evening. After 6pm, the almost deserted streets were suddenly busy, every street stall, café and restaurant heaving with people "stoking up" before dawn next day, when food and drink would be forbidden again until nightfall. Each day we were transported to the air base for the show, which went down well, then back to our hotel late evening.

Adana and Trabzon

Three weeks later we were on a Turkish Airlines flight to Adana. In the 1960's Adana was a small place, almost a village, with just one basic hotel and a bar/restaurant next door. The hotel would be our base for the coming month. Incirlik Air Base was, and is, a major USAF base with the standard three level entertainment centres, one each for enlisted men, NCOs and officers. We worked all three clubs on a four week booking. Next stop on our schedule was Trabzon on the north east Black Sea coast, on the old Silk Road which dates back to the first century BC.

"Right, kit up folks." We all donned combat kit and helmets. Armoured vehicles took us through rough countryside, at times driving through very narrow mountain passes, with a few bullets ricocheting off the armour- plating. Someone quietly told us that terrorists had a nasty habit of rolling rocks down onto US vehicles, but not this time, thank goodness. It was all a bit hairy.

We reached the outskirts of the village of Trabzon where the local policeman stopped us. "What's going on?" asked our interpreter.

"A public hanging in the square." Terrific!

Our only route forward was through the village square, so we sat and waited. Finally we were let through. As we drove through the market square, we saw a large wooden tripod affair with the body of a man dangling by the neck from a hangman's rope. Even as we passed, villagers were throwing stones at the body of the man, a butcher, who'd chopped up the bodies of his wife and mother in law, apparently. It was bizarre. Young children paused from their stoning to cheer and wave to us.

Ben the bear
The airbase was a collection of buildings surrounded by a high fence and barbed wire, with an inner high fence guarded by armed watchtowers. It felt like a prison camp. We could hardly miss the huge radar listening golf ball installations. Apparently there were a whole mass of missiles on base, all pointed towards Russia. The men were all confined to base, definitely no fraternising with the locals, living in self- contained units. They indulged in high class foodstuffs from the US. R & R in Adana was once every three months. I was soon surrounded by soldiers showing me photos of wives, children and girlfriends. They were all desperate to talk with us. We were from the outside world and they were eager for news.

Our 'stage' was in the clubroom, which doubled as cinema and pool room. The facilities were good. They had a gym, with mandatory work outs, and an outside recreational area for baseball. In a corner outside, I spotted a large cage and inside it was a big brown bear. As soon as I could, I walked up to look at that bear. I wasn't happy to see this beautiful animal caged, but it was obviously well fed and it looked content.

"Why is it caged there?" I asked.

"Well, ma'am, it was wanderin' about the place and sometimes it turned nasty. So we built the cage."

"How did you get it in there?" was the obvious question.

"It likes our food, so we tempted it in with some treats. It sleeps, mostly. But we give it a bucket of beer at weekends. Ben loves that, then he sleeps it off."

Maybe I'd found the original bear with a sore head.

I saw four guys clean out the cage, disinfecting the bear as it ambled around the baseball pitch. Everyone certainly loved that bear. It would sometimes lie on its back, legs in the air, or roll over on command, then stand on its hind legs to a round of applause. I'm sure I saw that bear smiling. It was truly happy. If only I'd had a camera, but I didn't own one.

Onstage, our usual routine, 'Anyone from Texas?' etc. We could have been on all night, but we left them wanting more. A crowd of the men waved us off, "Come back soon."

We drove back through Trabzon. The poor guy was still hanging there in the square, maybe as a deterrent. When we got to Adana we were tired, but happy. I sipped hot, sweet coffee and tea at the bar/restaurant next door, then slept the night through. One more week of shows in Adana, then back to Ankara.

Raki

At the Ankara Palace, I suddenly had a problem, "Please missy, you give me hand?" One of the hotel staff was asking me to help drag my pianist, Mike, from the rubble of some Roman ruins near the hotel. I found him bedraggled, unshaven and smashed out of his mind. I liked Mike, so I kept an eye on him and tried to keep him away from the booze. Besides, with no pianist there was no show and that would be a blight on my reputation. The whole incident made me edgy. Mike, my brilliant, crazy pianist, had taken a liking to raki, Turkey's anise- flavoured alcoholic drink. Similar to Pastis and ouzo, raki was generally served with coffee and a glass of water. Mike passed on the coffee and water, downing quite a few rakis per session, and would become quite belligerent and incoherent. Eventually I banned him from drinking the stuff on workdays. I challenged him a few times, "I 'aven't been drinkin'," but I could smell it on his breath. Something had to be done. I phoned Alan Blackburn in Wiesbaden. There was one month left of this tour, "Do you want to pull the dates?" he asked. "Hey, this is my livelihood. Find me another pianist."

He found someone who'd worked with me before in Germany. Problem solved. Now I had to face Mike. I let him get well and truly drunk. He missed a show. I let the club know beforehand what I was about to do. Then, deep breath, "You're finished, Mike." The look on his face was incredulous. He kept apologising, but "Sorry" just didn't wash with me anymore. He was his own worst enemy and drank himself out of a good job. I just stood up and walked away. I never heard from Mike again. He never returned to Germany, knowing there would be no work for him. The Blackburn's would see to that. With Dave, my new pianist, we finished the tour, exploring different ways of presenting my songs. We came up with a new light hearted approach.

Dinner with the President
I was invited to a special dinner at the Ankara Palace hotel. The hotel management sent me a personal invitation, "The dinner is for special European guests, Jackie. You will be our special guest."

I thought *'Oh, this is going to be a boring evening,'* but said, "Thank you that would be very nice."

I was sat on the left of an imposing character. Everyone was showing him deference, so he was obviously very important. I introduced myself.

"Tell me, Jackie," he asked, "are you happy in our country? What did you think of Ankara and Istanbul?"

So I described my head on encounter with Ramadan, me desperate for food. "I found Istanbul very interesting. Constantinople seems a more romantic name for the city, though.

"He chuckled, "Don't let Kemal Ataturk hear you say that!"

He asked me what it was like to be a singer, travelling the world.

Being Me

So I told him about Ben the bear in Trabzon and about the London scene. I avoided discussing foreign troops in his country and me singing for them. It just seemed the polite thing to do. We chatted on various issues, "I suppose this happens to you all the time, these formal dinners?" I asked.

"Well, yes, I suppose it does."

Someone eventually told me I was sitting with Celal Bayar, President of Turkey and a close friend of Kemal Ataturk, the country's founder. (In 1937 Ataturk appointed him as Prime Minister and in 1950 Celal Bayar was elected as President of Turkey.) Afterwards, I was really surprised to receive a beautiful, huge diamond and garnet ring from President Bayar, with a note, "Thank you for your company."

Celal Bayar

Izmir and Kemel Ataturk

We all took a tourist trip to Izmir. Open air clubs lined the seafront, all packed together, competing for customers. There were nut sellers pushing their carts, men carrying samovars like silver pagodas, the smell of kebabs roasting on portable grills, and fish of every kind.

"Come on, Jackie. We've found the best club for singers and belly dancers." Belly dancers were the main attraction in this cacophony of noise and particular gyrations of the body drew extra applause that I just couldn't fathom. To me they were all plump people with beaded bras and yashmaks, "shaking it all about". Definitely not something I could use it my act!

The Izmir/Smyrna waterfront was quite spectacular, with Kemal Ataturk's statue rising up, gazing out to sea, surrounded by a myriad of red Turkish flags. I found the Grey Wolf's house. It's now the Ataturk Museum. He moved there when the army drove Smyrna's Greek population into the sea and a great fire destroyed much of the city. I saw Ataturk's wooden bed, his stark furniture and, in glass cases, his velvet overcoats lined with fox fur. The house had a deathly feeling. Back to fresh air, the boys and the belly dancers!

The tour came to an end, so I flew back to Germany, entertaining US troops for USAFE. Which is when I met Private Presley...

Chapter 13 - 'One Night' when 'I Got Stung' Romancing Elvis

Back in Germany - I Spend Time with Elvis Presley.
We had a three night tour of an Army base in Friedberg. "Jackie, there's someone I'd like you to meet. How about you bring your musicians along for a musical evening?" We were being invited out by one of the American musicians.

I walked in through the front door of a house in Bad Nauheim, off base, to find the King of Rock and Roll himself smiling shyly at me, "Welcome, priddy lady. Come sit over he- ah. Ah'm Elvis."

As if I needed to be told. I nearly fainted. The whole gang of us spent a great evening together, jamming. Elvis loved his gospel and church music. We belted out a few songs together but when he went

Being Me

into "Amazing Grace" I hollered, "Can we have a key change? I'm singing in my boots!" The key went up a fourth. That was better. I could hit my notes again. "Girl, you got lungs!" said Elvis. I wasn't sure whether he meant my voice or my boobs.

We gave Elvis a private show, with him as guest singer. Beat that! All evening we filled that house with music. My muso's were really good, and blasted away as never before.

Elvis Presley had natural charisma. When he sang, it was straight at you, very personal and overpowering. He sure melted me.

We sat and talked, "How long y'all gonna be he- ah on- base? Y'all great. Will ya come back t'morra? Heck, let's all do it agin!"

"We're here for another two nights. Sure, we'll come back." Are you kidding? Who could refuse that invite?!

The Military Police drove us back to base at Friedberg. They watched carefully over Private Presley the whole time. They had to keep people away from him.

I always thought that Elvis was plain bored with the restrictions and the routine of daily life at that time. He had his distractions, fine cars and girls all around, I was told. We saw nothing of that. We only visited the house at night, after the show. Next evening, after our early show, the MPs drove us all over to Bad Nauheim again. The troops had early reveille, so our shows were early evening.

"Hi, Jackie. Hi guys! Great t'see y'all agin. How'd the show go? Y'all must be starvin' so I laid on some eats." There was a whole spread of pizzas, Southern "hushpuppy" biscuits and grits, huge hamburgers, salads and a big bowl of Cajun seafood gumbo, the whole works. "Let's git the pardie started," said Elvis as he grabbed a burger. We partied and sang as we ate. Elvis played his guitar and sang right along with me. "Hey, we work real well together, you an' me, Jackie!"

"As long as it's near my key, Elvis!"

We found time to talk. "Ya' know, this is a kind'a break fer me? When ah git back t' the States, all hell'll break loose. They got films lined up fer me right now. Ah'm jest a boy from the sticks. Ah'd really like t'be a straight actor."

We talked plenty, and I kind'a fell in love with Elvis. For a while we slipped off into a back room and canoodled a little. "Y'all should come visit me over in the States some time, Jackie." I swooned my way out of that house, and out of Elvis' life. We never did meet up agin - I mean again!

That chance meeting kind of took the shine out of my remaining time in Germany, but soon I was back in UK, planning my next move.

Chapter 14
The Road to Morocco

"Jackie, we've put together a great road show for USAFE and you'll be working with top pros. It'll be a great trip through France and Spain, even North Africa. You'll have a great time!" It was just after Christmas in freezing cold West Germany. The promise of warmer climes appealed. Well, it sounded good at the time.

'So we're off again, leaving the good life in London and lots of cash behind. For what?'

'For the travel and adventure, Vonnie, working with top pros, on the road.'

The Twinkling Tappers

The top pros were Syd and Max Harrison. As 'The Twinkling Tappers', stars of vaudeville and film, they were a fab tap, gymnast and comedy duo whose work went way back into the 1930s. (There is a Pathe News film clip of them onstage in 1933 on YouTube to this day!) Then we had "The Singing Saw", a Romanian who made musical sounds with a saw. A bass player and guitarist completed our ensemble. There were six of us in all, plus musical instruments and personal luggage, all crammed into a pale blue VW transporter. Max gave the VW a look over, "Don't rely on this old tub getting us there." Max was self- elected father figure to us. He carried the cash float and would be driving the 'bus'.

Being Me

One morning in the early winter of 1960, we set off, first stop Toul- Rosieres USAF airbase, close to the French/German border. Its bombers were capable of delivering tactical nuclear weapons against Warsaw Pact forces in the event of an invasion. Almost as soon as we set off, the inside of the transporter filled with smoke with bass player on pipe, Max puffing endless cigars and the Singing Saw smoking cigarettes that smelt like cow dung. In desperation, I opened a sliding window, "Jackie, it's freezing out there. Close it!". I sat quietly for a while but my eyes were streaming and I could feel a sore throat coming my way. So I declared, "Look boys, cut down on the smoking before I lose my voice. If I do, you'll have no singer, and no dolly for the GIs to coo at." They eased off on the smoking. After that, Max kept turning his head to make sure I was OK, which was a worry because he was driving erratically at the best of times.

We did two shows, entertaining the USAF 50th Fighter Bomber Wing at Toul- Rosieres. They were good shows, with lots of applause. We stayed there for three nights in BOQ (bachelor officer quarters) then headed for the Pyrenees and the crossing into Spain.

Partying in the Pyrenees

We approached the snowcapped mountains. "It looks cold up there. Are we OK for fuel?" I kept reminding Max about petrol. He and Syd were forever arguing and might just forget. We came to a small hamlet snuggled in the mountains and spotted a hand cranked petrol pump outside a small bar. Perfecto! The hamlet comprised just six tiny houses. Well, they were hardly houses, just two rooms on one level, one for sleeping, the other for general living, goats and chickens included. We entered the bar-cum- living room, scattering a few chickens from underfoot. Thank goodness, there was an open fire blazing away, but there was no running water or electricity. We sat on the few rickety chairs, set around two tables in the room, drinking local wine at two pesetas a glass. It tasted bloody awful but at least it warmed us.

Max was his usual full on self, always the entertainer, handing out photographs and signing them 'Humphrey Bogart.' He was the spitting image of Bogie and could play the character well. The

Harrisons used Bogie in their act. The locals were fascinated by him and pinned 'Humphrey Bogart was here' photos on the walls of the bar. The Singing Saw provided a few tunes and suddenly it was fiesta time, with one of the locals playing a battered old guitar as we all danced around the room, Ole- ing like mad.

I often think about that little bar with those photos slowly fading on the wall. I think of the weather beaten faces of the men and women, working the mountain lands in all weather conditions. I think of the kids, almost in rags, but polite and happy, their faces blackened by the fire smoke. Then I think of how lucky we are, enjoying the luxuries of life. We left that hamlet in high spirits, with a tankful of petrol, enough to reach Madrid.

Madrid
What a city. It was breathtaking with its grand buildings and wide, tree lined roads, and it was warm! We decided to stop over and explore.

"Turn down that side street, Max. Let's find a pension."

Max spoke fluent Spanish. "Do- o you know- o a cheap- o place we can stay- o?"

Luckily the first person he tried that on spoke English. The man pointed across the street at a pair of double doors. Max went in and came back saying, "You're not going to believe this place." We all trooped in with our gear to find sheer opulence, marble and gilt statues everywhere, even a grand sweeping staircase. My bedroom was unbelievable. The bed was on a raised dais, with luxurious window drapes and sunken bath. I'd never seen anything like it in my life. We were starving. A carniceria (butcher's) next door doubled as a tapas bar, so we all dived in. I had my first tapa of albondigas (meatballs in rich sauce) and a glass of anise, along with a glass of water. Back in my room, after a long soak in the tub, I slept like a baby in that glorious bed.

Next morning I explored the house, admiring the fine furniture and nude frescos hung on the walls and painted on the ceilings. Why such opulence? Later I was told that our incredible digs had once been a bordello, but a very high class one where clients had obviously been served refreshments, sat under beautiful crystal chandeliers. It was a far cry from Les Girls back in Cyprus.

I joined the gang for breakfast in the carniceria. We had homemade meat pies and delicious empanadas, parcels of pastry stuffed with meat and veg, then more albondigas, as we discussed our incredible ex bordello. In halting English, the carnicero explained that Generalissimo Franco, the Spanish dictator, had closed all the brothels some while ago. "OK," said Max, "we're staying another night." No one argued. It was too good to miss.

Two days later we were back on the road as we had to be at Torrejon USAF air base by mid- afternoon. But I had more space to myself in the VW. Where was the singing saw? We'd left it behind, on the pavement outside our bordello.

"You silly bugger, we'll have to go back," said Syd and Max together.

Problem was, how to find our way back to that side street. We drove up and down the maze of streets in Madrid. Panic started to set in. Suddenly I yelled, "Turn down there." I'd seen a building I recognised. The carnicero was pleased to see us again and what's more he had the saw in safe keeping. Off we went again, with the damned saw draped over my legs. For a while we all ignored him, 'sending him to Coventry' as they say. We never did learn the Singing Saw man's name. We knew he was Romanian, but little else. He remained 'The Singing Saw.'

The delay cut down my prep time for arrival at the air base. I was the pin- up and singer, so I had to look cute on arrival. *'In future,'* I thought, *'I'm travelling with a head full of rollers.'* As a general rule, if the hair looks OK, the face follows.

We stayed three nights on base in the BOQ, entertaining the 3970 Strategic Air Wing with two show nights. The show went down well and the airmen were great company. They saw little outside entertainment in their closed quarters, so a live show passing through made their day. "You're better than the last show we had" was the general comment. We were a lively troupe. We always, always involved our audience in the show. We never left stage without the whistling and cheering that told us we'd done a good job.

The facilities on some bases were not always good, but we somehow managed to cope.

Next stop was Gibraltar. But the Spanish border to the Rock was firmly closed. We had to go around the corner to Algeciras to buy passage on the ferry to Morocco. We were greeted with, "Perdone, visa necesario. Problema!" while the border guard looked me up and down.

Bloody marvellous. Now what do we do?

A diplomatic relationship

Max and I paid a call on the Spanish consul. "Party time Jackie. Jazz up a bit?" Dressed to the nines, I entered the consulate with Max, all smiles. Surprise, surprise, the consul invited me to lunch.

'OK, Jackie, now what have you got yourself into?'

'Yvonne, I can handle this.'

Lunch with the consul proved very pleasant. The restaurant staff obviously knew him very well. And he had this young blonde on his arm, and me not speaking Spanish. Imagine the lewd comments that would have been floating around. The food was good, my first formal Spanish meal. The consul very correctly delivered me back safely to our lodgings and next morning we were given our visas. We bought tickets for the ferry to Tangier and boarded ship, with the consul's lingering invitation still in my ears 'to do another lunch on the way back.' He was around 5ft 4in with horn- rimmed glasses. *'Never in a million years.'* I wasn't worldly wise, but I was learning fast. *'Don't stick your head out too far and you'll get away with murder.'*

That day the Straits of Gibraltar were not a millpond, so we had a bumpy ride. It's a short trip, but after rounding the Rock, the Atlantic wind whipped up the sea to a frothy mess, throwing the ferry around quite a lot. The Moroccan coast is surprisingly close to the Spanish mainland. It was an amazing experience, threading our way through the constant fleet of tankers and commercial shipping, passing east and west through the churned up waters between the Atlantic Ocean and the Mediterranean Sea.

We arrived in Tangier, stepping into a completely different world from Spain. It was a tacky, dirty place, the streets full of beggars and street traders who did your head in with their constant shouting and bawling. We drove straight through, heading for the mysterious Kasbah and Casablanca.

Casablanca

A medina or casbah, yep, it's spelled that way too, was built to defend a city, or stronghold, against invaders. That's why they have very narrow lanes and high walls. The Casbah lanes of Casablanca were "invaded" with stalls, mostly offering the same range of rugs and "hubble- bubble" pipes or hookahs as each other. I haggled for a beautiful leather travel bag for five shillings, it lasted me for many years. I also bought a hookah for my parents, just for fun. We were plied with hot, black tea and coffee wherever we went. Haggling was standard practice and Max was a bugger at haggling for an item, right down to the absolute bottom price, then moving on to the next stall, without buying anything, just to prove he could do it.

Our 'hotel' was the absolute pits. It was in a side street. The cockroaches and the constant noise rising from the street below meant no sleep for us that night. We were on a tight budget from the Blackburn's, so next day we escaped, hopefully to the comfort of Nouasseur air base and the usual USAF hospitality. "Come on Jackie, I need your help here," said Max, on arrival. We persuaded the USAF to find us accommodation in the BOQ.

Escape from death

Agadir was our final destination, before heading back north to Germany. "Let's change the show. We can try out new ideas in Agadir." We all agreed. Syd and Max came up with an act with "The Singing Saw". The Harrisons would run through their act as the Saw played, frustrating them to the point where they finally took away his saw! It proved a good comedy sketch. Syd, Max and I did a version of Peggy Lee's 'Fever' as comedy, with me playing the straight man while they mucked about behind me until I walked offstage, fuming. The new show went down well. Well satisfied, we took a break, delaying our return for three days.

We set off north on 29 February 1960. Two hours into the drive, around midday, the road started to shake. It was terrifying. I sat behind Max, watching him trying to drive in a straight line, but the road ahead was heaving and moving around. We were in the middle of an earthquake, a big one. We pressed on, even walking beside the van at times to lighten the load. It was that serious. The road surface was opening and closing in gigantic cracks beneath our very feet. We were terrified, but had to keep moving at all costs, simply to survive. At times we walked along in utter silence, praying for firm ground, with just the VW engine noise for company above the eerie silence. Then the earthquake suddenly stopped, so we were back in the van for a few miles. Then it started again, not as severe as before, but still violent. After that, silence...

That day a 5.7 magnitude earthquake shook Agadir virtually to death, killing a third of the population, injuring a further third of its people and destroying the bulk of the whole city. An initial quake, just before noon, was a precursor to the disaster. That would have been the tremors we felt when we were just two hours drive north of the city. We were very, very lucky bunnies that day. We'd left just in time.

Agadir

The disaster was instant news, worldwide. My recent letters to Mum and Dad had spoken of being in Agadir, so they knew I was there. Later, they told me of anxiously watching news of the disaster unfold on the BBC news on their new 12 inch TV. Mum was convinced she'd seen a blonde girl being pulled out of the rubble on a stretcher. They were worried out of their wits, and even contacted the Foreign Office for information. At the next town along the road I phoned my old school pal Val Ward, whose number I had for emergencies. "Hi, Val, it's Jackie. I'm in Morocco. There's been a big earthquake in Agadir. We just left there and we're safe. Tell Mum and Dad not to worry."

Travelling north to Casablanca, we moved back into the Nouasseur USAF base for a few days. They'd come off quite lightly from the quake, with just a few minor casualties. The base sent men and equipment to help with the rescue and recovery programme. We praised Max, our hero, for driving us safely through. He liked that.

Back on base, Max worked the sympathy angle well. He and I were invited to the Officers' Club for dinner. Last minute, we excused ourselves and joined the rest of our gang in the OM restaurant. "Oh, slumming it now, are you?" said Syd.

Our very worn VW

Our transporter was failing by the day. We made it to Tangier and re-crossed the Straits of Gibraltar to Algeciras, safely back on mainland Europe. No way dare we face the mountains of the Pyrenees with this old bus, so we followed lowland main roads in case the VW gave up the ghost completely. Max nursed her along. By now we were down to around 35mph (60kph). The old girl was clanking along like a tractor, drinking oil and water by the gallon. "The big ends on its way," said Max. He phoned the Blackburn's and shouted down the line, "This van is knackered! It shouldn't have taken this trip in the first place. And we're running out of cash. If we make it back to Toul-Rosieres, we'll need picking up for Wiesbaden." He was raising his voice by the minute, "We've been through hell. No visas in Spain! If it wasn't for Jackie we wouldn't have got them. Then the bloody earthquake disaster. It's a wonder we're still going. Sort it, and sort it out now! Call you tomorrow." He slammed the phone down. "Bloody agents, they're all the same!"

Syd and Max had been top of the bill for years in the UK, USA and Canada. They deserved more respect, but to booking agents we were just another troupe on the road. "Right, let's go," he said, "We'll nurse the bloody thing back, then I'll set fire to it." We believed him. We crawled along the final autobahn. Somehow we made it to Wiesbaden. Back at base, Max dismantled the engine while we trooped off to the bierstube to eat. Max turned up, hands covered in black grease, "I just phoned the Blackburn's and told them to come and get the damned thing. I've dumped the engine on the pavement." Then he had a beer and lit up a cigar.

Romance - at last
It happened in Adana. Through 1960 I sang in nightclubs across the UK, and for the Blackburn's and USAFE in Germany and Turkey. Which is where I met Bill...

A USAF officer invited me along to his family home, "Jackie, we're holding a barbecue at home. Will you come?"

"That would be nice. Thank you."

Came the day, and I was introduced to a handsome, tall young officer. "Hi, I'm Bill. I took in your show last week. You were great!"

"Thank you, kind sir," said I coyly. We hit it off right away, so I agreed to a date. We dated lots, and I fell in love. Of course, we were in the middle of yet another tour, so I had to keep moving. We stayed in contact by letter.

Chapter 15
1962 – a Roller Coaster Year

Proposal of marriage

"Jackie, I'm gonna take some leave. I'm gonna fly over to be with you."

"Oh Bill, that would be wonderful."

He flew from Adana into Frankfurt and we spent two blissful weeks together.

"I reckon I should meet your parents, Jackie," he said. It was that serious.

A few weeks later, when I was back in the UK, Bill turned up at our door to meet Mum and Dad. They both liked him. This handsome American air force officer formally proposed marriage to me, right in front of my parents, real old fashioned stuff! He slipped a ring onto my finger. I was engaged to be married! Oh heaven!

Then the cracks started to show. Bill was adamant that we would set up home in Omaha, Nebraska, my singing career at an end. "Jackie, I really don't want my wife to be up onstage performing. You'd be at home with me, of course."

I couldn't believe it. My parents were horrified. Maybe we'd find a way through this? I loved him so, but I hadn't struggled, scrimped and saved towards the career I loved, just to sit on a green John Deere tractor in Omaha. I was heartbroken. Worse still, my parents made it impossible for Bill and me to talk and sort things out between us. One or both of my parents sat up with us every night of those two precious weeks, when we really needed to talk openly to each other. We were trapped in a time warp, a world of chaperones and early to bed, not the night life to which I was used. Bill and I both felt suffocated in that house. Time passed and Bill's R & R was soon over. We said our fond farewells. He returned to Adana and I flew back to Germany.

No more word came from Bill until a letter saying, "I've been speaking with a pianist working here in Adana. He says that he took you to bed when you were sixteen. I'm breaking off the engagement. You can keep the ring."

I wrote back right away, "What! I don't even know the man you describe. I've never met him. I've never done that. And you don't even ask what I have to say? Damn it, I've always kept to myself, and you know it. The man's a liar."

I had a reputation of being straitlaced and off limits with men, other than for friendship. Then another girl in our troupe, another Jackie, admitted that she was the girl in question. She wrote to Bill, enclosing a photo of herself to prove the point. But my mind was already made up. If my fiancée could be swayed by idle men talk, then he wasn't the man for me.

'There's plenty of fish in the sea, Jackie. Forget him.'
'Thanks Yvonne. But I really did love him.'

I let Bill go out of my mind. Lord knows what happened to the ring.

Evelyn Taylor

A few weeks later I was back in London, appearing at the Astor Club. A message came backstage, "Would you like to join me at my table?" It was signed "Eve Taylor". Evelyn Taylor was probably the most dynamic, certainly the most feared, of all showbiz managers. Artists she represented at various stages of their careers included John Barry, Val Doonican, Adam Faith, Larry Grayson and Sandie Shaw. She didn't suffer fools gladly, had a formidable reputation and was certainly a force to be reckoned with.

I found her sat alone in a quiet alcove in the club. "I was told you were good," she said, "so I came along to see for myself. Let me tell you, you *are* good. You can be one of the best, so I'm going to manage you." Just like that. Eve spelled out her terms, there and then. Non-negotiable. "Come in to my office tomorrow. The contract will be ready to sign."

"I still have commitments in Germany with the Blackburn's. I have to complete my contract with them first." Eve knew the Blackburn's well of course, and agreed.

Next day I signed on the dotted line. *'Ooh, I'm signed up with a top manager. Big time, here I come!'* Eve Taylor had a big reputation and I knew she would be good for me. First, she booked me to appear at a few upmarket clubs in Blackpool. And that's where I met the next 'fish in the sea', one Drew Harvey. On reflection, more like a dogfish?

'You absolute pillock, Jackie!'
'Thanks, Yvonne.'

Marriage — on paper

Drew Harvey and I met at a guesthouse in Blackpool. We were both lodging there and his group was in showbiz too. We became friends. I felt happy in his company and we laughed a lot. The group was short of work. "Maybe I can find work for you in Germany," I said. I was due to return there and I could probably put in a good word for them. We left it at that, but stayed in touch.

Back in Germany, I did find them work, so they drove over in their Bedford van and found a cheap static caravan to rent in Frankfurt. Eventually, I found time to travel over and visit. "I'm off back to London shortly, lads. I've landed a management contract with Eve Taylor."

"That's big time, Jackie. You're on your way!"

Drew Harvey started courting me. He came on strong. His group said, "You two should get married, you get on so well together."

I'm still totally ashamed of myself. A few weeks later, Drew and I turned up at the British Consul's office in Frankfurt and were summarily married. I really was emotionally "on the bounce" from Bill. Then I had to break the news to my parents. I phoned them, "Hello Mum, I'm married. I'm Mrs. Harvey now." Oh my word, did the shit hit the fan! But in my own mind, I partly blamed my parents for the break up with Bill, denying us any privacy to sort ourselves out.

A few days later, 'Mrs. Harvey' was back in Wiesbaden at the White Horse, working out my final USAFE contract. Then I flew back to UK, to reconcile with my parents. They were so pleased to see me, alone. I moved over to Blackpool to work my first bookings for Eve Taylor. In all that time I had no letter, no phone call, nothing, from my new husband.

I caught the train to London. Eve had bookings for me in the clubs. I moved in with my new in- laws, Len and Eileen Harvey, in their ground floor flat in Forest Hill. I treated myself to a new bedroom suite and redecorated my bedroom, wallpaper and all. The whole lot cost about a quarter the price of just one stage gown. I've always spent big on stage gowns.

Drew Harvey was now touring Sweden with his group. How did I know that? Almost daily we received mail at his parents' flat from his many girlfriends in Sweden, recalling their intimacy together. "What's this about?" I asked. "Doesn't he know he's married?"

"Oh well, boys will be boys," said Eileen.

Jackie, how low can you stoop? You shouldn't be with these people. You were brought up better than this!' '

Yvonne, they're nice people. I have to forgive.'

'No, you do not.'

Pregnant pause

I had to tell Eve I was pregnant. She was very matter of fact. (My God, I thought, how often does she have to deal with this?) She made me an appointment in Harley Street, loaning me £350 for a 'termination.' I sat on the steps of that clinic, not afraid of the procedure but thinking deeply that I would be taking a life. I got up and walked away.

Eve was bloody furious with me, "I've got you booked for a summer season!"

"I'm perfectly fit and capable of doing it. Don't worry." Back at Forest Hill, my errant husband reappeared. He saw a roll of cash in my handbag. "Where did this money come from?"

"I'm pregnant, thanks to you. My agent loaned me the money for an abortion, but I refused. I couldn't do it." Drew Harvey gave me no words of support, no fatherly warmth. He was the professional shit.

I'd bought a piano on tick, paying back the money by installment. It stood in the Harvey's sitting room, where I worked at various songs. "Look Drew, you can help me out, I'm tied up with work. Take this money along to the piano shop and pay off my loan. I'm going to give life to our baby." I handed over the £350.

A while later I asked for the receipt for my final payment. "They didn't give me one."

"That's daft. Of course they gave you a receipt. Where is it?"

The damned man just walked away from me and left the house. I went to the piano shop myself, "May I have my receipt for the final payment on my piano?"

"Jackie, we've not received a final payment. The £350 balance still stands."

When would the heartbreak ever end? I confronted my new husband, "I've just been to the piano shop. They say you didn't make the final payment as I asked you."

The wretched man said nothing.

"What have you done with the money, for goodness' sake?" He refused to answer. I asked him again. "I've spent it," he finally admitted.

"On what?" He didn't answer.

"Do you realise what you've done to me? I now owe double - £700. You are one sad person. Get out of my sight." He slunk off without another word. After that, times proved a bit thin for me, paying back Eve plus paying the balance on the piano. At least I was working, earning money. It took me quite a while but I did it but with no thanks to Drew Harvey. The word "bastard" became part of my vocabulary.

Now my summer season was approaching. I parted from my in-laws, "I'll be living and working in Great Yarmouth all summer. I'll keep in touch with you both, but your son is not welcome in my life." During that whole summer, true to form, Mr Drew Harvey never once contacted me.

Happy times with Lonnie, Des and Billy Fury

Great Yarmouth 1962 sticks in my mind as one of the most memorable times of my whole life. Oh Lordy, we had such a happy show, with Lonnie Donegan as headliner and Des O'Connor, then me on the billboard.

Lonnie was a wonderful character and Des was a really easy going guy. His wife Gilly was pregnant and Des carried her around as if in cotton wool. I kept my pregnancy very secret. Lonnie, Des and I really hit it off. We added slapstick comedy to our own acts, throwing ourselves all over the stage together. But I had to come clean when my "bundle" started to slow me down, "I'm sorry, guys, but I'm pregnant." They were not happy.

"I'm perfectly fit and I'm not leaving the show." They were content with that. "If I have a problem, you'll be the first to know."

Luckily I had none of the usual women's problems of morning sickness and so on. I lodged in a small hotel, just a few hundred yards from the theatre. It was Italian owned, with a great little restaurant on the ground floor. The pros often piled in there after work for supper and there was always a great atmosphere in the restaurant as we all unwound after work.

Harry Secombe would sometimes throw in a little "Neddie Seagoon" act for laughs. In 1962 Great Yarmouth was probably the greatest showbiz arena in the UK. There was our show at the ABC theatre and the Harry Secombe show on the pier. On the promenade the rock and roll theatre was going great guns with a show presented by Larry Parnes, the music promoter. Larry managed most of the rock acts, including Billy Fury.

Billy Fury

From the moment we met, Billy and I became close friends. We were the same age and had a lot in common, including a passion for Sunday lunch. Billy rented a house in Yarmouth for the season and Sunday lunch at his place would become a ritual for us. Each Friday, one of his minders would pick me up and we would shop big time. Come Sunday, we would all tuck in to roasties, Yorkshire pudding and a big joint of roast beef, the whole deal. I did the cooking and Billy paid for it all. Once I tried to talk him into a leg of lamb, "No, Jackie. Your beef and Yorkshires are the best, and the apple pie and custard are the highlight of my week." Leftovers for Monday too. Billy Fury and

Jackie Trent

I became real soul mates. He told me how having rheumatic fever as a boy had left him with a heart murmur. Whenever Billy was enjoying himself, I would see his pallor suddenly change and his lips turn blue. I'd make him lay down for a while and I'd talk to him quietly, "You're good for me, Jackie," he would say, "You calm me down."

Obviously, he was far from healthy. The Billy Fury I knew was a beautiful person, very down to earth and not at all what the press made him out to be. He was adored by his many thousands of fans. We became like brother and sister. We were that close. Often on those weekends he would ask me to come into his room, just to stroke his head and talk to him. And each Tuesday there were always fresh flowers delivered to my dressing room at the theatre, with a card, "Thanks, Jackie. See you Sunday. Luv B."

Sunday nights I always stayed overnight at Billy's, in my own room. The inevitable question came up, "Are you two an item?" And I would think, *'If you only knew of my shambles of a marriage, my so called husband and my lump, now starting to kick inside me.'*

I kept fit by walking the promenade every day, apart from weekends when we had an afternoon matinee plus an evening show. Don't let anyone tell you that showbiz is glamorous! On Saturdays I would stoke up with a small pasta dish at the hotel, then be straight into the theatre for the day. It was OK for the guys, a bit of slap on the face and they were ready. I was the female star and the audience expected glam, so I had a two hour routine prepping my hair and face. As my pregnancy advanced, I slowly grew wearier. I checked in with the local clinic, "Miss Trent, you really should be taking it easier."

"Thanks, but I have to work as long as possible. It's the only income I have." I had to push this to the limit.

I had a meeting with Lonnie and Des. "I've been to the clinic," I said. "I'm fine to work." Lonnie was OK with that, but Des was more sceptical. Gilly was struggling with her pregnancy and needed a lot of rest. "No two women are the same, Des," I said. "Maybe I'm just lucky."

I was still wearing my usual dresses, but a girdle was on the horizon, to ease my back. The clinic said I was OK to use a girdle.

Baby might end up with a flattened nose,' I giggled to myself. They added, "By the way, you're three weeks more advanced." Damn. Three weeks less pay!

I bought baby clothes on the market in Yarmouth, including a load of terry towel nappies, all on the cheap. Mum, knowing I was pregnant, had gone into baby mode, crocheting for England. So far, so good. What could go wrong?

Everything, actually.

Disaster

I heard a fire engine race past the theatre, bells frantically ringing. I was sat in my dressing room, window wide open to let in a cooling breeze. The bells suddenly stopped close by. I thought no more of it until later that day, when a message arrived at the stage door, "Miss Trent, there's been an accident. Unfortunately your room caught fire. Would you like to review the damage between shows?"

For a fleeting moment, my world came crashing down. *'Kick back, girl!*

I sent a message back, "No, I'll face it after the second show. I don't want to be more stressed than I already am. As long as I have a bed for the night, I'll be fine."

After work that night, I had a real shock when I saw the damage. My room was completely blackened on one side, there was water damage everywhere and my everyday clothes and precious baby clothes were ruined. I'd carefully wrapped those baby clothes in tissue paper, dusting them with baby powder. Every day I'd picked them up, just to smell the aroma, imagining my baby wearing them. Now they were all ruined. "How did it happen?" I asked.

"The maid had been ironing in your room. By mistake, she left the iron plugged in, face down on the carpet when she left the room"

Thank God my stage clothes were safe and sound in my theatre dressing room. For the time being I did my daily washing at the theatre. I did my Sunday stint at Billy's. It was a relief from my nightmare. Come Monday, I had to shop and start again. I didn't dare look for baby clothes, just basics, that was all I could afford. The hotel owners were great. My food and lodgings cost me nothing from then on. My original room was gutted and redecorated, all within two weeks. Being back in my big room cheered me up no end. I tried to resurrect some of the baby clothes but it was impossible to remove the smell.

'OK Jackie, into the bin they go,' said I, out loud. I had to make myself do it. There were a few weepy moments as I threw those little things away. Then I started again. I visited second hand shops and bought quite a few baby things, in lovely condition, carefully washing them in Dreft pure soap flakes. With new ribbons, they looked as good as new. I had no husband, no financial support and soon a baby to care for. With my working future uncertain, I guarded every penny.

A helping hand

A supper was organised by the pros at my hotel, but I wasn't invited.

"Sorry Jackie, men only." I was a bit miffed.

The following day, Lonnie and Des gave me an envelope. They both seemed very emotional. I opened that envelope to find it full of money, around £2000. "All the pros have chipped in, Jackie. That's why you weren't invited last night."

Those wonderful professional entertainers had all stumped up to help me out. The hotel had chipped in with the food as apparently they'd done a roaring trade with wine sales. Lonnie had sent out invites to the dinner, so I asked for the list and wrote to everyone,

Being Me

thanking them personally. Showbiz is a tough trade, but those pros came through for me that night. Lonnie and Des were all smiles and I cried a lot. I was so overwhelmed.

Mid- August, height of the season, and Yarmouth was heaving with holidaymakers, but audiences were falling as good weather and light evenings kept people away. We entertainers prayed for rain, especially on Saturdays. The matinee crowds were shrinking by the minute. There would soon be more of us onstage than in the audience. And there was another factor of course. UK summer holidays for many were dictated by traditional factory closure holidays, when whole industrial towns would close for 'holiday week.' Changeover day was Saturday, when people would be on the move right across the country, so matinee attendance slumped dramatically. It's very difficult to maintain timing, especially in slapstick, with no audience reaction to play off.

It was also nearing my time. My stage dresses were becoming uncomfortably tight, so I knew my days were numbered. Lonnie gave me his dressing room for my final three weeks. No more climbing the stairs to my first floor dressing room. Lonnie and Des were relieved I was leaving. They had visions of me dropping my bundle onstage. We were all sad to part, but it gave them peace of mind. I hung on until my birthday, 6 September, and a final Sunday with Billy. We had a glorious lunch, with all his friends around us. Billy organised a driver to take me back to London and my in- laws. More tears, plus his final gift, a great big teddy bear, "Keep him close, Jackie."

Billy Fury really was one of the most beautiful people I ever met. We wrote for a while, but we would never meet again. He passed away on 28 January 1983.

Rest in peace, my lovely, adorable Billy Fury.

Chapter 16 - Birth and Betrayal

Back to Reality

In the car back to London I rehearsed meeting my in-laws again, with the possibility that my repulsive husband might be there. I didn't want a scene, but I was alone in the world. I had to front-up, as if everything was fine and dandy.

Len and Eileen Harvey were pleased to see me. "You look really well," said Eileen. I was nicely tanned, a deckchair on the beach, sunshine and a paddle in the sea had seen to that. I chatted about the season in Yarmouth, then went to bed exhausted. Later that evening I was woken by someone climbing into my bed, Drew Harvey! I leaped up and switched on the light. "Don't even think about it, you bastard. Just get out, now!"

"We'll talk about it tomorrow."

"Oh really! You can talk all you like. You should have thought of that months ago when you left me high and dry to cope on my own while you were screwing around. You're no husband and never will be. You're shallow and empty and a complete taker. I'm not supporting you any longer. Get out."

I felt better, telling him to get lost. Then I heard raised voices in the hall. His father was confronting him. I heard the front door open and close again. "Are you OK, girl?" asked Len.

"Yes I'm fine."

"Do you want a cuppa?"

Being Me

"That would be lovely."

I rose, still shaking, but he insisted I went back to bed, "Just try to relax." Easier said than done, with baby kicking like fury for the rest of the night, and the lingering "smell" of my so-called husband hanging in the air.

The following morning I felt as though I'd gone through a wringer and junior was kicking my rib cage to hell, obviously restless. I'd read that babies in the womb enjoy music. Mine had *lived* music, seven performances a week, onstage. So I sat at my now paid for piano and sang to myself as I played. Peace at last in the womb.

I had to address reality, so I told Len and Eileen, "Your son is gone from my life. He's no part of my future. I'll have to find my own place." They couldn't argue with that. I saw an ad in the local grocer's shop: "Flat for rent." I phoned the landlord and said, "I need a long-term rental."

"OK, go and see it. Number 78 Woodvale." That was just up the road from Eileen and Len! "Speak to Joan. She has the ground floor flat. I'll tell her to expect you."

Joan Podd showed me around the flat. It was perfect. "We've been here for fifteen years," she said. "The landlord's a real nice guy. Ring 'im, but offer ten shillings a week less than he's askin'." I did just that, offering three months' rent in advance, £66, for immediate occupation.

"Yes girl, that's fine," he said. "Get your name on the gas, electric and phone bills."

Oh my! My own phone at last. No more disinfecting public phone boxes! I felt part of the outside world. I could do business from my own home at last. Anyone who's had to run their business life from cold, smelly public telephone boxes will know how I felt right then. I spent the next couple of hours with Joan Podd. Over a cup of tea and biscuits I told her I was expecting shortly. She couldn't believe it. "You don' look it. Anyfing I can do to 'elp, I'm there for you." I'd seriously dropped on good neighbours and friends in Joan and Ted Podd. Maybe they would keep a lookout for Drew Harvey bothering me. I told her all about him. I'd given Len a key to my place to help out with DIY. It was possible their son might just "borrow" it.

Now I needed to set up house. I found a young American couple selling up and going back home. They had everything I needed: Westinghouse fridge, baby things, boxes of pots and pans, even a lovely Silver Cross pram and all for just £25. I struggled around the apartment, painting and decorating like mad. I was determined to have everything ready for baby and me.

Deliverance
Eve Taylor rang me, "I've got you signed up for a tour with the Shadows at very good money. I hope you give birth on time!"

"You can't order babies on time, Eve." She'd had no children apart from her adopted son. I knew I would have to work after giving birth. I tried a hot bath to maybe speed things along. That didn't help, but a lot of hard work around the flat did the trick.

One night, after a very hard day, I went into labour. "I've left my brushes in soak. Check them for me, love?" I shouted to Len as they wheeled me into the ambulance. I still hadn't moved in to the flat yet, what with all the paint fumes. Off to Kings College Hospital, Denmark Hill. I was well advanced, so they gave me a shot to slow me down and put me to sleep. Just before giving birth they cut me open. Apparently I kicked out at the theatre sister and she hit me straight back. I carried the bruise on my face for days.

It was 30 October 1962. I gave birth to a *13lb 12oz* baby boy! He looked three months old when he was born. My only visitors were Len and Eileen, "Sorry, Jackie but Drew's taken a booking for tonight. He won't be coming." They sent Mum and Dad a telegram, announcing the birth of their new grandson.

Drew turned up the following day with flowers. "Bugger off and stick your flowers where the sun doesn't shine. Your parents know how I feel. I'm moving into my own flat after I finish the next tour and you're not welcome."

Next day I was introduced to my brand new baby son. I decided to call him Darren. I was so weak, and he was so heavy, I could hardly hold him. I lay in my hospital bed for three days, sedated and very weak. My in-laws visited again, "Eve Taylor's phoned, asking how you are and will you be fit for the tour?"

I asked the hospital staff. They said, "You have to be here in ten days' time to have your stitches removed."

"But I'll be on the road then, in the north of England."

"Well, we'll not be responsible for you if you don't turn up."

Mother- in- law came to my rescue, "We'll look after little Darren while you're on tour, luv. He'll be safe with us. We've arranged for the health visitor to come along to make sure everything's OK." A whole week passed before the hospital would release me, then I had three precious days at home with baby Darren, Eileen and Len before I had to be back on the road. It was tough, fighting to recover my health. Even tougher, leaving my baby behind.

Back on the road again
On the Sunday morning, I treated myself to a cab into London, meeting up with the Shadows in Baker Street. We all started our road tours from Baker Street, opposite Baker Street tube station. The tour buses would be lined up by Madame Tussauds waxwork exhibition. That's what Gerry Rafferty's song "Baker Street" is all about.

Our coach was a really comfortable job, with a loo, light years away from travelling rough in that old VW van across Europe and Africa with the Twinkling Tappers. We had room to spread out, with me sat on my inflatable rubber ring to ease the pain, while the Shads constantly teased me. We were headed for the Liverpool Empire theatre. Lordy, that trip seemed to take forever. En route we had the radio blasting away. Somewhere near Northampton, we heard the Beatles announced for the first time, singing "Love Me Do". Hank Marvin said, "What a strange name for a group. That'll never catch on." We all agreed.

In Liverpool we stayed in top professional digs, quiet and hidden away. Had we booked into the Nelson Hotel, directly behind the Empire, the Shads would have been swamped with fans. Believe me, those girls got in by whatever means.

I woke next day, still feeling beat up from the trip, but more or less OK. I could move, but not freely enough to work the stage properly. My stitches had to go. I found the nearest Boots the Chemist and bought sharp pointed scissors, a magnifying mirror and a bottle of antiseptic. Don't read on if you're squeamish…

I stood over that mirror, took a deep breath, then somehow cut away those stitches, one by one, then put myself straight into a warm bath with lots of salt.

I never want to live through that surgical experience again. I never told anyone what I'd done.

On opening night, the noise out front was crazy, all from a theatre full of screaming girls, pleading for the Shads to come on. The audience was maybe 20 per cent boys, at most.

'Think fast, Trent. This is new territory. They're not here for you.'

I fell back on my old 'entertain the troops' tactic. Between numbers I'd shout, "Who loves Hank? Who loves Bruce? Who loves Brian? Calm down, they'll be on soon." If you can't beat 'em, join 'em.

It was my first performance in a pop show, but I did OK. I closed the first half of the show. The audience worked themselves nicely into a frenzy during the 20 minute interval, then the Shads walked onstage. It was bedlam out there. No one could possibly have heard them play. The theatre loudspeakers were just basic Vox amps, turned up to 10. The Shads closed, then we all did a runner for the stage door, almost as the curtains were falling, before the theatre started to empty. We were into our little bus and away. Every night, the poor stage door keeper was besieged by hundreds of screaming girls, banging and shouting at his door. Of course, 'Elvis had left the building.'

We were home, safe and sound, having a lovely supper in peace and quiet. "You did a good one, Trent," said the Shads, knowing they were really the main attraction. That made me a very happy girl. After supper, there was a call to Bible class. "Liquorice" Locking, who had replaced Jet Harris as bass player, was a devout Jehovah's Witness and tried to encourage us to attend. I went to a couple of meetings. Brian kept clear, but Hank eventually became a Jehovah's Witness.

Our tour of Stoll- Moss theatres took us right across the country: Liverpool, Manchester, Nottingham and Edinburgh, one week at each. But finally the tour was over and I could go home for a month to recover. I settled into my flat, enjoying the sheer pleasure of playing with my baby son. I told Eve, "No more work until I'm ready and don't put me on the road, just a few London clubs." I needed time to make adjustments, to change my life pattern.

Being Me

Recovery

I had to be on the road again to earn a living. I couldn't afford a nanny, so I decided to try an au pair to help look after my baby. *Lady* magazine had lots on offer. I phoned a few and invited one to come along to meet me. She had sound letters of reference which seemed OK, so I hired her. And I always had Joan downstairs and my in-laws along the road as back up to watch over little Darren.

Now I needed to be more mobile. I needed a driver, someone I could trust. My kid brother Les, back in Stoke, was into motors. He started out with a "pop-pop" motorcycle, as Dad called it. The drive chain tended to fly off the back sprocket. I knew Les had progressed to driving an old car and apparently, whenever he stopped, the doors would fly open. Les had left school. His first job was bread lad for Embrey's bakery, working for Harry Evans, Dad's ex workmate from the pit. But Dad insisted that Les took an apprenticeship, so he was currently an ironmonger's apprentice. Les and I were always really close, really good mates. It would be nice to have his company on the road and I'd be sharing my success with family. "Do you fancy working for me, Les?" I asked. "I can double your pay, all found, if you want to come down and work for me."

I made his day. "That's great. I'll hand in my notice right now." I bought a mini car from a local garage. It had had one owner and was in good nick. I gave Les a cosy job for life and a real life apprenticeship. And I had a friend by me to enjoy the good times.

Eve Taylor booked me some television spots on all the top shows: *Sunday Night at the London Palladium* with Mike and Bernie Winters and *Two of a Kind* with Morecambe and Wise were the top two. In the middle of a big song Eric's face would appear from behind the camera, leering at me. At times, he did everything he could to distract me or make me laugh. It was their show, so he could do almost anything he liked. We always had great fun together, Eric, Ernie and I, on and off stage.

Evie fixed my first recording contract, with Oriole Records. Everything was moving fast. She booked me up north so Les drove us to Manchester and Newcastle-on-Tyne to great nightclubs, working week about. Once there, we had no travelling during the week. I enjoyed every minute of it all, and Les kept me company. I phoned home every other day to check all was OK, but I couldn't wait to drive home to my baby.

The final shows were in Tyneside. I was so desperate to set off home that we loaded up the mini before the final show and then set off south, almost as the final curtain fell, driving through the night.

We arrived home in Woodvale around 4 a.m. As I entered the flat, I heard my baby screaming. He was stood in his cot, wet through from head to foot, his bottom seriously blistered and bleeding. I found the au pair asleep in her room. I hauled her out of bed, violently, and gave her until 6 a.m. to get out. Purely out of politeness, Les dropped her off at the nearest train station. We packed Darren, the cot and baby stuff in the mini and drove north again to my parents in the Potteries. They had the shock of their lives when we turned up at their door at 10 a.m. We had been continuously on the road for more than 10 hours.

"I *have* to work," I said. "We need the money. Les and I have to travel all week."

"Just give him to me." That was my Mum, coming to the rescue. For this to work, I had to give up possession of my baby son to my parents. But Mum and Dad loved having their grandson around them, "It's given us a new lease of life," she said later. Little sister Mally helped out too. She'd just started senior school, aged 12.

We rested up for two days and then made the painful trek south again, to London. We drove almost in silence, while I did a lot of soul searching. Back at my apartment, Les dismantled the Silver Cross pram and crammed it into the back of the little mini car. Then we had one more trip north with baby clothes. Lily's eyes lit up when she saw the pram. She couldn't wait to polish it. They'd never been able to afford a Silver Cross, but now she could proudly parade the shiny Silver Cross and grandson along the street. We bought a second-hand high chair that Dad rubbed down and varnished. Voila, brand new! Baby Darren quickly settled in, sleeping all night. "He's a real sober sides," said Dad.

Back in London, I threw myself into work at the nightclubs, three weeks on and one off, to be in Stoke. Meanwhile, Les learned to set up my stage sound and lighting. At home we set about the flat, Les painting while I made new curtains from material I bought on Peckham market. I replaced the furniture and fittings with smart secondhand gear and treated 6ft 2in Les to a double bed. No more feet dangling over the end of bed for him, and no more falling out of bed. Our final treat was a Rediffusion 20 inch rental TV. And then, after all the work was finished, I made cheese on toast for our little "topping out" party.

Chapter 17
1963 – Rome with Mussolini Jnr. London with The Beatles

I needed some home time with my baby. I asked Eve to book me into clubs in Manchester, Birmingham and Liverpool, if possible, so that I could commute from Stoke and spend time with baby and Mum and Dad. Club land up north was very strong. I played the Piccadilly Club in Manchester many times. The club was run by Joe Marlow. Joe had someone make a monogrammed suit bag for me to carry my stage costumes around. He was a Manchester City fan, even though Alex Ferguson, who later became manager of rival team Manchester United, was his friend. In 2003 Alex was at Joe's funeral in Manchester. I sang for the congregation. I also met Harry Goodwin at the Piccadilly Club.

Harry Goodwin
Harry gained fame as resident photographer for Top of The Pops. His photography portfolio included every major American and British star, other than Elvis, because they all appeared on TOTP. Harry became a close friend. "I never had formal training in photography Jackie. I learned my trade on RAF photo reconnaissance flights over Japanese occupied Burma during the war. I used RAF gear to take photos of local girls in Kuala Lumpur that I sold to my mates."

Back in Civvy Street, Harry found work in Manchester as a stage hand. His first celebrity shoot was of Ken Dodd, the famous comedian, also famous for stashing cash under his bed. Harry's big break came in late 1963, when Johnnie Stewart invited Harry to be the photographer for the fledgling TOTP. The show became an overnight success and moved to London. The six week trial ran on for Harry until 1973. By some accounts, Harry's photographic collection of the stars of pop, boxing and beauty queens amounted to some £7m and several of his photographs are in the National Portrait Gallery.

Like me, Harry never forgot his roots. His favourite dish was always fish and chips. Some of his final words were, "I want Jackie and Colin to write my biography." Too late! And what a story lost...

One night, Eve Taylor double booked me, saying, "You'll be at the Levenshulme club early on, with time to get back to the Piccadilly club."

"Oh really," was all I could say at the time. I would have plenty to say afterwards.

I turned up at the Levenshulme and changed into my stage dress. The compère said, "Stay in your dressing room till we call you. I don't know why they booked you here. It's a stag night and there's a lot of blue jokes out there right now."

So I stayed in the dressing room. I didn't even know what a stag night was. When I was called, I walked to side of stage and looked out at the audience. All men!

"I told you it was a stag night," said the compère, "Just do me twenty minutes." I thought *'Well, I'm here now, 'I might as well get paid.'* As I walked onto the stage, the compère warned the audience, "If I hear anyone shouting 'Ged 'em off,' I'll take her straight off stage." I went into a load of punchy numbers. It was a bit noisy out there at first, then they settled down. I won a standing ovation at the end of those awful 20 minutes. "I'm not doing that again!" I said to anyone who cared to listen as I stormed offstage.

Back at the Piccadilly, I told everyone what I'd just been through. "You should never have gone there," Joe said. "They have stag nights at the Levenshulme mid- week."

"But Eve's booked me for tomorrow night into the Devonshire club. Is that the same?"

"Yes, and you're not going there," said Joe very firmly.

Next morning, absolutely fuming, I phoned Eve Taylor, "There's no way I'm playing the Devonshire tonight. It'll be another stag night."

"But I've signed the contract. I didn't know it was a stag do."

"Well, you should check first. You go onstage if you like. I'm not." I stayed firmly put at the Piccadilly that night.

Some of the clubs up north could be pretty blunt in their approach. One night Alma Cogan was top of the bill at the Wakefield club in Yorkshire. In the 1950s, she was the highest earning female singer in the UK. Alma was renowned for her voluminous dresses and her giggling through a song. Right in the middle of a big number, she had a powerful voice, the Entertainment Secretary cut in on the PA: "t'pies 'av cum, best get 'em while they're 'ot!" Just like my first outing at Longport WMCIU in 1951.

One week, I was playing the Wookey Hollow, a big nightclub in Liverpool, travelling from home each night. I suddenly suffered the most awful pain and shouted, "Call an ambulance, and make it quick." When the ambulance turned up, Malcolm Reynolds, one of the ambulance men, recognised me. "You're Jackie Trent. Would you sign one of your photos for us?" he asked as he wheeled me out the door. I grabbed a photo, signed it "Thanks for the lift!" then off we went to the hospital, bells ringing and blue light flashing. I was in hospital for a while after my operation for appendicitis. The following week I was due to appear at a Birmingham club. Evie cancelled it. The club didn't believe I was laid up and sent a doctor to my home to make sure I'd really had an op! "Here, take a look at my nice new scar," I said. The doctor went away, satisfied.

When I was back on my feet, I phoned Eve Taylor. "I need you down here in London," she said. "You have to work the London clubs and keep a high profile in the south for radio and TV shows and record promo. I can pick up northern work for you anytime." She was right. I had to come to terms with my career. I had to admit, it was good being back in the London scene, in my flat. I was able to sit at my piano and work. I also bought a new cassette recorder that

Being Me

I could sing into. It was expensive, but worth every penny. Now I could record my voice with piano and be my own critic.

Educating Les

I recorded some of my songs in German, Spanish and Italian as I had lots of fans in Europe. Obviously I had a good audience in Italy, because Radiotelevisione Italiano (RAI) invited me over to a major TV gala in Rome. I took Les along for the experience. He'd been working for me for only a few weeks then. We were in good company, with Alain Delon, Bertice Reading, Alain Barriere and Al Martino, all of us having fun with a mixture of Showtime and soirees and all of us chattering away in our mother tongue, simultaneously!

That evening, our hotel was full of priests attending the Vatican Council. I met up with Les in the bar, half an hour late, to find him with a BA crew, who'd plied the silly bugger with a mixture of Sambuca and Coca- Cola. He giggled through dinner in the hotel, especially at our 4ft 6in waiter.

"Steak for him and a Dover sole for me. But first we'll have spaghetti Napolitano."

Les couldn't face the spaghetti, "It looks like worms."

Then his steak arrived. He cut into it, "I can't eat this. It's got blood coming out of it. It's not like Mum cooks."

"Look, lad, this is steak, not roast beef."

My fish was beautiful, so we swapped plates. He soaked the fish in vinegar, "It tastes funny."

"Of course it does, you've ruined it with vinegar. Use the slice of lemon next time. You can eat it now."

And then The Bluebell Girls found Les.

The Bluebell Girls

The fabled Bluebell Girls were in town. They of the impossibly long legs and legendary elegance, who normally graced the stage at the world famous Lido Variety Club at 78 Avenue des Champs Elysees in Paris. The tourist edict was, "When in Paris, first see the Eiffel Tower, then visit the Lido!"

That night, a group of the Girls took Les on the town. They thought he was fun. Apparently they poured red wine down him as they toured Rome. In St Peter's Square the Vatican police brought the happy party down to earth for making too much noise, "Il Papa is asleep." Next day, Les couldn't understand why he had a thumping headache. He'd never experienced red wine. His tipple at home had been a half of mild beer. I had no pity. I dragged him along to the TV studio, looking very grey faced and hopefully a little more worldly-wise, "Learn on your feet."

And my God, was I kept on my feet! At the TV studios by 6 a.m. for make- up and costume, then orchestra calls. It went on and on. So it was a welcome relief when we were invited out for dinner at a restaurant jazz club in Trastevere, in the old part of Rome.

Bartolomeo Patacca was the greatest swordsman in all of Rome. In 1683 he raised a band of mercenaries to save Vienna from siege by the Turks. As they were about to set off to do battle, word arrived that Vienna was saved. Patacca immediately spent the war funds on a celebration party.

In 1963 they were still celebrating as we walked into the restaurant in the Piazza dei Mercanti that was named after Patacca. I was introduced to a wild eyed, handsome American, Remington Olmsted. "Hi, ma'am. I'm Rem Olmsted. Welcome to my humble place." Before me stood a wild, long haired bohemian American football player, actor, singer, dancer. The very man who, in 1959, created this mad, happy place, where the chefs and waiters all joined in, singing along with the patrons and musicians. The food was fantastic, the music was out of this world and I was in seventh heaven. And as for the pianist, Romano…Could he play!

"Yeah, Jackie. That's Romano Mussolini, Benito's son, the Italian dictator!"

On the second night, I couldn't help myself. I got up and sang a few numbers, both jazz and blues. And Romano Mussolini was my pianist! Les and I were special guests for three nights at Da Méo Patacca. We were spoilt rotten. On the third night, shock, horror, Rem Olmsted's straggly long hair had gone. He'd had a haircut and he was even wearing a suit!

"Guess it's a bit tight? I ain't worn it in years," he admitted with a smile.

"That's fine," said I.

Les laughed, as a 17 year- old would do. Les laughed a lot. As that final evening came to an end, Rem Olmsted quietly presented me with a beautiful gold Rolex watch. He gave Les one too. God, I sure must have impressed him. The watch weighed a ton!

Beatles Night Out

My life in the 1960s changed dramatically. Eve Taylor saw to that. She taught me deportment, "Just do as I say." I totally believed in Eve. She said, "You're a star now, so act like one."

I often think of those early times in the swinging 60s. They were exciting times. One, long roller- coaster ride, working with now legendary names, all on the merry- go-round, madly promoting ourselves. There was a pecking order, and the Beatles always won preference. They were the group of the moment. One day Eve said, "Jackie, I've booked you for Mike and Bernie Winter's *Big Night Out*. You'll be working with the Beatles. It's a big one, but you'll need to wrap up warm. One scene will be on the Thames in an open boat." She was right. It was bloody cold and windy. After filming on that windy river, we all dashed from the boat back into the warmth of the studio.

In our early days, the Beatles had been just part of the music scene, one group among many. I'd cross paths with them sometimes,

Saturday Club, that sort of thing, at a time in their career when they were accessible, when most of us were just striving musicians. In the trade, the Beatles were known as "The Likely Lads from Liverpool". But Lennon was different, as if the others were below him, going off to sit in his 'sulking seat' if things didn't suit him. Personally, I found him condescending.

I had a great rapport with the other lads though. Ringo caught me holding a packet of cigarettes, "Got any ciggies to spare, Jackie?" I gave him the whole packet. Brian Epstein kept the lads on a tight budget, £25 a week, so they were often short of cash. I had discovered smoking as the in thing to do, a packet of 20 a fortnight. At the end of the week, just as we were finishing filming, Ringo slid up to me, "We've clubbed together & bought you these, Jack." He gave me a whole pack of Benson & Hedges Gold. I'd never seen a whole pack before.

The show was broadcast on the ITV network on 29 February 1963: the Beatles, Billy Dainty, Lionel Blair…and me. After the recording sessions, we all went to a party together. Alma Cogan was our host. Cary Grant was in town and Alma loved Cary, so she threw a party for him and the Beatles. Everyone was invited. "Jackie, you should have been there when that Entertainment Secretary shouted, "t' pies 'av cum ", there was a mad scramble. I almost stopped singing. I think I choked on a few words. What a place!" said Alma.

Another time, we all ended up at Eric Mason's Starlight Club. Eric was a close friend of the Kray brothers. He was throwing a party for the Dreamers, the boys who backed Freddie Garrity. Everyone seemed to be there: P.J. Proby, Ray Davies and the Kinks, an 18- year-old Elkie Brooks and Eric Burdon, who asked if a kid he'd brought along could do a spot onstage. His name? Steve Marriott, later to be a member of the Small Faces. As I said, everyone seemed to be there. We were all part of Soho club land.

Broad Meadows school group. Mrs Mills on the left. Me 2nd row, 6 in from the right. Photo courtesy The Sentinel.

Early Stardom for us All!

The Unnamed Society, Bignall End

North Staffordshire Coal Queen 1955

*Fun with the camera –
Courtesy the Sentinel*

North Staffordshire Coal Queen - Age 14

*Winston Rowley,
Under-manager, presenting my
Cola Queen award at Brymbo
Colliery. Courtesy Ken Rowley*

My USAFE band – great Mussos!

Onstage for USAFE – Having a Ball!

Alexandria in the 1950's, with the US Navy.
(One of them is tickling my back..!)

Cyrus 1950's with Jack, Master Diver and the Royal Navy dive team

Peter Herretts TR3, before I knocked down the traffic sign! Cyprus 1950's

With 'The Gypsies'

Entertaining British Troops - Aden - 1956

Early morning arrival in the desert for a Panarama TV programme, entertaining the troops

'The 2 o'Fus'

The Card

Alan A Freeman & Petula Clark - Variety Award

Oh Mi-Lord!

Wedding of the Year 1967, with Tony, Adam Faith & Jackie Irving

This Is Your Life and The Big Red Book, with Michael Aspel

Blackpool 1960

Germany 1961

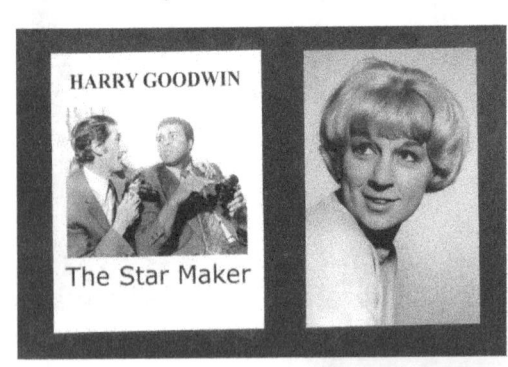

A postcard gift from Harry Goodwin – Top of the Popographers

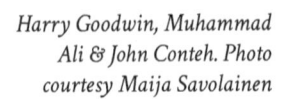

Harry Goodwin, Muhammad Ali & John Conteh. Photo courtesy Maija Savolainen

Mexico 1972

The Rock of Gibraltar, for a Gala Performance
Taking the sun with resident baboon

Cyprus 1959 – The Acropol Hotel Team
Sylvia on left, me, and redhead Gloria, with Muriel on camera

Happy times with South Wales Police, Canton, Cardiff, guesting at a Road Safety exhibition. Roger Duffy, 2nd from right, remained a friend for life

... and 40 yrs later

The photograph was taken outside the old Stoke City Victoria ground. Jackie was there to promote the song, I think she and Tony Hatch had co-written, 'We'll Be With You' which was adopted as the Stoke City anthem at that time (and is still sung from time to time at matches). It was taken in 1972 either just before or just after the 1972 League Cup Final at Wembley when Stoke City beat Chelsea to win the cup (the only trophy they've ever won). A large crowd had gathered outside the ground knowing that Jackie was inside and were hoping to get a glimpse of her. Jackie, being Jackie came outside and crowd surged forward and the photo was taken with me and another colleague trying to shield her - and I had my moment of fame!

PC Roger Owen centre. Courtesy the Sentinel newpaper

Turkey 1958 - With Mick the pianist    *The Windmill Theatre, London - Age 15*

Sister Sheila's salon, Tunstall for TOTP No 1 Session 1965

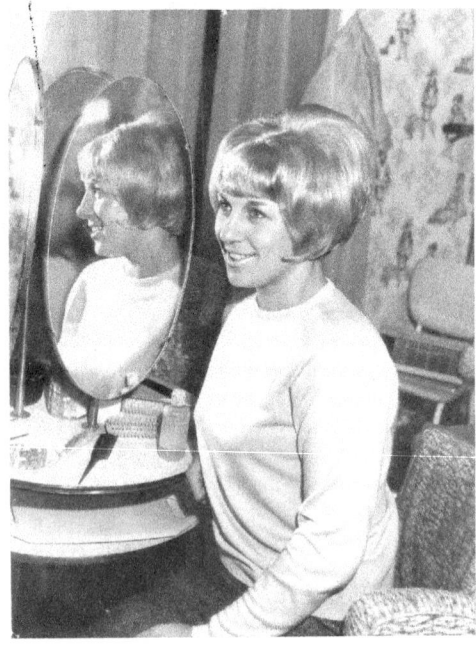

The Piccadilly Club, Manchester with Joe Marlowe

HRH The Duchess of Kent - Batley Variety Club

1965 - Pye Studios, signing my first album

Gifted Musicians – with Suzi Quatro & The Bee Gees

Suzi Quattro flattering me - Maurice Gibb nearby

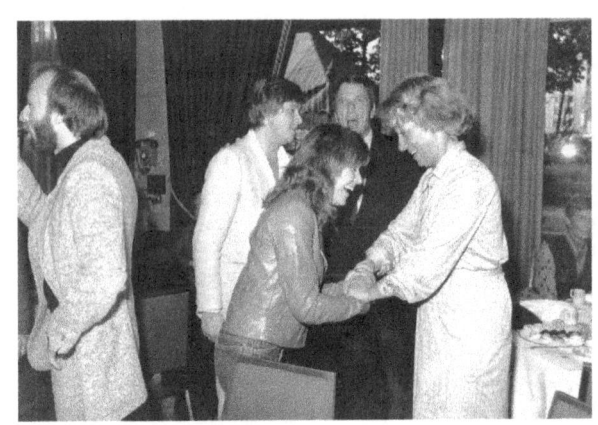

With my adorable Danny La Rue

Fronting Up, with Bea Arthur of 'Golden Girls'

Pet, Me & Maureen Arthur

2 Classic Gold Stars...

Australia Day Concert 1983 *Australia Day Concert 1983*

1995 – Australian Citizenship – a great honour.
Photo courtesy Margo Thatcher, my friend.

Carols at Xmas - Sydney

Cruising the Pacific, starring on the cruise ship Mahsuri – out of Sydney.

1989 – touring Australia with my 'Best Friend' Sammy Davis Jnr

*Neighbours Original magazine –
with Kylie Minogue and Jason Donovan*

Me at work in Australia

Capital Community Radio, Perth, W.A. 2013 with Oliver McNerney & Stella

The Indian Pacific trans-continental train - Sydney to Perth in 3 Days

With Sydney Police, New Year 2012-13. And one of them is a UK Brummie!

2013 - Back Home in Sydney, by the harbour bridge

A reunion at the Sentinel newspaper SoT, with Roger Owen, Pete Conway and John Pye

Me in Menorca

*My Favourite Oysters at my Favourite Menorcan restaurant,
Casa Sexto in Mahon*

*Wedding Day,
24 November 2005 in St Lucia,
West Indies*

Chapter 18
Soho Nightclubs and Tony Hatch

Soho

The name supposedly originated as a hunting call.

Soho in daylight was really quite stark. A land of greasy windows and peeling paint, with litter lining the gutters from last night's high class frivolities. But after 9 p.m., Soho was transformed and was suddenly alive with bright coloured lighting, the streets lined with bouncers and touts, all encouraging the punters to "Step in, step in for the time of your life."

But there was another Soho. The world of black tie clubs and supper clubs, where chauffeured limousines and London cabs swept up to the door, spilling out the rich and famous, and the infamous, to be greeted by a uniformed concierge in top hat. A warm greeting, a handsome tip, and the doors would swing open into another world of glamorous hostesses and deep pile carpets. The hostess was a main feature of most London clubs, all good looking, high class ladies on commission, sitting with clients and encouraging them to open their wallets. Of course, the hostess "would prefer champagne" to maximise commission. If whisky was ordered, the girls would be served cold tea. Commission and tips were the name of the game, which made 'toilet attendant' a sought after position. We all need the loo.

Being Me

I had become a regular top of the bill at the best clubs. Front of house, they were glorious and glamorous, many with glass stages and dance floors where the under lit stage would change colour to suit the mood of the music. Backstage was basic, very basic, but that's par for the course in show business.

'Nothing's changed there then, Jackie. It's not much different to that store/changing room at Longport Working Men's Club, back in '51.'

'Sure. It's all a bit of a giggle isn't it really, Vonnie? The punters just see us stepping out into a world of glamour every night. But at least we're earning a damn sight more than 30 bob a night, and we've seen the world.'

It's good to reflect on life sometimes, to keep a perspective on things.

I was always writing little songs to myself. As I walked through life, I took mental pictures of people, places and events, all to be linked in lyrics for the future. It seemed the most natural thing in the world to do. I was born with melody inside my constantly foot-tapping self. And I was simply blessed with the voice that I have. I had plenty of daytime for reflection and songwriting, at home in my flat in Woodvale, Forest Hill, near my in laws. But it was a busy life. Before Les worked for me, as evening approached, I'd have a quick clean up, pack my stage clothes, grab my battered leather music case and set off across London. I'd leave the flat around 7.30 p.m., armed with gown bag and music case, taking a London Transport bus to Peckham, then a No 12 to Victoria and finally the Tube to the club. I always made sure I was in my dressing room at least two hours before a show, to prep myself.

After work, the late night buses would bring a few of us club performers home. 'Hello Bar, how did the show go, tonight?"

"Ello darlin'. It went all right. An' you?"

Barbara Windsor and I sometimes shared the late night bus home. If I was working the Celebrity, Churchill's or Embassy clubs, Bar and I would often cross paths. Around that time she was working with Danny La Rue and Ronnie and Annie Corbett at Winston's Club. They followed Danny when he opened his own club Danny's, in Hanover Square. Danny's minder, Frank Kurylo, went along with him. That's how daily life was, then. No taxis, I couldn't afford taxis.

I usually arrived back home around 2 a.m. Life became a whole lot easier when Les joined me. It was nice to be driven to work.

Welcome to the club — 1963
I used the standard songs as openers, just like everyone else: "Everything's Coming Up Roses", "Got A Lot Of Living To Do", that sort of thing. Then one afternoon in my flat in Forest Hill, I thought, *'I can do better than this.' Why not write something original as my intro that will fit every club?* I put the basic chorus together in my head, then out came my notepad and the words and melody just flowed onto paper:

> *Every single generation wants to join the celebration*
> *To get out on the town, just to be seen.*
> *There are night spots for toffs and intellectual boffs*
> *With the most outrageous outfits to prove you've been.*
> *Just one picture in the paper that can make you or just break you*
> *Show a leg as you step out of the car*
> *It's your big chance now for fame and no one even knows your name*
> *And the man behind the camera doesn't care.*
> *You're a nobody, with a somebody that sadly has to make the news*
> *And it doesn't matter if they're the worse for wear*
> *Welcome to the Club*
> *All the night spots hit the high spots; the days of yesteryear have gone*
> *The style and the grace where every star was a face that everybody knew*
> *Welcome to the Club. Always welcome at the club.*
> *I miss you - yes, I still miss you all.*

The Duke of York Club was owned by an outrageous Russian lady and her clients really *were* the toffs and the Royals. Outrageous things sometimes happened too. One night in the Astor, as Eric Mason tells it in his memoirs, he met the former finance minister of a small African republic. The meet involved money laundering. The infamous Richardson firm (gang) were there too, sat around a table of 20. All hell let loose after a few bottles were smashed on heads. The clubs could be volatile places, but I myself never once saw any violence.

Being Me

'Welcome To The Club' worked well for me at clubs right across the UK. It was also my intro to Anthony Peter Hatch.

Tony Hatch

One evening in February 1963, I was working at the Astor. A message from Eve Taylor arrived backstage, "I'm here in the club. Join me at my table." So after my performance, I did. "Jackie, this is Tony Hatch. He's a producer at Pye Records."

I'd learned to assess men quickly. It was part of the survival package for single women in show business. This one was smartly dressed and, from his first words, I could see he was very cocksure. We shook hands. "Great performance, Jackie. By the way, who wrote your opening number? I've never heard it before."

"I did."

"Well, it's very good," said he. We all chatted awhile and I agreed to call in at Pye studios for an audition.

The following week I walked into Studio 1 control room at Pye Records. There was no reception area on the ground floor, "Hi! I'm here to audition." Ray Prickett, the sound engineer, took me down the steps into the recording booth, set me up with a mike and left me to it. I sang Kander and Ebb's song, 'Colouring Book' for the demo. (They wrote *Chicago*, by the way.) "That's great, Jackie," said Tony.

A few days later, Eve phoned me, "Pye want to sign you to a recording contract. I'll let you know when it's ready for signing."

In due course I called in at Eve's office, and there it was, a three year recording contract for Jackie Trent, three singles a year, with the possibility of an album. I signed up. A few weeks later I recorded my first single for Pye, 'Melancholy Me'. I hated the damn song. I still do, but that's what they wanted. A while later, Pye called me in to routine some stuff. Mum, Dad, Mally and little Darren were staying with Les and me at the time. "Come on," I said, "If Mally will look after Darren, Les can show you the sights of London while I'm working in studio." We pulled up outside ATV House between Marble Arch and the Edgware Road. Pye had the whole basement area of ATV House. Just then, Tony Hatch turned the corner, walking towards us. "That's Tony Hatch," I said, pointing him out.

"Is that him, then? He's a bit short. Not much to look at," said Mum. Dad couldn't comment as he couldn't see him, crammed in the back of the mini car. I left them to enjoy London while I did my stuff at Pye.

Later that week Les drove the family back home to Stoke. Mally was due back in school and Dad's pit holiday week had finished. Dad worried me. He was having breathing problems, paying the price for working down a coal mine for most of his life. I still had that secret wish to help him escape the damned pit. Would I be in time?

"Jackie, I've got this melody for a song. Do you want to write the lyrics?"

"Love to." And that's how it all began...

Tony Hatch is quoted in *This Is My Song*, Andrea Kon's unauthorised biography of Petula Clark, as saying, "Jackie had a gift for it. I got ravelled up." Whatever, we quickly became a successful songwriting team.

Tony and I wrote, 'Somewhere In The World' together, our first joint effort at songwriting. Pye put it out as the B- side to 'Melancholy Me', but 'Somewhere In The World' was a better production altogether. From the start, Tony and I developed a system. He would give me an acetate of the basic melody, with him la- la- la- ing. The very thought of it now makes me giggle! Then I would find a direction for the lyric, in reality often my own private thoughts:

I know there'll be a love, be a love
One love for me alone, me alone
And when he comes along, comes along
He'll be my very own, very own.
I would give all that I have, just to find him
Somewhere in the world, there's someone for me.

I found those lyrics in my "Blue Room" in Forest Hill. I created a writing mood, painting the ceiling of my apartment navy blue and hanging deep blue curtains. I always felt safe there in the semi- dark, away from traffic and people. I phoned the completed lyric to Tony's wife.

The following week we had a green light from Pye to record 'Somewhere In The World'. In studio we had a couple of run throughs for sound engineer and orchestra balance adjustments, then one take. I became known as 'One- Take Trent'. Why? Because the muso's and sound engineers were used to singers not being able to get it right with just one take. (One famous group had multiple takes of what would become a hit song. At one point the sound engineer, working with them through the night, became so tired that he accidentally deleted all the recorded tracks.)

Throughout 1963 and '64 I was mostly UK based. Les drove me to the gigs, then back to Stoke at weekends. Mum and Dad had become foster parents to little Darren. That was the best I could do. I had to keep working and earning what I could. For instance, I finished a show in London on Saturday 3rd August, then Les drove me down south to Bournemouth for two concerts at the Winter Gardens, matinee and evening. I was paid £30, before Evie's 20% management fee and her husband Maurice Press's 10% agent's fee, 30% in all. Sometimes it was a hard slog, but we were young.

Chapter 19 – A Few No 1's...

Where are you now?
I was invited to Pye Records' 1964 Christmas Party in London. There was lots of music, dancing and hilarity all round. Tony took me to one side and said, "Granada have asked me to write a feature song for their TV drama series, *It's Dark Outside*. The female lead will be seen playing a record of the song to herself. I've got a melody, but I'd like you to write the lyric and record the song. They want someone not too well known, who hasn't had a hit record. And we have a four day deadline." Tony sent me his melody acetate so back to the Blue Room. This time we had an exact script to fit. The female lead would play the song and the words had to fit the storyline and her memories of an absent lover, haunting and wistful:

When shadows of evening gently fall, the memory of you I still recall.
We walked in the rain, you kissed me, whispered my name.
Where are you now, my love? Where are you now, my love?

So the song wasn't even aimed at the charts. In fact Evie Taylor, my manager, tried to stop it being released as a single. She even threatened to take out a Court injunction to stop Pye releasing it! Why? Because Granada paid us nothing for the song, saying, "Consider the free publicity you'll enjoy." That was standard practice with TV companies. As with 'Somewhere In The World,' I called Tony's wife and simply dictated the lyric of 'Where Are You Now' to her over the phone. At the time, Tony and I worked independently, just as Bernie Taupin and my old mate Elton John did, a few years later. After that, Tony booked the big Pye No 1 recording studio, session musicians and the Breakaways, Vicki, Margot and Betty, as my backing group. They were the top session vocalists of the 60s and featured on a lot of my songs. We made that four day deadline. Job done. And Granada had their free background song.

After that I was due to fly out to South Africa on a three month tour. But it was Xmas and my parents had come down from Stoke to spend time with me in London before I flew off. While I was at the hairdressers, Tony turned up with a massive basket of flowering plants as a gift for me. An ominous sign, Mum and Dad thought.

Dad confronted Tony, "You can stop messing about with our daughter. You have to work together, but you're a married man. She can get over you."

So next day, Boxing Day, Tony wasn't there at Heathrow to see me off to South Africa, as agreed. I thought, "Bugger you, mate!" He'd broken a promise. "I'll show you."

I phoned Evie Taylor, "Tell the people in South Africa I'll be there tomorrow. I'm staying over at Heathrow tonight." I didn't contact Tony at all.

South Africa
Next day, surprise, surprise, Graham Hill, the handsome, mustachioed Formula One driver, sat next to me on the plane. I was surrounded

by his BRM racing team, all on their way to the South African Grand Prix, first race of the 1965 season. We were all travelling 'back of the bus.' "Graham always travels with us," the crew told me.

"So you're a singer?" said Graham.

"Yes, and a songwriter." I told him the story about 'Where Are You Now'. We agreed that the song title could fit both our lives, always on the move, never settled in one place. Besides chatting up the young blonde, Graham told me some of the realities of racing. The dangers, racing friends he'd lost and of his family and how he missed them when he was away. In Johannesburg we parted company, changing planes. The BRM team headed for Cape Town and me to Durban: to a bit of a shock. My backing group for the tour, Alain and the Stereos, couldn't read music! The promoter broke this news as we drove from the airport to my hotel. "But yu'l reerly liike them, Jaackiee!" in his rich Afrikaans accented drawl.

"We've practiced some of your songs, Jackie," said Alain de Woolf.

"We'll be good," chimed in the Stereos: Hymie, Manfred, Darryl and Paul. And they were, after we'd worked out a few routines together.

Then another shock. As I unpacked my case, giant cockroaches dived out of it. And boy, were they big! I stood on the bed, screaming down the phone for the manager. Later, onstage under glaring spotlights, I tried to keep a straight face singing, while massive cockroaches scurried across stage right in front of me. Durban really was 'cockroach alley'.

Adam Faith was top of our bill. He lasted five shows before doing a runner and beetling off back to the UK. He couldn't stand the cockroaches so I became top of the bill. As I fought cockroaches onstage, my new friend Graham Hill was busy on his stage, racing his BRM at the East London Race Circuit in Cape Province. He came third. Jim Clark won that day. It was also Jackie Stewart's debut Formula One race.

One day I took a stroll from my hotel. I sat at a bench on the street, nervously reading a sign 'Whites Only'. Then I saw a young African boy bowled over by a car that failed to stop. He was bleeding and looked to be unconscious, so I walked towards him. "Don't touch him!" shouted a voice from somewhere. "If anything goes wrong, you'll be held responsible." I was so shocked by the whole thing that I admit, I did walk away. I couldn't wait to leave Durban.

I was three months in South Africa, so I wrote a few letters to Tony Hatch at Pye Records. He was my recording manager and I was contracted to make further recordings, so I felt he should know what was happening on the tour. No reply whatsoever. Perhaps he was still smarting at being put in his place by Dad. Meanwhile the show moved on to Cape Town, a beautiful city. Peter and Gordon came out to replace Adam. Let's just say they were less than dynamic onstage. I once again became top of the bill.

Fun at 40,000 feet
The tour ended and I flew back to the UK with South African Airways. Mid-flight, the senior steward brought me a message, "The captain asks if you'd like to join him in the cockpit."

Why not? They sat me in the jump seat, right behind the captain and the steward brought me a glass of wine. "Good evening, captain. I'm Jackie."

"We know," he chuckled. "Have you flown in a 707 before?"

"No. It seems a lot noisier than the BOAC plane I flew down on. Why is that?"

"Because you'd have been in a rear-engined VC10."

I sat looking at the night sky and the stars, the mass of control dials, all dimly lit. Suddenly the radio crackled into life, another SA Airways plane, heading in our direction. The pilots exchanged greetings. Then our pilot, apparently SAA's senior pilot, announced, "I have a most beautiful blonde young lady here with me in the cockpit tonight."

"Sure. Pull the other one!"

"Jackie, say a few words to my fellow pilot, would you?"

I whispered my huskiest, "Hello boys" into the microphone as the two planes shot past each other at 1000 mph plus, headlights flashing…

Alain de Woolf later came over to the UK. I introduced him to Tom Jones and London club land. In 2013, he wrote to me recalling fond memories "and Tom forever flirting with you, Jackie".

Fun with Tom Jones

In March 1965 I was back working the theatre and club circuits while 'Where Are You Now' was going out onscreen, playing in the background of the TV series, *It's Dark Outside.*

One day Tom Jones's wife Linda phoned, "Jackie, they want Tom at a function to celebrate his first No 1. You know me, I'm not comfortable with those dos. Would you go along for me, with Tom and Gordon?"

"Sure Linda, I'll do that." I was good friends with Tom and Linda. Gordon Mills, a very Welsh man with black, curly hair, was a singer with the Viscounts and doubled as Tom's manager, both families sharing Gordon's flat in Holland Park. Gordon had discovered Tom in the Welsh valleys and brought him to London where we crossed paths.

After the function I careered around the streets of London with Tom, Gordon and Gina, a friend of mine, all madly shouting and waving to people from Gordon's knackered car, which seemed held together with rubber bands. We had a crazy time, crashing in on various bars and nightclubs, me in a jazzy number and Tom still in his stage gear, all of us looking a bit surreal. Now that was a night!

Eve Taylor called me, "Jackie, the BBC want you for a show in Germany, for the troops. It'll go out live. Then you'll be on *Two Way Family Favourites* with Jean Metcalfe at the London end."

"OK Eve. I'll do it." I liked entertaining the troops. They were always a good crowd.

Two Way Family Favourites

"The time in Britain is noon, in Germany it's 1 p.m., but home and away its time for Two Way Family Favourites."

Every Sunday for more than 30 years, up to 16 million people tuned in to the BBC Radio Light programme to hear that message, followed by the theme song, 'With a Song in My Heart.'

TWFF was a BBC national institution, succeeding the wartime *Forces Favourites*, where servicemen and women, mostly based in West Germany, could swap messages and greetings over the air with loved ones in UK. There was however to be no daring messages of passion to fiancées or girlfriends, and certainly no noisy jazz music. Oh no, Auntie Beeb wouldn't allow that sort of thing. Jean Metcalfe in London and Cliff Michelmore in Germany were the regular hosts. *TWFF* brought Metcalfe and Michelmore together. They married in 1950, but had to remain just platonic friends on air. Can you imagine all that happening now?

I flew out on a civilian flight direct to Hanover. The military collected me from the airport. I was to stay with the regimental commanding officer and his wife. The show was held in something like a big hangar and my band was the regimental brass band. My audience was the whole regiment, a tank regiment. The show went down well.

Tanks and trouble

I was on base for four days. A tank commander saw me looking at a line of fearsome looking battle tanks. "Would you like to drive one, Jackie?"

"Me? I don't even have a driving licence for a car."

But in no time I was kitted out in combat overalls and helmet and taken to a safe area. Safe for everyone else, that is; an open field. "Right, up you go!". I climbed up and slipped through the hatch into the steel hull. "Sit in the driver's seat, if you will, and we'll fire her up."

A horrendous noise erupted as the massive Leyland engine started up. It was impossible to speak without headphones and a mike. And there I was, crammed into a tight metal seat, with two massive clutch pedals at my feet, holding a joystick to steer by, peering through a narrow slit of a view. The regular driver watched over me as the commander gave directions from the turret. They were having a laugh at my expense, but we didn't hit anything. Years later, an ex- serviceman told me that local German people encouraged the military to knock a few things down so they could claim generous compensation from HM government.

There was a gala dinner on my last night. The C.O. said, "I've organised an escort for you," and a titled officer in full dress uniform and sword escorted me to the dinner. At table I sat in disgust, watching the childish antics of our brave elite, passing the port to the left whilst hurling flaming bread buns across table at each other. They used the table candelabra wicks to ignite the buns.

'Jackie, these are British officers? They're a disgrace to the uniform. US officers would put them to shame.'

'True, Vonnie. But it's nearly over.'

Not quite. On the way back to the C.O.'s house my escort pompously propositioned me. No, it was more like a command, "You're with me tonight, of course."

"Indeed I am not!"

"But you're in show business. Aren't you supposed to be loose girls?"

"Some might be, but I'm not. Take me back immediately or I'll report you to the C.O."

"What! You're not serious?"

"I'm very serious. You may be an officer but you're certainly no gentleman!"

Next day I quietly asked the C.O. to arrange another escort to drive me to the airport. I think he got the gist...

My first limo

I needed a bigger car. Les and I were travelling long distances, crisscrossing the UK to wherever Eve had booked me, then driving home to Stoke, late on Saturday night to spend Sunday with my little boy. After a hectic week of driving long distance, of lugging suitcases into hotel rooms, then two hours of make- up and the glaring spotlights onstage, the cheering audiences, the very late night suppers, come Sunday morning, I needed a break. It was just so precious to sit quietly on the floor at Mum and Dad's playing with little Darren and his toys. Those moments really made me realise what I was sacrificing for my career. But the constant bills, always waiting to be paid, soon brought me back to reality,

'Head up, Trent. Go do it!'

I needed a comfortable long distance car, big enough to carry my family as well as myself, so I part exchanged the mini car for a gorgeous midnight blue MkII Jaguar I saw in a Forest Hill car showroom. One night I was sat in the front passenger seat of my

Being Me

Jag, travelling overnight to Stoke after a show, when an approaching lorry flashed his headlights at us. Les didn't slow down. A broken down lorry suddenly appeared in our headlights. I shouted, "Look out, he's stopped!" Too late. Last minute, Les steered the car hard to the right, losing control. We slid broadside into the back of the lorry. My side took the full impact, flattening the car roof right above my head. The shock of the impact knocked me unconscious. As I slowly recovered, I could hear Les shouting, "Jack, Jack, are you alright?" My head cleared as Les exchanged details with the lorry driver.

The following week I was playing the Dolce Vita nightclub in Newcastle, run by David, Marcus and Norman Levey, a great club that drew international artists. "Been making an impression, Jackie?" they chorused, looking at the Jag. The car was repaired in Newcastle while I played the nightclub.

My No. 1 surprise!

In April 1965 I was at the Palace Theatre, Manchester. Eve Taylor phoned me at the stage door, "Are you sitting down? I think your record is going to be a hit. It's sold several thousand copies just this morning. Pye are in full swing and there are orders for it all over the country."

I did sit down. I was completely shocked! Viewers had written in to the *TV Times* asking where they could buy a copy of 'Where Are You Now'. The *TV Times* printed the letters and the rush was on. Pye Records quickly made a single of it and rushed supplies to shops across the country. Yet still no word, no contact from Tony, the very man who co- wrote 'WAYN'. I thought, "Bugger you, mate. If you want to be mardy* and unprofessional, get on with it!"

'WAYN' steadily climbed the charts while I was busy appearing at theatres all over the UK. Evie rang, "I've booked you for *Sunday Night at the London Palladium*. I'm having a special dress made for the show. You'll have to come in to London for fittings." Of course, I'd have to pay Evie back for the dress. So now Les and I had even more

---

* *Mardy is a northern English slang word meaning childish/sulking behaviour.*

travelling to do. Daytime driving to London from wherever, then back to the next provincial theatre for the evening show. They were long days, but hey, it was fun!

For the Palladium I chose to sing 'Let There Be Love' and of course 'WAYN'. I needed orchestral arrangements for the Jack Parnell Orchestra, but each time I called Tony's office I was fobbed off by his secretary, "He's busy in studio. I'll take a message that you rang." That went on for two weeks. Two weeks! What was going on? In frustration, I phoned Louis Benjamin, head of Pye Records, and said, "Tony won't return my phone calls. We need arrangements for the Palladium."

"Sorry, Jackie, I didn't realise he was ignoring you. I'll deal with it."

Next day Tony called. "Tony," I said, "Don't fob me off with your secretary. Grow up, you're the co- writer. We need orchestral arrangements for the Palladium." I told him the key and the arrangements I needed.

'WAYN' took the No. 1 spot from Roger Miller's 'King Of The Road', the Beatles' 'Ticket To Ride' had topped the charts for three weeks before that. I was in heady company indeed.

That week, the final week of my current tour, I was appearing at the Theatre Royal, Nottingham. Evie phoned. "You'll have to come down to London again, for a final fitting." At least we had the new M1 motorway to cruise down, direct from Notts to London and back. I was closing the first half of the show in Nottingham, so Les could drive me down to London, staying overnight at my flat in Forest Hill before the fitting, then back up the M1 to Nottingham next day. There were two shows per night, so I had to be back in my dressing room around 5 p.m. On the Saturday there were three shows, including the matinee, and after my final curtain went down, Les drove me straight over from Nottingham to Stoke where we collected Mum and Dad, then drove on to my flat in Forest Hill, arriving between 2 and 3 a.m. We all caught a few hours' sleep. At 11 a.m. Les drove me to the Palladium for camera, lighting and sound checks. We ran a full show. Then Tony turned up during band call with the song arrangements. "Nice to see you at last," I said, sarcastically...

Being Me

June Woodbridge turned up. She was my hairdresser. She recalls:

"My little bit of fame was once appearing in a Nescafé TV advert, otherwise I was a hairdresser. I did Evie Taylor's hair and Sandie Shaw's. Then Evie introduced me to Jackie. The main occasion that sticks in my mind was the amazing day I spent with Jackie backstage at the London Palladium in 1965.

Norman Vaughan was the compère that day. Also on the bill were the Bachelors, the Rockin' Berries and Hope and Keen, a comedy/juggling act. During the morning Jackie and I sat with Tony Hatch in the stalls and watched other acts rehearse. We all went out to lunch in Tony's dark blue Jag and found a small backstreet café. I recall Jackie saying to Tony, 'Whenever I ring your office I get told you are too busy to speak to me.' After lunch it was time for Jackie to get ready and I did her hair in her dressing room, backstage. Evie Taylor was there and it was a special time, one of exciting anticipation. I vividly remember standing in the wings with Norman Vaughan, watching with utter awe as she sang 'Where Are You Now' so beautifully. It was a wonderful and magical day that I have remembered with fondness for fifty years."

That evening Les drove my parents to the Palladium for the show. Mum and Dad went front of house while Les came to help me in the dressing room backstage. "Mum and Dad are really nervous," he said.

"No more than me, Les."

The London Palladium

Sunday Night at the London Palladium had been running on ATV since 1955, attracting every star performer across the globe onto its famous stage. I had a very nice dressing room, side of stage.

"Miss Trent, this is your half hour call."

"Come on Les, button me up."

"Miss Trent, this is your five minute call. Overture and beginners."

Someone came to fetch me to the wings. A final check of my hair and dress as I stood watching the compère doing his thing. Then, "Here's a lady who's reached the top of her tree this very week with her No. 1 hit 'Where Are You Now'. Will you welcome the lovely Miss Jackie Trent!"

The curtains were already open as I walked onstage and into those spotlights.

And that's what we all dream about, isn't it?

To be stood in the spotlights, in front of the TV cameras, about to sing to the world. I was honoured with closing the first half of the show, earning me extra applause as the curtains rang down. Wow, wow and triple wow. I was in heaven! I walked back to my dressing room with stars in my eyes, to find my errant husband, Harvey, already there. He'd blagged his way past the stage door by saying, "She's my wife."

"What the hell are you doing here?" I exploded. "Who let you in?"

"You were great. Congratulations on your record," he said, offering an armful of red roses.

"Well, you can get out, right now. You're no husband and no part of my life. And you can stick your roses up your backside!"

"No, no. We can make this marriage work."

I laughed in his face. The smell of fame and fortune had obviously attracted the little rat. Then, "Phone call for Miss Trent at the stage door," came over the tannoy. I left the room. It was Tony Hatch, "Congratulations. You were fantastic!"

"Thanks, Tony."

Being Me

Back at my dressing room, Harvey had gone. "Phone call for Miss Trent at the stage door." This time it was Eve Taylor. "You were absolutely - *pause* - "fabulous!" Praise indeed.

After the show, I met up with Mum, Dad and Les. They were all bubbling away as we drove back home to Mally and little Darren, who had watched me on TV. We had a pot of tea, Mum made cheese and onion sandwiches, and then we all went to bed. How about that for simple family values?

Footnote:

Hope and Keen who were on the bill at the Palladium that night. Well, their fathers were Max and Syd Harrison, The Twinkling Tappers, who shared that memorable trip to Morocco with me and the Singing Saw, years ago...

Chapter 20
1965 - Indecent Proposal

The Isle of Man

I slowly came out of the clouds from being No 1. Evie Taylor had me booked to work with Val Doonican, first a theatre tour of UK, then the summer season in the Isle of Man. She managed us both at the time. "How about some more money, Evie? I've just had a No 1."

"Can't do, Jackie. I really don't want to go back and ask the producer for more money." Val later told me that Eve Taylor *was* the producer.

Les and I took the Jaguar over to the Isle of Man by ferry and I rented us a two bedroom apartment in Douglas for the summer, near the Palace Theatre. We had a powerful cast lined up for the show: Val Doonican, who was very easygoing and nice to work with, as headliner, me as second top billing, Des Lane, 'The Penny Whistle Man' and the Jones Boys. There was also Les Dawson, who had his wife and young baby over with him. Les was being paid just £40 a week so he was always short of cash. I often treated them to fish and chips on a Friday night. Pete Brady, the Radio Caroline DJ, was compère, always with a gin and tonic in hand, offstage. I was riding the crest of a wave. I had my No. 1 hit and I was second billing in the summer show. I was a star at last!

There was life offstage as well. Another star, Geoff Duke, the motorcycle racing world champion, made a point of saying hello. The

Being Me

world famous TT Races were held that June. First Graham Hill, then Geoff Duke, both No 1's in their own worlds. Both would be awarded OBEs, and I met them both in 1965. There were parties galore that season. Someone even drove me round the TT circuit, all 37 ¾ miles of it!

Les's friend, Pete Sidoneo came over to join us for two weeks holiday and stayed for the whole summer. Les was assistant stage manager at the Palace and found him work in the flies. "But I don't like heights," Pete said. Working in the flies meant being way up in the roof of the theatre, lifting backdrops and stage gear on and off stage during the performance. Pete coped pretty well. He liked being around the theatre so we let him stay with us in our flat. Audiences probably never realise the hidden, real life humour and drama played out in the wings.

One day Tony Hatch phoned me from London. "Hi, Jackie. We need a follow up to 'Where Are You Now', something in the same vein with the la- la- la's, something haunting. I've got a melody worked out. I'll send it over. By the way, I miss you."

"Miss you too, luv."

'Oh dear, what are you doing, Trent?'

Tony sent over the melody for 'When the Summertime is Over' on an acetate. Then another acetate arrived with the melody for a bright tune and the working title 'Love is Me, Love is You'. I wrote a happy, bouncy lyric to fit Tony's melody and my life at the time:

Come on baby let's tell all the people we found a way to end the blues
Let's get together and just start a rumour that everyone will think is news.
Love is warm, love is fine, love is yours, love is mine.
Love is free, love is true, love is me, love is you.

In a way, I suppose I was subconsciously writing Tony Hatch into my life. I posted my bright lyric to Pye Records over on the mainland. After that, Tony flew over to run through a few song routines with me for a new album to be recorded in the autumn. "I don't really want to stay in a hotel," he said. "Can I stay with you?" He shared my bed for the night. After that, Tony suddenly became more accessible by phone at Pye. He even phoned me a couple of times every week. Is that how it works?

Jackie Trent

Summer season on the Isle of Man came to an end. Back in London I called in at Pye studios and recorded my new album, *The Magic of Jackie Trent*, before flying out to Israel for a month's cabaret at the Hilton Hotel, Tel Aviv. Eve Taylor called me in Israel with a message, "Jackie, will you buy a bale of cloth for Tito Burns while you're there?" I had met Tito Burns in Germany when he and his wife had an accordion act. He always wanted to be an agent, and was fond of saying, "I will always treat my acts with respect." He had since become a booking agent. I didn't really like the man, and his reputation as a managing agent wasn't the greatest, but I said OK.

I was contracted to sing for the Ladies' tea afternoons every Thursday. I hated singing for so many overdressed, pretentious women who obviously were there just to *talk*. I felt like an accessory to their trinkets. I learned to hate Thursdays. Give me the troops in the desert anytime!

The two of us

A telegram from Tony arrived, "I want to leave my wife for you. I've told Jean. Letter following."

What the hell? This came completely out of the blue. I was shocked. I had not led him on at all. After that, he wrote to me twice a week. What to do? What to think? I knew I was falling in love with him, but could I trust him?

'Jackie, why do you do these things? We don't need this. Remember 'the fish in the sea'?

'Yes, Yvonne, but I love him. Really I do. With our love and our music, what can go wrong?'

PART 2

Chapter 21
New Life, New Music

A New Life

My contract in Tel Aviv finally came to an end, no more 'ladies tea afternoons.' *'Whoopee!'* But what next? I was 25 years old. I'd been semi- professional, singing on stage from age 11. For the past 9 years I'd sang and travelled my way across Europe, the Middle East and Africa. I liked that independent way of life. I could do what I like, go where I like. It was me. Yes, I had my little boy back home, from a marriage that never happened. So I had to think of him too.

The problem was men! Twice I'd let a man into my life and twice I'd been screwed up. I really didn't want it to happen a third time. I held that telegram from Tony Hatch in my hand, "I love you. I want to leave my wife for you. I've told Jean."

Almost without trying, we'd written my No 1 song together, so maybe I'd found my musical soulmate in Tony Hatch? I loved music. It was my life. I was a born entertainer. And he'd slipped sideways into my life, and my bed, in the Isle of Man, just months before. Maybe I'd found the right man at last? Back home, how would I deal with Tony's advances? Could I trust him? How would I fit in his future plans? How would he fit into mine? Staring out of the 'plane window, I checked in with my conscience: *'I'm free as a bird, OK? I can go wherever I want.'*

'Oh really! And what about roughing it across Europe on trains and in VW vans. What about the whorehouse in Famagusta and the topless ballet? Be honest, you don't always make the right choices in life, including men!'

'Yes Vonnie. But Tony loves me. We write great music together. Surely, this time will be right?'

My mind was spinning as the 'plane flew westward, back to UK. Suddenly I was back in reality and to dear old Les at Heathrow airport.

"Hi Jackie. Nice to have you back home. Did you have a good flight? And what's this bale of cloth? Going into the hosiery trade, are you?"

"No Les, it's for Tito Burns. Maybe he'll have Dougie Millings make him a suit."

Tito Burns was born Nathan Bernstein. Better known as Cliff Richard's manager, he set a new style, dressing Cliff in jazzy stage costumes tailored by Dougie Millings. The Kinks, The Stones, The Beatles, Tom Jones, they all 'followed suit'. And boy was his shop in the right place, right by the stage door to the London Palladium. Dougie must have made a fortune!

Les drove me home to my apartment in Wood Vale. Tony turned up next day and was all over me. "Hello Jackie, welcome home. I've been so desperate to have you back." He gave me a big hug and a massive bouquet of flowers.

"Look, I've already moved out from home. I'm staying at a hotel near the studio. The future is ours, but some American artists are over here, so I've taken on extra sessions. I'm really busy."

We embraced, whilst Tony eagerly talked of our future plans together. One thing led to another and Tony stayed over that night. So the decision was kind of made for me. Love and music all the way...

Next day it was back to business, and Evie Taylor. She called me, "I've signed you up for lots of bookings in London and the provinces." Well she would of course as she took 30% of my earnings, even 30% of my songwriting royalties. Yes, Evie Taylor owned 30% of *me*! The success of 'Where Are You Now' suddenly made me realise the significance of the small print in my contract. Big money was involved here.

But for now I had to be back on the road with Les. Now and then we called in at Pye's London studios to finish off my first album, 'The Magic of Jackie Trent.' Everything was looking good. Tito Burns returned the favour for his bale of cloth by telling porkies behind my back. He told Eve Taylor I'd had an affair with the hotel band leader in Tel Aviv!

"But that's just not true, Eve. I was covering for someone else. The band leader fell in love with the Swiss ambassador's daughter. Daddy disapproved, so they had to meet in secret. I helped out by making a show of leaving the hotel with him, then disappearing so they could be together. What a load of nonsense! And Tito Burns didn't have the decency to ask me about it. I hope that bale of cloth chokes him!"

Tony found us an apartment to rent in a brand new block, just built, on the Edgware Road, off Marble Arch which was very handy for Pye studios, just a few hundred yards away.

"Jackie, come and look at this apartment I've found for us."

Les drove me over there. The apartment looked fine.

"Will you move in with me? I want to spend the rest of my life with you, Jackie."

"Look Tone, I've been let down twice already. I don't want a third time. That means more women behind my back."

"I'll never let you down, Jackie."

"OK, if that's what you want, Tony. I do love you. Listen, we'll fit this place out great! I can afford it." And I could. At this point in our careers I was very much the principal breadwinner. I toured constantly. One week I even commuted from London to Cardiff every day, to spend as much time at home as possible. A good engagement in 1965/66 would earn me between £700 and £1000 a week, a very large income in the mid- 60's, plus my royalty earnings on top. Wowee!

Dress Code
Tony was still a back room boy. He started accompanying me to functions, but his dress style was really old fashioned, "Can't have that Tone. You're with me now." I threw out a lot of his stuffy cardigans and suits and had Dougie Millings bring Tony up to date with new gear. He got to like his new image. I set to, choosing furniture and fittings for our new home together in the Water Gardens. Tony was too busy for that, working long hours at Pye. When I'd finished, the apartment looked fab. I kept my Wood Vale apartment for Les to use.

This Is My Song
In 1983, Andrea Kon published her 'unauthorised' biography of Petula Clark's life: 'This Is My Song.' She interviewed Tony Hatch and Pet Clark for the book, but not me. She wrote:

'[In 1965 Jackie and Tony] had decided to take up 'a trial residence' together. Tony was unsure about marrying again after his disastrous marriage to Jean.'

'Claude's [Pet Clark's husband] reaction was predictable,' [Tony] says. 'He told me he knew something would happen the moment I had success.'(pages 168/9)

The cheek of it! I'd been earning far more than Tony - for years!

I bought a copy of that book when it came out in 1983. I could hardly believe what I was reading. *I* was the established stage star, *I* was financially independent and Tony Hatch was chasing *me* in 1965. My goodness, was he chasing me...

And by his own admission to me, Tony's 'disastrous marriage' was entirely of his own making. Looking back now to the 60's, I wonder if Claude and Pet were being given a false impression of me behind my back.

'My Love' – US No 1 Hit
We finished furnishing the flat. Just two weeks later, around November 4th 1965, Tony flew out to America for a recording session with Pet. He took with him a new song we'd written together: 'Life And Soul Of The Party', a bright and breezy song, to follow up Pet's success with 'Downtown.' High up over the Atlantic, a fellow passenger on the 'plane, an American, put doubts in Tony's mind about the song. "We Americans understand 'Life of the Party' and 'Soul of the Party,' but not 'Life and Soul of the Party. It's un-American." Apparently Tony moved to another seat to think again.

He landed in NY with a basic new melody and a working title. At his hotel he excused himself, retired to his suite and called me urgently, in London, "We've got a problem here with 'Life & Soul.' I've written another song melody on the 'plane, 'My Love', but no lyric."

He la la'd the melody down the 'phone to me and I la la'd it into a tape recorder. New York was 5 hours behind UK, so I had a few hours in hand before Tony had to produce the finished song to Petula, next day. I worked through the night, writing about the joy of love, of how I saw love, what it meant to me right then:

My Love is brighter that the brightest sunshine
Softer than a sigh

Tired, but content, I dictated my lyric over the 'phone to Tony in his NY suite, just in time for his morning appointment with Petula.

The whole song was very bright, but low key. Amazingly enough, Pet wasn't crazy about the finished job. She didn't think it strong enough to be a hit, but the session was booked and the recording went ahead. 'My Love' was finally released and went straight to No 1 in the US charts. Incidentally, Pet did finally record 'Life And Soul Of The Party.' I confess, I've never really liked the song.

My Avaricious 'Husband'
Within days of Tony leaving for NY, almost like magic, black magic in his case, Drew Harvey turned up at my door. He'd obviously heard that Tony was away. Drew and I hadn't crossed paths since he gatecrashed the Palladium on my No 1 night. I was really shocked to see him again. "What are you doing here?" Foolishly, I let him in.

"How did you find me?" He'd obviously found my forwarding address from his Mum and Dad.

"What a lovely place you have."

"Yes we do, Tony and I." I made the point of including Tony. "I'm having a cup of tea. Would you like one?"

It was a very strained meeting. Drew had a good look around the place. He was obviously there to find out how well I was doing. I told him very little, but he obviously smelled 'money.' As soon as I could, I showed Drew Harvey the door.

Would you believe, shortly afterwards a letter from Drew's solicitors arrived on our doorstep, giving notice of a court action against Tony, seeking £100,000 for 'enticing' me away from him? Pardon me, Drew Harvey had kept a long distance from me, almost since we'd married. And he intended issuing divorce proceedings against *me* for adultery!

'Lordy, Lordy. What sort of world does that man live in?'
'What man, Jackie? Take no notice.'
'You're right, Vonnie. Stuff him.'

Tony arrived back home from America. I told him, "Drew Harvey turned up at my door. He's threatening to sue you for enticing me away from him. He wants £100,000."

"Jackie, he must be joking. He's in the wrong, not you."

Right then, Tony was my hero. He knew all the sordid details of how Drew Harvey had treated me. We were both really upset by the injustice of it all.

"We'll fight this together, Jackie."

A few days later, I just happened to call in at Darnells on Bond Street for a dress fitting.

Douglas Darnell and his partner Eric Plant were world famous couturiers to Marlene Dietrich, Joan Collins, Zsa Zsa Gabor, Dusty Springfield, my close friends Di Dors and Dot Squires, and me, of course! Over the years, Douglas would make many show dresses for me. It wouldn't do to be seen on stage in the same dress too often. Stage dresses were always a big expense for me. I believed the public needed to see us look the part, up there on show.

I once bought an ex- Shirley Bassey dress from Darnells, "Jackie, this outfit of Shirley's is just right for you, only used once." Douglas simply had to remove the hip pads for it to fit me perfectly. Sometimes we worked so hard onstage that, after just one performance, the dress would be soaked in sweat as the body salt ruined a dress.

Douglas finished his work, measuring me up for a new dress. "Oh! Your ex- husband and his fiancée were here, shopping. He bought her expensive items - around £2,000." £2,000 at the time was close to *double* the annual wage of a coal miner. Drew Harvey was obviously out to make a big impression.

"Fiancée indeed! Right, I'll play detective on this one."

I asked to see the shop receipt, which just happened to list her address and 'phone number. I wrote the details in my ever ready notebook. "Fiancée, eh!"

I tracked Drew down at his parents' flat. "Persist with this and I'll go see your new *Yvonne* and her parents. I'm sure they wouldn't want to hear the truth about you."

Yes, he'd found another Yvonne. Then *I* started divorce proceedings against Drew Harvey.

Now it was time to help my parents. My singing and songwriting success was bringing in the cash I needed to help Dad escape the pit. I had Les drive me up to Stoke.

"Dad, I want you to stop working. I want you out of that pit. Would you do that for me? I want you and Mum to move down south to be near me. I can afford to give you both an allowance. I really want to do this."

He sat quietly in his chair and said nothing, but I could see tears in his eyes. Dad was still in his early 50's, but already he was having breathing problems from all those years down the pit. "Only if Lil and I can help out in any way down there, for you and Tony."

Dad was true to his word. They settled in to my apartment in Wood Vale and redecorated the place throughout. With Les, they hung 18 rolls of wallpaper in the huge hall alone. Mum was a dab hand at wallpapering. Then they set to at Tony's ex- marital home. As part of their divorce settlement, Tony and I bought his wife Jean a new home and we raised a mortgage against my earnings. The marital home was by the river in Hampton Court. It was up for sale, asking price £13,000, but there'd been no offers.

Mum took one look inside, "This'll take some scrubbing out."

"Well, Tony's always so busy, Mum. He almost lives at Pye studios."

Mum, Dad and Les redecorated the house, in and out. When they'd finished, the house sold within a week, for £18,000.

"Dad, you've all done so well, Tony and I want to pay you for your work."

"No, you're giving us enough already." Dad was still Dad.

Petula Clark
Tony took a call from Claude Wolff in Switzerland. It was Christmas time. Afterwards, Tony said, "Claude needs new material for Pet, Jackie. He's invited us over to spend a few days with them."

"That's great Tone. It's time I met Pet."

We arrived late at night, tired and hungry. Pet and Claude had apparently already eaten, then gone on to a disco bar in town. I was excited to meet Pet, so we passed on eating and went straight over. I spotted her right away. She looked at us, then turned away. Oh dear! I had bad premonitions. We sat and waited…

Finally I prodded Tony into going over to Claude. Almost reluctantly, they invited me to join them. It was clear we were hardly welcome in their party set. Or was it just me? Over the next three days I tried my best to befriend Petula Clark, but she truly acted like a cold fish and put a barrier of almost silence around her, as far as I was concerned. It got worse, a whole lot worse. On the second night we all four sat together, to eat. Tony told Pet of an idea he had for a medley for a forthcoming show at the London Palladium.

I said, "Pet, it's a great idea. It really would work well."

I was horrified when the lady went white- faced and stood up, with anger I assume, then stormed off, totally ungracious. I was close to crying. Tony later met Miss Clark. He came back with the verdict, "It's either me alone, or not me at all."

Looking back, I can only think that I posed a serious professional threat to Petula Clark. After that I tried once more to speak with her, but then gave it up as a bad job. *'Live with it, Pet,'* were my private thoughts at the time.

I won in a way. Unknown to her, Petula Clark was belting out *my* lyrics to her hit songs. Tony had persuaded me, reluctantly, not to reveal that I was writing the lyrics for her songs. For the time being...

And Claude Wolff rather let himself down. In 'This Is My Song,' Claude is quoted as saying, "I find Jackie Trent rather vulgar and uninteresting." Fair comment, we're all entitled to our opinion. He then went on, "I felt that a person like that couldn't write good songs. Pet had nothing in common with Jackie (how very true, sir!). I was afraid that if she was going to write all the lyrics, they weren't going to be terribly good."

I wonder, even now, from where Claude and Petula drew their conclusions about me. We hardly knew each other. We were almost strangers in the night. Only Tony had direct contact with Petula Clark and Claude Wolff. Andrea Kon wrote *about* me but she never *contacted* me for her book and Tony never spoke up for me when the book was published in 1983. And where was the biographer's professionalism, slandering me without even speaking with me? I strongly suspect she was told not to interview me.

In all, Tony and I would co- write 22 hit songs for Petula Clark and some 400 songs together in total. So I didn't do such a bad job, did I, Claude? At Petula's invitation I would even later write the lyrics for several joint Clark/Trent songs.

Tony Comes Good

I remember when Tony came good with his sensational hit 'Downtown.' He was finally matching my earnings and it came as a big shock to him. I remember, he'd just brought me a cup of tea in bed, then he opened the mail. I saw his face go white.

"This can't be right, there's too many noughts." He was holding up a Performing Rights Society royalty statement. Tony 'phoned PRS right away, "You've made a mistake, there's too many '0's' in my cheque - £55,000." There was no mistake. Today - 2014 – including my earnings, that would equate to around £20m between us in a year. The national average wage in the UK at the time was around £1,250 per annum.

Chapter 22
Lyrics and Leisure

A Few Good Songs - The Golden Years

People have often asked me, "Why didn't you record the Pet Clark songs yourself, instead of giving them to her?"

My answer has always been, "Well, Pet was hot property at the time and, putting it crudely, she was the best horse to back with some of our songs." And, of course, some were written to order, specifically for her voice. The exception being, 'I Couldn't Live Without Your Love'. That one was written for me. I probably gave away a hit song there. Of course, the first of Pet's hits that we co- wrote was 'I Know A Place.'

Once Tony and I we were living under the same roof, song creation became the fabric of our relationship. Tony would constantly 'play around' with musical phrases and melodies. Once he'd planned the bones of a new melody, he would invariably play it to me, principally to ensure that he had not inadvertently borrowed it from another composer. I have a very retentive memory for music and lyrics. Once the melody was firmly in his mind, I would put on my 'singers hat' and help him take the melody in the right direction for the type of voice he was writing for. This was important. We never wrote speculatively, but always for specific singers. Although Tony can sing, (our stage show together has included various duets), he is not a natural singer. The kind of practical changes I suggested to a lot of the compositions would not have come naturally to him. Once the music was complete, I would then write the lyrics.

At the time, we didn't work together on stage. We wrote songs together, but that was it. For stage work I had my own pianist- cum- musical director. Besides, we had plenty to do and were usually on a deadline. An example is, 'Sign Of The Times,' which we wrote as a follow- up to Pet Clark's US No 1 Billboard hit, 'My Love.' Although 'My Love' had reached No 1 in the States, we knew that Pet wasn't particularly happy with the song. We needed something bright and breezy, more along the lines of 'Downtown' and 'I Know A Place.' I found the inspiration for 'Sign of The Times' from everyday sayings, 'Do you know, butters gone up by thruppence?'

'Well... it's a sign of the times...'
It's a sign of the times
That your love for me is getting so much stronger
It's a sign of the times And I know that I won't have to wait much longer

Once we'd focused on a subject matter, we wrote the song in about a day. And always, Pet seemed to need the new song 'now!' That's probably good chemistry. It's certainly a great motivator and we always came up with the goods. But I never went to any of Pet's recording sessions. I was the outsider, not included in anything, not even by Tony who, looking back, never gave me the support to feel like a human being. And emotion was ever me.

I wrote the lyric for 'If You Ever Leave Me,' whilst I was going through the trauma of divorce. My head was spinning, but I was in love, committed to this new man in my life. While Tony was busy in studio, I sat in our brand new home and simply poured my heart into the emotions of the moment:

If you ever leave me, I won't show the tears
If you ever leave me, I'll hide all my fears

Tony set the piece to a beautiful, haunting 'gypsy' melody. That's what we call the orchestra string section: gypsies. Before I'd even stepped into Pye No 1 recording studio, I knew this would have to be a 'one take' session. My eyes were streaming with tears after that recording. Yes, 'One- take Trent' again. I recall Pat Halling, the fab New Zealander violinist, together with all his 'gypsies', pouring into the control room after that recording to listen to the playback, along with Tony Hatch & Ray Prickett, our sound engineer. Ray always had a studio tan, white as a sheet! We'd nailed it, of course. The rest of the orchestra had cleared off to the pub.

I think one of my best recordings ever was 'There Goes My Love, There Goes My Life.' My lyric was probably the most challenging lyric I ever wrote. It had to fit the dynamics of a very French song. I made no attempt to translate the original lyric and simply followed the emotion of the song itself, which was very, very powerful. Tony came up with a blinder of an arrangement, 'busying itself' around my voice with an electrifying intro, like a bush telegraph, urgently tapping away:

Tap, tap, tap, tap... Tap, tap, tap, tap...
How could you forget the taste of love, when I can still remember
All the words we said are wasted, now it's just a dying ember
Every thought we shared together, disappeared without a warning
As the book is closed forever, so the truth is slowly dawning
There goes my love; there goes my life

I *lived* that recording session, with the orchestra playing live in my ears through the cans (headphones). It was probably one of my best recording works ever. That's certainly how I felt as I finally stepped out of the recording booth, exhausted and weeping. I could write lyrics anywhere. I wrote 'I Couldn't Live Without Your Love' on my ever present notepad, travelling somewhere in the back of the car. 'I Couldn't Live Without Your Love' was a statement of how I felt about my growing relationship with Tony:

'Didn't like you much when I first met you
But somehow I couldn't quite forget you'

I wrote how it was, living together, yet things not exactly ticking the right boxes.

A Touch of Jealousy?
'Don't Shit in the Custard.' That really *was* our working title for Pet Clark's hit song, 'Don't Sleep In The Subway.' We always had the American market in mind when writing Subway. After all, 'Don't Sleep in the London Underground' really doesn't have that magical sound, does it? The New York Rapid Transit, that's the subway's official name, was almost a world of its own. Down there things happened. Take 1981, for instance:

- the subway carried 3.5 million fares a day;
- there was a 'man under' incident every day; one suicide every week and 13 murders a year. Plus 'space cases', people getting themselves jammed between the train and the platform.

The NY subway really was, and is, a vibrant, living community. People lived down there. They were called 'skells', not quite the station

Jackie Trent

dwellers of India, where the traveller almost has to step between them, but people all the same. At Flushing Avenue a stream actually ran between the tracks, right along the length of the platform. And of course, there was the daily drama. At Broad Channel, some kids once filled a fire extinguisher with petrol, then injected it into the token booth and set it alight. Two ladies were in there and both died. Why? As an act of revenge, that's why, after one kid received a summons for 'Theft of Service,' i.e. not paying his fare.

And there were rules for survival down there:
- don't sit by the door, to avoid bag snatchers;
- avoid empty cars;
- and the No1 Rule for the NY subway? Don't ride the subway if you don't have to.

A real life New York plain clothes policeman told me this. He worked the subway daily.

And my lyric for 'Subway' was actually based on a real life event. Simon Dee, the TV interviewer and DJ, called me one day, "Jackie, would you like to come with me to a London film premiere?" In 1966, Simon Dee was arguably the No 1 radio DJ in the UK. His girlfriend was a singer. Simon was keen for us to write a song for her, so he invited me to join him at a private screening in Soho, where all the small preview cinemas are, 100 people or so capacity.

"That would be nice, Simon."

I enjoyed the afternoon. It was a good film in good company and Simon obviously enjoyed showing me off in a harmless sort of way. Afterwards, he drove me home in his customised black Mini Cooper. We pulled up outside the Water Gardens.

"I've just seen Tony steam off round the corner, by your apartment. He didn't look happy."

We were both a bit surprised. It was broad daylight, 4 o'clock in the afternoon. Surprise, surprise, a jealous Tony Hatch. I went into our apartment to find him packing a bag.

"What are you doing?"

"I'm going. What were you doing getting out of Simon Dee's car?"

"He phoned me this morning and invited me to a special showing of a musical in Soho. Good God, it's only 4 o' clock in the afternoon.

Being Me

We saw you walk past us and around the corner in a hurry. What are you trying to say? You know damned well that Simon's trying a get an audition with you for his girlfriend. You're being absolutely ridiculous." Tony refused to listen. He stormed out of the apartment with his bag.

You walk out on me when we both disagree
'Cos to reason is not what you care for

A while later the doorbell rang. A sheepish face looked at me as I opened the door. "I've forgotten my shaver." Tony had sat in the pub for an hour or so. The Masons Arms was a regular watering hole for Pye Records' people. "Come in, you silly bugger."

You try to be smart and you take it to heart
Cos it hurts when your ego's deflated
I've heard it all a million times before
Take off your coat my love and close the door.

We made love. That seemed to straighten his head again. 'Kisses and cuddles' indeed, as Tony later related on an album sleeve! I wrote it all down in my ever ready notebook. I'd probably have been a good policewoman, 'Notes made at the time, etc.' Later I showed Tony my lyric for the song, including the line:

Don't stand In the pouring rain.

"It's a bit fifth rate Ivor Novello- ish," says he.
"Well write something better, then. Please do that."
He couldn't. The lyric stood, and the song became a worldwide hit.
I found the lyrics for 'Who Am I' in New York, staying at the Waldorf Astoria, off 5th Avenue. Tony had a recording session with Pet. Once again I wasn't invited, so I wandered off along 5th Avenue to Central Park. The whole pace of the city left me breathless. The very atmosphere seemed charged with electricity. Everyone seemed to be in such a hurry. And the buildings:

The buildings reach up to the sky...
The traffic thunders on the busy streets
The pavement slips beneath my feet
I walk alone & wonder, 'Who Am I?

Just standing there, staring up at the buildings towering over me, I thought, '*Who am I? Just one tiny ant, trapped amongst millions of other ants, all scurrying madly around?*' My thoughts ran on, '*Maybe I could escape from all that; maybe I could fly...*'

I close my eyes and I can fly
And I escape from all this worldly strife
Restricted by routine of life
But still I can't discover,'Who Am I'

Pet Clark's version had a gentle arrangement but that's certainly not what I had in mind when I wrote the lyric. I had Johnny Harris ring its neck for my version, with jazzy brass. Johnny was a great trumpet player himself, and a hot song arranger. Tony Hatch would often ring Johnny to ask advice on brass arrangements.

Johnny Harris
Johnny Harris was a lovable eccentric. As a kid, he'd suffered polio, leaving him one leg shorter than the other. He wore a surgical boot, which he'd swing around madly whilst he conducted. One time, Johnny worked in America as musical director and arranger for Tom Jones, until Gordon Mills, Tom's manager, decided that Johnny was drawing too much attention. He of the shoulder length hair and the swinging boot was drawing more audience attention than Tom!

We called Johnny Harris, 'The Boot.' So many times we'd find holiday postcards in our mail from 'The Boot on ski's,' with ski goggles, or on a beach somewhere, wearing sunshades, with a bottle of suntan cream nearby. I can still vividly picture Johnny Harris in studio when we were recording, 'Who Am I,' pushing Ronnie Verrell on drums and Peter McGurk on contrabass to pull out all the stops, his long hair flying madly and 'the Boot' swinging wildly to the tempo. I pulled out all the stops myself on that one. They say I should have recorded more jazz and brass numbers. Needless to say, the brass section poured into the control room afterwards to enjoy what we'd put together.

Johnny Harris would be best man to Tony at our wedding in 1967. He 'retired' to LA, where he took on rearranging Disney's cartoon music, a job for life. God bless you, Johnny Harris.

Summer Holiday

My very first summer holiday, age 26. In the summer of 1966 we took a villa at Forte dei Marmi, situated on the Italian Mediterranean coast. We drove down in style, Tony at the wheel of our Pontiac Parisienne convertible, bought from Lendrum & Hartman in London, the UK importers. Les drove his Ford Cortina. He loved that Cortina. We packed both families into the two cars, stopping in Calais the first night, then somewhere in Switzerland on night two. The brakes failed on the Pontiac on the way down.

Forte dei Marmi - 'Fort of the Marbles'

Forte dei Marmi is a coastal resort in northern Tuscany. The area was fabled for its quarried marble which was exported all around the world. Queen Paola of Belgium was born there and Gianni Agnelli, head of Fiat and Ferrari and owner of Juventus FC, had a holiday home in Forte dei Marmi too. In 1940, in a bar in North Africa, Agnelli was shot in the arm by a German officer, arguing over a woman. Gianni Agnelli was known as 'The Rake of the Riviera.'

In 1966 my family descended 'en masse' on Forte dei Marmi. We hired bicycles. Mum and Dad chose a tandem to ride around the resort whilst my sister, Mally and Tony's sister, Ninette went out together with two Swiss guys. All hell let loose with the parents, who did not approve. Tony's Mum, Eileen, thrashed three year old Darren after he locked her in her room, another big bust up. "Don't you thrash my son again," said Tony, feeling responsible for Darren. Mum and Dad were fuming too. In truth, nobody liked Eileen. On the return journey home, in Calais, Darren trapped Mum's hand in the Parisienne car door. Eileen thrashed him again. She had a problem that woman. Or maybe it was just with Darren?

Hit and Miss
We bought our first Rolls Royce in 1966 from ATV. The Parisienne was just too big to drive around London. The RR looked a bit sombre in its dark blue and black livery. Maybe that made it accident prone. Insurers have stats on accident prone car colours, you know? It was previously Lord Renwick's car, but was damaged in a collision with a London bus. After repair, the car looked brand new again, so we bought it. Tony proudly drove the Rolls Royce home and parked it in the garage. I remember being in the kitchen, next to the garage. I heard a 'clunk,' then a face appeared at the kitchen window, white as a sheet. It was Tony, standing quite still. He beckoned to me to come outside. *"The fucking little battery charger has fucked up the Roller."*

I went out to look. The long, shiny car was now not so shiny, with a massive dent and paintwork missing, where the battery charger had landed on the bonnet, after falling from its shelf. Off the car went, back to Jack Barclays for repair again. We kept that car for two or three years.

In the autumn of '66, Les and I were back on the road. One night after a show, driving down the M1 near Watford Gap, we were suddenly confronted by a van, right in front of us. It had slid nicely through the central barrier from the opposite carriageway, right across our bow. Then, just as if a conductor had magically raised his baton, cars, vans and lorries orchestrated themselves across the carriageways, sliding and smashing into each other, even piling on top of each other.

"Oh shit!" said Les. He was still a novice driver, and in a big Jaguar car.

"Black ice Les, don't brake. Just steer to the hard shoulder. We're coming off at the next exit." Thank goodness, we were virtually at the Watford Gap exit. That was an eye- opener for Les, driving on black ice for the first time.

Chapter 23 – The Two Of Us

Tony and I wrote 'Open Your Heart,' aimed at the European market, a big Italian- style ballad, very much in vogue at the time.

So darling, open your heart to me
Give me a love we can share
Open your heart to me
Just let me feel your warmth everywhere

I wrote the lyric in the style of 'O Sole Mio'. Did you know, the Walls ice cream version, 'Just One Cornetto' was once voted the most well known jingle of all time? Obviously we hit the right buttons. 'Open Your Heart' brought an Italian producer over from Rome and he brought Italian lyrics for me to record the song in Italian. And boy, was he gorgeous. I fell for him, and I told Tony so! But that was as far as it went, just a dream.

The song proved so popular in Italy, I was invited along, just me, to a big TV Gala show in Rome, to perform the song. In my dressing room, before the show, my makeup artist stuck *cardboard* eyelashes onto my own lashes.

"What's this? I'm starting to look like Sophia Loren."

"Yes, I did Sophia Loren's make- up for film," she said.

I have to say, the result was fantastic! I couldn't bring myself to take those lashes off for days afterwards…

Bomb Scare

Bombs seemed to just pop up in my life. I was born just four days after that Luftwaffe bomb exploded in Chesterton. And twice I escaped injury from EOKA terrorist bomb blasts in Cyprus. So a bomb scare at the London Palladium was almost par for the course.

I was closing the first half of 'Sunday Night at the London Palladium,' Engelbert Humperdinck was top of the bill. Just as I was finishing my second number, a helmeted policeman came on stage and into the spotlights. He just walked up to me, as the orchestra slowly fizzled to a stop. "Pardon me," said he, as he took the mike from my hand:

"Ladies and Gentlemen, I must ask you all to calmly leave the theatre, *calmly* please? There's a bomb scare, so we have to take the matter seriously. Just walk out if you will, nice and orderly."

That included us. For almost two hours, the cast and crew stood on Argyle Street, before we were allowed backstage to collect our gear. I did have a few giggles. My glittering stage dress drew more than a few looks from passers by, I can tell you! Of course, our audience had long gone home.

The Two Of Us - 1967 - the start of our legend...

We were constantly writing songs for other artists. In the 60's we seemed to write something new every week, a string of hit songs for other artists plus my own No.1 hit, 'Where Are You Now.' We even wrote the opening number, 'London' for the 1966 Royal Variety Command performance, which I performed in front of HRH Queen Elizabeth II. So it was a bit of fun to write a song based on our own lives, just Tony and I. I think we came up with the title together, 'The Two Of Us.' We just sat and wrote:

> *The Two Of Us*
> *There'll always be for you and me, the two of us*
> *We'll always be together like the cat and the cream*
> *For we're in a dream of our own - we'll go it alone*
> *There's just the two of us and we'll always be travelling on*

And that's how it really was for us at the time, easy going but having a ball!

We wrote a simple song, livened up with a brassy middle 8 for me to go for:

And in the evening when the day is done
I'll turn down the lights when all our friends have gone

I stepped into Pye No 1 recording booth. The arrangement worked beautifully, but there was something missing. A harmony voice! Surely this was a duet, if ever there was one. Over the mike I said, "Tony, this song's about two people. We need a harmony and it's not in my key. I'll be singing in my boots. Come down here and have a crack at it!"

'The 2 o' Fuz'

The last time Tony had sung on a record was backing Eddie Fisher in the early 50's. After a few jibes from me, and a couple of whiskies, Tony finally came down to the booth, looking very unhappy. He had a few goes at it, with me singing along to help him whilst the muso's teased him. Finally, Ray Prickett gave us the 'thumbs- up' from the control room:

"Just come up and listen to it," is all he said. We'd nailed it. Only to see the recording shelved at Pye Records, gathering dust...

I mentioned Ray Prickett, one of the best sound engineers in the UK. He was sound engineer on all of my recordings. Ray was unflappable and worked long hours. He was a very unassuming man.

Being Me

Pat Halling, a New Zealander, was lead violin on a lot of my work. His 'gypsy work' was some of the finest. Ronnie Price was my pianist on 'If You Go Away', not Tony. Ronnie could play anything. And finally Ronnie Verrell on drums. Ronnie was a real character and a flamboyant drummer. He was band leader Ted Heath's regular drummer.

Early in 1967 we bought Eve Taylor's flat at 3 Malvern Court, South Kensington. I admit, she advised me at the time, "Don't marry Tony, he'll just use you." In truth, quite a few people said that to me, even Marlene, one of the girl dancers from my Cyprus days, back in the '50's. She would remind me of that when we met up again in 2013, "We warned you Jack, but you just couldn't see. We knew what he was about."

Jean's divorce from Tony came through around the end of 1966 and mine was proceeding. We never really discussed marriage. Tony never formally proposed, we sort of slipped into the assumption of marriage, as and when my divorce came through. And I never realised what a major production our marriage would prove to be for the media!

My divorce was always confrontational, yet Jean's divorce of Tony proved far more painful for me, believe it or not. I liked Jean and she had their two young children to care for. Jean and I stayed friends and Sharon and Amanda would visit us. In time, I would become almost their adopted mother. My divorce of Drew Harvey proved melodramatic, almost a Gilbert & Sullivan comic opera:

*'I'll never throw dust in a juryman's eyes,
Said I to myself, said I,'*

Iolanthe

*'Oh, I was like that when a lad!
A shocking young scamp of a rover,
I behaved like a regular cad'*

Trial By Jury

In Court, even Maurice King, Drew's own defence witness, spoke up *against* him.

Judge: "Tell me Mr. King, how would you describe Mr. Harvey's behaviour during the marriage?"

"Well your Honour, I have to say that Drew Harvey carried on the life of a single man. He was a cad, a 'Jack- the- lad.'"

"Does that mean he had relationships with other women?"

"Yes, your Honour. Constantly, and lots of them."

Maurice knew exactly what Drew was up to at the time as he worked for Maurice King as a talent scout, with some success. Drew discovered The Rockin' Berries in Birmingham. I finally won my divorce petition, freeing me from the damn man. Thanks to him I could never now have a church wedding, but wed I would be!

Wedding of the Year!

I was working onstage almost up to our wedding day. Then, just before the big day, I spent two whole days settling in family and friends from up north at a hotel we'd booked, just around the corner from our apartment. Most of the family had never seen London before.

"Hey Jackie, the traffic never stops running here, even through the night. Wouldn't do for me, all this noise," was the typical reaction. Over the years, I suppose I'd just become used to the constant background noise of London.

On the eve of our wedding, Tony stayed over with Johnny Harris, his best man. My sister Mally stayed with me in our Kensington flat. We spent half the night laying out our Darnell's beautiful wedding dresses. I'd kitted Tony out with a wedding suit made especially by Dougie Millings.

Wedding Day – 18 August 1967

At 7am I had a 'phone call from a friend, "Have you heard your new single on the radio?"

"What single," I asked?

"You and Tony - 'The Two Of Us.'"

Unknown to me, Les Cox, a Pye producer and our good friend, had pulled our recording off the shelf and brushed off the dust. Pye circulated all the radio DJ's with demo copies. 'The Two Of Us' was released on our Wedding Day. The timing couldn't have been better and we had unbelievable airplay throughout the day, I'm told. Of course, I didn't hear it, I was busy myself, getting wed…

Being Me

At the appointed hour a white Rolls Royce, loaned to us by my friend Gina's godfather, collected Mally and I from home, to make the grand arrival outside Caxton Hall. The pavement outside was packed with TV and press cameramen. Pathe News filmed our grand arrival for their national cinema news feature. I kept my head down and tried to smile, and not trip over, whilst camera lights flashed all around me. The cameras stayed with us inside Caxton Hall, capturing the scene of some 300 guests, mostly celebrity guests, packed inside the Hall. ATV filmed the whole event, billed as *Wedding Of The Year* in the national press, and every guest was given a copy of 'The Two Of Us.' Perfect marketing, Mr. Cox! ATV presented us with a personal copy of their wedding film production. And it *was* a production, a commercial exercise almost. Frankly, the event lacked sincerity. Evie Taylor brought Adam Faith and his future wife Jackie along. They were to be married the following day, so the cameras grabbed a shot of us all four together. I gave Jackie my wedding garter for her big day.

Take 2. The wedding reception, plus cameramen moved on to a hotel in Grosvenor Square. The cameras flashed again. They never seemed to stop. The cine's panned in on us as we cut the cake. Journalists, madly scribbling notes, seemed to be everywhere.

In no time at all it seemed, Tony and I were airborne, up front on an Alitalia flight to Rome. There were just two other passengers in First Class. The man was a dignified Arab gentleman dressed in traditional thawb and kaffiyeh with gold trimmings. During the flight I saw him reading the London Evening Standard. A wedding picture of Tony and I filled the whole front page. He looked over at us a couple of times. Finally he spoke, "Congratulations."

"Thank you," I replied.

I later asked one of the stewardesses who he might be, "Oh! That's Prince Faisal of Saudi Arabia."

I quietly reflected on his refined persona, compared with that brash local Sheik, years ago in the desert sands of Doha. He who'd served a younger me with the sheep's eye on a plate of couscous...

We finally arrived at the Cavalieri Hilton hotel, the finest hotel Rome had to offer, set in 15 acres of lush Mediterranean gardens, on one of the seven hills overlooking Rome, only to find the cameras already there. Surely not, but the penthouse floor corridors were strewn with tangles of cabling, movie cameras and tripods. But not for us! Edward G Robinson was also resident in the Cavalieri Hilton. I crossed paths with him a couple of times in the hotel corridors. A gruff "Hi" was about all he offered, as we passed each other. Apparently Edward G. was starring in a spoof film, 'Operazione San Pietro' - 'Operation St Peter's.' It obviously involved 'Centurions,' who constantly wondered past me in the hotel corridors. Quite bizarre!

Our personal paparazzi cameramen arrived next day. So there were lots of 'coin in the fountain' posing sessions and other such things. After two days of it, Tony could stand no more, "Jackie, isn't it time we consummated this marriage?" We finally called a halt to the cameras. 'Just the two of us...'

'The Two of Us' went straight to No 1 in Australia and stayed in the Australian top 10 for six months. The loving family theme appealed to the Aussies. But we never realised how much the song would change our lives forever.

Back in UK, after the honeymoon, there was no time for me to be on the road. I was too busy recording and writing song lyrics. Everyone wanted a Trent/Hatch song. But Sundays were sacred and that was my special 'Billy Fury Sunday lunch' day. I would prep everything on Saturday night, so I could have a lie in on Sunday morning.

Being Me

The 1967 Showbiz Xmas season in London was a heady climax to a brilliant year. We were still 'Wedding of the Year.' We seemed to be writing hit songs for everyone, so everyone wanted us at their party. I felt trapped in turkey world. Everyone had turkey on the menu.

Finally at home over Xmas, this 'turkey' finally blew her top on Boxing Day. We had both families staying over. The house was filled with family, and yes, turkey was on our menu too. And I seemed to be doing all the work, along with Mum. "Bugger this Mum, I'm off out for a walk in the fresh air."

I pulled on my boots, threw a coat around me, and walked out in the snow. The open space was a real tonic. I seemed to walk for miles, ending up on Bromley High Street, which is where Tony turned up. He'd been driving around, looking for me. He found me walking aimlessly along empty streets, looking at all the Xmas lights in the shop windows. At that very moment I was smiling, thinking of the marauding shoppers who'd soon invade the town, next morning.

"Jackie, get in the car. You've being doing too much. You're very tired, so I'm taking you home to a hot bath and bed for a couple of hours. You're not doing any more."

"Oh Tone, I've just had it. Mum and I have been doing everything. Eileen hasn't even washed a cup. I've waited on her hand and foot. And she openly calls my family working class. How dare she!"

Back home, I had an hour's sleep, then joined the party again. Mum, my sisters and my niece had tea all laid out. I suddenly felt hungry.

"You've not looked well for a few days," said Mum. "And you've not eaten enough. You're definitely pregnant."

"What!"

I remember feeling strangely embarrassed at the thought. Tony opened champagne and there were congratulations all round, which made me feel worse.

"But I might not be pregnant, Dad."

"Well your Mum should know. She's had five of you," said Dad.

Of course, Mum was right.

Married life certainly didn't slow things down. In fact the pace doubled with lots of songwriting, recording and of course Tony's Pye workload. Eve Taylor was overloading me with work too. She was certainly getting her pound of flesh. And boy, was I writing! I just couldn't stop writing song lyrics, in the car, on buses, in the kitchen. I kept travel sickness pills on hand as writing in the car made me feel sick.

We needed help and we needed more space. Shortly after Xmas we bought 'Shortlands' in Kent. The house was advertised in the Times. We moved in to this gorgeous 10-bedroom Tudor style mansion, set on a big corner plot with enough space for a pool in the 'back yard.' To keep us both free to work, we employed a cook, a nanny and my darling Madge. Madge Rogers and her husband Jim stayed with us for 13 years. I miss her level headedness, even now. "Yes, Mrs. H, No, Mrs. H." Madge was from the old school of life. In 13 years, she never once called me 'Jackie.' Madge was my good friend.

Eve of Departure

Eve Taylor was busily sending me to bookings all over the country. Of course, she signed the booking contracts on my behalf: 70% my behalf; 30% her behalf. How could I have signed such a contract? Well, of course aspiring young people hope and trust, don't they, never reading the small print. I certainly didn't read the small print. But now I was married and I had my husband and family to consider. We had a beautiful home and staff, but I was enjoying none of it. Eve was showing no consideration for my change of circumstances. I felt like a piece of meat being sold off a slab, so I wrote a firm letter, asking her to agree future bookings with me first. "Don't go signing any more contracts for me. I shall not honour them."

Eve's reply was a screaming 'phone call, "You'll work wherever and whenever I say."

Being Me

"No Eve, not any more. You can take me to court. Enough is enough." Then I put the 'phone down. It never went that far. I bought myself out of Eve's contract for £15,000, one hell of a lot of money at the time. But we did stay firm friends and I honoured her final bookings for me. Eve tactfully took just a 10% agents fee, not the previous 30%, but she did raise my charge out performance fees to compensate herself. So now my royalty monies were just mine.

Michelle is Born

I gave birth to my daughter, Michelle, by caesarean section. As soon as they wheeled me out of the operating theatre, I knew something was wrong. Tony's unsmiling face told the tale of disappointment: another daughter. He never was to produce a son. The look on his face actually made me apologise to him as I lay on the gurney. How sad is that? It should have been a shining moment for us, but he already had two daughters from his first marriage…

Chapter 24
Far Away Places

'The Guvnor' - Frank Sinatra Calls

I love surprises. Who doesn't? One evening the 'phone rang.
"Hi, is that Ja'ackie? This is Frank Sinatra."

"OK Mike, stop mucking about." We were good friends with Mike Yarwood, the famous voice impersonator.

"No Ja'ackie, this really is Frank Sinatra. I'm calling from LA. Is Tony home?"

"He's out watering the dog, Frank."

"OK, I'll call back in a while. Love your work. I'd like you to write an album for me."

"Sounds great. We'd be pleased to do that, Frank." Who wouldn't?

"Lovely speaking with you Ja' ackie. See you soon in New York. I'll call back in an hour or so."

I just sat there, stunned. Frank Sinatra, America, write an album for him? I poured myself a stiff gin and tonic, spilling most of it, I was shaking so much.

Tony arrived back, "Are you alright? You look shocked."

"I am shocked. Guess who's just rung... Frank Sinatra!"

"Who's taking the piss?" Tony's reaction was like mine.

Being Me

The 'phone rang later and it was the man himself again. We were definitely going to New York and he wanted songs for a new album. Forget the G & T, champagne was in order. We'd hit gold, writing for 'The Guvnor;' so it was celebration time for us.

The scary part would be writing the songs. Yes, we'd written for wonderful artists, including Petula our Golden Girl, but a personal call from Frank Sinatra was a very special moment for a couple of 20 something's, especially for Yvonne Burgess from Newcastle- under-Lyme. And we were to travel in style across the Atlantic Ocean, to meet the great man.

Taking 'The Queen' to America - September 1968

Came the day, we took the train from London to Southampton, Tony, Les, 6 year old Darren and me. A short taxi ride brought us to the port. I remember looking up in awe at our ship, the RMS Queen Elizabeth. She dwarfed her berth and everything around her. Then I remembered another time, October/November 1944, when the US 345th Infantry Regiment had marched past our house on Talke Road, Chesterton, preparing for war. The same 'Queen Elizabeth' had brought them safely over the Atlantic to do battle. Now she was to take us to America to write music.

Our on board suite was grand. The first class dining room was even grander. I must admit, at dinner I did enjoy making my grand entrance each night, feeling like a queen myself as I glided down the sweeping staircase to the dining room, trying not to fall as the ship swayed madly about. This was showbiz grandeur in the extreme. The first class dining room was a stage set with gentlemen in dinner suits and ladies in their finery, all wearing lots of baubles, bangles and beads. Each table was surrounded by white gloved waiters, hovering in a dazzling atmosphere of silver service. An elegant string quartet played music that just floated through the air.

I wasn't overly impressed with some of my fellow passengers. I'd learned, over the years, than appearances can be false and money doesn't buy good manners.

'A bit different to our rust bucket trip on the Med, ten years ago eh, Jackie? No leering sailors; no fishing for dinner over the side of the ship, and no rabbit hutch sweaty cabin.'

'Too right, Vonnie. Let's enjoy, and flaunt it, eh!'

After dinner, we changed into casual gear, joining the Swinging Sixties in second class. Even the ship was rocking and rolling. Out on deck it was blowing a force nine gale. We finally gave up and headed for bed. The Purser suggested brandy and ginger ale to allay queasiness and it worked. Les laid horizontal for most of the crossing. He'd been seasick in his own bathtub, our Les. One day we tried a dip in the indoor swimming pool. This was not for the faint- hearted. One minute I was in 3ft of water, the next as the ship rolled, the water was over my head. The pool was eventually closed to avoid casualties. A shame, it was exciting fun. Six year old Darren adopted our lift attendant. He spent hours in the lift listening to sea stories. The attendant had a peg leg. Maybe he'd prove to be Long John Silver? We kept checking on Darren. At least we knew where he was.

"Is he being a nuisance?"

"Not at all. He's full of questions and I'm enjoying it."

And off they went again, chattering away.

The Commodore's Reception

Tony and I were invited to a formal reception in Commodore Marr's quarters. We unknowingly disgraced ourselves by first attending a reception thrown by the Midland Bank. It really was a matter of business and pleasure. Strict foreign exchange limits at the time meant we would quickly run out of cash in America and £500 was the limit at the time.

"Don't worry. If you need extra cash, we can help," said a senior bank man. Job done, but we couldn't just leave, and the bankers were great company. So we were late for Commodore Marr's reception. Big mistake.

As we entered the Commodore's suite, a steward formally announced everyone present. There were so many Lords and Ladies. The other guests were understandably a bit miffed with us as protocol demanded that no drinks could be served until *all* 12 invited guests were present. The Commodore received us graciously. He also graced the gathering with recitals of his poetry...

Commodore Geoffrey Trippleton Marr DSC RD was Commodore Captain of the Cunard Fleet. As Geoffrey Marr, he went to sea, aged 14, first serving in the Merchant Marines. In WWII he joined the Royal Navy, seconded to the battleship King George V, Admiral Tovey commanding. He was also at the sinking of the Bismarck in the North Atlantic. The Bismarck finally sank at 10.10hrs on 27 May 1941.

Since the war, Geoffrey Marr had risen through the ranks of Cunard, finally becoming Commodore of the whole Cunard fleet. RMS Queen Elizabeth was in her final year of service and her last Atlantic crossing was on 5 November 1968. She would be sold to the City of Long Beach, California. In 1971 Commodore Marr would enjoy a final reunion with 'The Queen,' taking her to her final resting place, in Hong Kong.

New York, New York
Our arrival in New York City was spectacular, not to say a relief to be out of the Force 9 Atlantic gale and into the calmer waters of the Hudson River. We slowly glided by the Statue of Liberty. On shore, Mr. Sinatra had everything organised. A super limo took us to the Americana hotel where our suite was bigger than the combined ground floor area of four average houses back in UK, with TV's everywhere. Darren ran amok, "There's a TV in the bathroom," he shouted excitedly. The panoramic views of the city were amazing. We were all kids in paradise, awaiting instructions.

We met up with Claus Ogerman, the renowned orchestrator and conductor. He worked a lot with Frank Sinatra. We met him for lunch one day, in Manhattan. "Look, I'm gonna warn you. It's gonna be hard work with Mr. S. You don't know where you stand with the man until you have him stood in front of a mike. And he cancels recording sessions like anyone else would cancel lunch."

"Why?"

"Because he's Mr. S; because he's Mr. Sinatra and because he can do that."

Claus Ogerman, born Klaus Ogermann, worked with many, many fine artists. I loved his arrangement of Solomon Burke's 'Cry To Me,' that eventually hit the screen in 'Dirty Dancing,' the low budget film that became a box office smash hit. We were in special company that day. Three days later came the big shock. Mr. S was not meeting us in New York. We would have to fly to Los Angeles, then possibly Palm Springs, to his home. I wasn't feeling in great shape after the caesarian op, then having to leave my new four week old baby daughter behind in UK with my parents. The swings and roundabouts of life, all my emotions, came into play as we boarded the aircraft. I smelled the food in preparation and almost threw up. Then I suffered a panic attack and refused to fly. That caused a stir, I can tell you and I was not exactly flavour of the month. Four of us hurriedly disembarked, as our luggage was dragged from the 'plane.

Being Me

We took the USS United States back to UK which was a faster, more modern ship than the 'Queen'. She'd recently won the Blue Riband for the Atlantic crossing. The Atlantic was still unforgiving and the force nine gale was still blowing. My pills to stop me producing breast milk had gone AWOL and two of our suitcases went to Honolulu. It was all a bit of a fiasco.

The social atmosphere on the American ship was completely different to the 'Queen', far more relaxed. The first class dining room was serviced by African- American waiters. Our fellow passengers, mostly white, were seriously rude to them. We took exception to this and felt distinctly uncomfortable. A waiter was assigned to us. I recalled the 'Snake Pit' in Frankfurt, 'whites to the right, blacks to the left.' I resolved to break the barrier and make our waiter smile and talk to us. Ours was the only table with an English accent. We enjoyed wonderful service. And yes, he finally smiled...

Back home, Tony was now joining me in the recording booth. Pye released our latest LP, 'Live For Love'. We wrote four of the songs together and dueted on all of the tracks. I was anxious to know my fan reaction, no longer being purely a solo singer. I read John Gibson's critical review in The London Evening News of Friday 11 October 1968:

'... chummy sound...tends to bore and if they can tear themselves apart I'd prefer Jackie to go it alone in several tracks. After all, she IS the singer.'

Not good, but a bit late now. Tony had the taste for being on stage. John Gibson goes on to note that we were finally due to meet up with Frank Sinatra, who planned an LP singing our songs exclusively. Wow, that's more like it!

A message from Sinatra came, "I'll be flying over to UK soon in the jet. We'll meet up at my apartment in Grosvenor Square."

We finally met Mr. S face- to- face. Frank Sinatra was a small figure of a man, but with a magnetic personality and the bluest eyes I've ever seen. He had me swooning, without even trying. Frank welcomed us with open arms. There was no entourage, just one guy who obviously looked after him. Mr. S was really apologetic for the problems we'd had, "I went to my hacienda in Acapulco to be out of the way, somethin' to do with the Mafia. Look Ja'ackie, I apologise. I never realised you'd just had a cesarean birth before you came over to the States. I'm real sorry for asking that of you. And we missed a swell party in your honour."

Frank was totally charming. He was dressed casually, in white open neck shirt, black trousers, no socks, just slippers. He ordered drinks, a Jack Daniels for him and we followed suit. Why not? I'd never tasted Jack Daniels in my life till then. The 'phone rang. It was his pilot, on speakerphone, "Mr. S, if we don't take off before 11pm, it'll have to be after 6am in the morning." Frank was quite happy about this and he'd spend the night in Crockfords, the classiest private casino in London. Frank spoke a lot about Nancy and Frank Junior, which broke the ice nicely. After a while we talked music and what he was looking for. He had an open mind.

I said: "Would you take exception to me writing about your personal life? I have an idea for a lyric."

I was thinking of Ava Gardner and their well-known angry exchanges together. Ava was his wife, and I believe, the love of his life. She was a very beautiful woman who I saw as a bit of a gypsy. I met her once at a social function in London. She had a passion for bull fighters. That wasn't good for Frank's ego, of course. Despite all that, Frank simply said "No, that's OK. Go ahead."

And that's where I found inspiration for 'The Auction':

What am I bid for this beautiful love.
What am I bid for this pure work of art
Then the climax of the song...
My love is going, going, gone

So Tony and I were now in full flood, studio booked with the finest muso's in London also booked, but *no Sinatra!* Just as Claus Ogerman had warned us, Frank Sinatra had flown back to the USA. The song was great. All we needed now was a singer. We found Mike Medway who possessed a wonderful singing voice. Imagine Mike's feelings, standing there in Sinatra's role, backed by the best muso's in town!

That was one expensive demo. We were deeply disappointed not to have Frank Sinatra's voice on the recording, but Matt Monro eventually did a beautiful version and sang the socks off it.

'The Two Of Us,' 1969
Tony finally became part of my act. Up until then we'd never performed onstage together. Tony wasn't even my musical director. Ken Flower was my pianist and musical director, brother Les handled the lighting and sound and drove me around. We had a nanny and a housekeeper. It wasn't easy, having six old Darren and Michelle just a few months old. I was away a week at a time, sometimes two weeks, working at one club, then straight on to another. I had a busy life, writing and recording. But in May '69 Tony finally became my pianist on stage. We did a short season at the Palladium, a 'Mr and Mrs TV Spectacular' for Yorkshire TV and then toured the UK.

Judy Garland
It's been said that Judy Garland was perhaps the greatest entertainer ever born, so it was quite an honour to have her in my home. It was June 1969 and Judy had just officiated at the opening of a new dress shop for Tony and me. We chatted about her recent wedding to Mickey Dean and her five week appearance at The Talk of The Town in London. She also told me of her disastrous tour of Australia in 1964. Mum joined in the conversation and Judy visibly relaxed, away from the public eye. She obviously had problems. They say her character was strongly influenced by film executives, constantly manipulating her image. Just four days after being in my home, Judy passed away. She was just 47 years of age.

Trombones and Trumpets
Maurice King booked us for a Yorkshire Television TV Spectacular, a Mr and Mrs. Colour TV Show. Matt Monro and Scott Walker would be our special guests. The show featured all of our music. The set designer went wild, creating a creamy, pink stage set. Backstage, at band rehearsal, I suddenly heard a lot of shouting and cursing. I

walked onstage, to find the frontline brass boys going at each other, "Jackie, do you have any plasters? We need plasters." The set designer had seated the trombone players too close behind the trumpets and trombone slides were hitting trumpet players smartly in the back of the head! The clock was running and showtime was approaching so, for a while there was absolute havoc, with saws and drills going it, extending the set, whilst rehearsals went on. Happy days...

The Monster who made Scott Walker
Scott referred to Maurice King as 'Boris;' or 'The Monster'. "Jackie, Boris really scares me." Which didn't help Scott Engel's confidence. "I hate performing live, Jackie," Scott also told me one day. Maurice King reportedly dealt with someone looking to move in on him managing Scott. Apparently he put a gun to the would- be manager's head...

At one time, Maurice managed Shirley Bassey, the Walker Brothers, the Rockin' Berries and me of course. Maurice had other interests. He owned the Starlite Club in Soho, where I used to hang out in the early 60's. A strong fan of mine, Eric Mason, provided security at the Starlite. Eric, a big friend of the Krays, made close friends with the Rockin' Berries. They even visited him in prison, when he was 'banged up' himself. Yes, Maurice King lived close to the underworld. In the summer of 1977 he was found dead, in the flat above his offices, an empty box of pills and whisky bottle nearby. 'Suicide' was the official verdict.

Australia calling
We had a call from our London agent. "There's an offer come in for you to go to Australia. Are you interested in doing a few shows there?"

We looked at each other, "Why not?"

Then the doubts followed, "But how would we present ourselves?" It would be a major test for us with the Aussies, and not at cricket! And I recalled Judy Garland's bad experience when she toured Australia. Would we make it? And could Tony have time off from the recording studio? He was in his last year of a ten year contract with Pye. We'd never done a full show together and I was still the stage star. So we came up with the idea for a new show. We just couldn't go on stage and sing songs. There had to be patter between us. We agreed from the outset that I would always call him a little short- arse and that always drew a laugh. We hired a couple of comedy scriptwriters to write some banter for us to use on stage, in the style of the Sonny & Cher TV show.

I said, "We'll need a backing group. Let's take 'Two Of Each.'"

"No, they're not good enough," said Tony. "And they have a girl drummer."

"What's wrong with a girl drummer? I firmly believe they are up to it. Have you ever seen them onstage?" He hadn't, of course.

"And we can set up their gear at home to practice the routines," I added.

And that's exactly what we did. We gave them constant practice. They were fine. Mally, Jackie, John and Mick even went along to Pye studios to audition. Tony gave them a contract for a couple of singles. Job done!

Now to test the new show on a live audience. We took 'Two Of Each' along with us for a week's gig in Middlesbrough, then to Newcastle- on- Tyne. If you can't make it work in the North East then God help you!

Show night. This was it. Believe me, we were all shaking, even me, even Les on lighting and sound.

'Come on Jackie, you've done all this before. Remember that act, back in 1960 with Syd & Max Harrison. It went down well with US servicemen in Morocco and Germany; why not here?'

'True enough, Vonnie. It'll be OK.'

And it was. We had standing ovations all week and great local press reviews. There were queues outside the clubs from early evening. We were onto a winner again! This was a complete learning curve for me, a solo artist for all of my life. Now I was adapting to be part of a show of 6 voices, with a whole new presentation: Tony, my sister Mally, her friends Jackie Daniels, Mike Castro and John Conran, plus the added frontline brass. It was all very exciting and a different new sound for all of us. I did the major vocals and ballads, backed by the others to give it depth. We rehearsed constantly, stretching ourselves vocally.

Around this time we bought our personalised car registration 20 FUS. I'm told it came off a moped, registered in Scotland. Anyway, it went onto our gold Rolls Royce Silver Shadow.

Down Under 1969

We wrote, 'Thank You For Loving Me,' which was released just before we flew out to Oz. We took the Kangaroo Route on this, our first tour of Australia. In 1947, the Kangaroo route took 77hrs 30 mins from Heathrow and an unbelievable 168hrs 55 minutes by flying boat from Bournemouth/Hurn airport. In September 1969 we faced a 38hr trip, a quick jaunt by comparison? Not so! The flight seemed to drag on forever.

At Heathrow we all boarded Pan Am 1, Tony and I up front, courtesy of the sponsors whilst 'Two of Each' sat close behind. The 'plane seemed to stop everywhere. The last 9hr sector was Jakarta to Sydney. I sat with a head full of rollers. What a look.! We knew there would be a press conference to face at the other end with TV, radio and the national dailies.

'Just like stepping out of the beat up VW van in Morocco,' Jackie; G. I.'s, squaddies, the press, they all want you 'lookin' good!'

'Sure Vonnie, but I can't control the hair in this rarified air, at 40,000 feet.'

Being Me

Just before landing, I took out the rollers. Oh Lordy, I looked like Harpo Marx, with my hair standing on end. In the VIP lounge we met the Aussie media for the first time, national TV, radio and newspapers. "What's with the hair, Jack?" I heard at least one wag shout out. The press did mention my unusual hairdo in their write- ups.

In Sydney we did a TV spot for Channel 9, a guest spot on lunchtime TV. Pre- show, the group were really nervous as they'd never faced a live TV camera before. We chose to sing 'Danny Boy' Acapella (no music, just voices). The six voices had to blend in perfect timing, and they did. The reaction was amazing and 'Danny Boy' became one of the big numbers in the show. The audience would shout for it, so we'd struck gold there. And a medley from the musical 'Hair' went the same way. We choreographed loads of movement for onstage action, Tony wrote great brass breaks and the group had it all nailed too. We were booked for three weeks each in Sydney and Melbourne, and then Sydney again for a TV special. But first the world- famous Chequers nightclub in Goulburn Street, Sydney.

Keith and Dennis Wong owned Chequers. Top class performers played there, but only if Dennis approved, "I like you - OK," or "I no like you." (Goodbye). One night at Chequers, Australian Prime Minister John Gorton caused a minor sensation by suddenly disappearing backstage with Liza Minnelli. In 1969 Chequers hosted a notorious party for Chicago mobster, Joseph Dan Testa. The place was full of 'heavies' that night. Our three week slot, also in '69, saw packed houses every night.

"You come again. I invite you back. You OK," said Dennis Wong, warmly.

Don Lane

Another invite came our way. "Don Lane would like you all to join him for a barbie, at home?"

Don 'The Lanky Yank' Lane arrived in Australia as a comedian talk show host for Channel 9. He replaced Dave Allen, the Irish comedian and made the show his own. Tony and I really liked Don, so we wrote a song for him, as a surprise. The shows in Melbourne went down very well, then we were back to Sydney for Channel

9's TV Special, 'Tonight with Don Lane.' We had a meeting with Don before the show. Tony sat at the piano, and I sang 'You're Everything.'

"Oh, I like that," said Don.

"Well it's yours. We've written it for you," we both chorused.

"For me? Morton Donald Isaacson from the Bronx? Wow, thanks guys."

That evening during the show, we formally intro'd the new song on stage. Tony doodled at the piano and I stood nearby as Don walks into camera, "Is that my song? You said you'd write a song for me."

"Well yes, this is your new song," we chorused (again).

Don performed 'You're Everything' that night and he later recorded it. The song became his signature tune. My lyric told of Don's life, his loves, his trials and tribulations and of just being himself, the joker in the crowd, who laughed too much, but just couldn't help it. That was Don Lane's personality. As the lyric says:

And the man becomes a King, now you are everything to me.

I adored Don Lane. I could have run away with him. Don passed away in 2009. I wish I could have given him one last hug. And we shared the same mentor in Frankie Laine. You recall I started my career singing Frankie's hit song 'I Believe?' Don Isaacson took Frankie's professional surname, becoming Don *Lane*.

That 1969 visit to Australia and the runaway success of 'The Two Of Us,' introduced us to a new life, touring the Southern hemisphere. We topped the bill at shows in Sydney and Melbourne and made friends with a whole new bunch of people. A lithe young Rex McClenaghan came into my life as one of the dancers who worked with us and we've remained firm friends ever since. We were so surprised, even flattered, that Australia had taken 'The Two Of Us' to heart. That's why we'd written 'Thank You For Loving Me.' It was dedicated to Australia, not to each other. I can quite see the thought that we were simply drooling over each other, but we truly wrote that song for our fans in Australia and said so onstage.

Thank you for loving me
Thank you for being so kind
Thank you for loving me
'Cause I can't get you out of my mind.

Then we upped the pace, using my solo voice:

My Mama told me, don't you worry, child
Everything you planned will work out in a little while
I've been waiting for you baby, such a long, long time
I've gotta tell the world that your mine, mine, mine

Yes, Australia and her forthright people suited me fine. But it would take a massive financial crisis in UK, then a life threatening incident in the Republic of Ireland, to set the final scene for emigration to Oz in 1982…

Chapter 25
Clubland and Cup Fever

Nell

Back in the UK, I played "lead" in the musical, 'Nell.' Yani Skoradalides, alias Johnny Worth, wrote the music and lyrics for 'Nell.' Johnny started out in the business singing in pubs, a bit like me I suppose. He wrote 'What Do You Want,' Les Reed arranged a demo of the song and Adam Faith took it to No 1 in the charts in 1959. Johnny asked me to play the hearty Eleanor 'Nell' Gwyn, King Charles' busty mistress. Tony Hatch would be musical director. The production manager on 'Nell' was ripping us off with false accounting so a young Cameron Mackintosh was brought in to replace him. Cameron had just graduated from RADA, forever condemned by the famous words, 'He'll never be a producer of anything.' As he became evermore successful, Cameron enjoyed making that early judgment of him public knowledge.

To play the part of Nell Gwyn true to life, I read everything I could about her. She was a Cockney; bawdy, hard-bitten and pathetic, a kid from the gutter. She was voluble, yet in some ways she was quite shy. Nell was only an orange seller for a short while, though her love affair with King Charles lasted a long time. I'd say Nell was a real character.

I started my rehearsals from January 1970 onwards. I even worked out physically in a gym, getting into trim. By 2nd February I'd lost a stone in weight and was ready for the stage. We rehearsed in rooms next to Richmond theatre. On 8 April 1970 we opened at Richmond playing for three weeks, then went on tour. Sadly, we couldn't find a London theatre available, so the show ended after just a few months, but not before I'd had my fill of garlic.

Stuart Damon, an American who loved garlic, played opposite me as Charles II. He ate garlic with everything. He absolutely reeked of garlic, and I had to kiss him every night.

"Johnny, you've got to have a word with Stuart. I like garlic, but there's garlic and garlic, and that's way too much garlic!"

One night we suffered an impromptu romping session onstage. In one scene we had to chase each other around the bedroom, even across the bed itself. Until one night, when the bed broke. We both ended up stuck in the collapsed bed, ad- libbing until we could manage to climb out.

That year, 1970, we toured the theatre and nightclub circuit with 'Two Of Each' and our invited guest singers. On 4 July we had Scott Walker with us, appearing at the Brighton Dome concert hall, two performances. The Astor Club in London gave us repeat bookings. Previously they'd always booked solo artists, including me. Groups were new to the Astor and Jackie Daniels, the second female singer, was certainly an eye- raiser. She was also the drummer, with red hair streaming right down to her waist, and boy, did she prove a great attraction! We 'took the roof off' to standing ovations every night.

A Little Vanity Slips In

"Jackie, don't move around the stage so much. Stand by me, at the piano."

Tony was getting the taste for being on stage and he wanted the spotlight more on himself. And our height difference bothered him, "You shouldn't wear such high heels. They make me look small."

"Tone, you are small. I married you for what you are, y'know? This is business, out on stage, my business."

Nevertheless, he took to wearing platform shoes, as the critics noted in their write- ups. And, whenever possible, Tony would stand on a higher step, behind me. At first I accepted it as I understood his concerns. But gradually, I saw through his vanity. And newspaper critics commented on Tony's lack of voice power.

Danny La Rue

For nights out, we often relaxed at Danny's night club. Danny La Rue moved from Winston's club to open his own club, 'Danny's.' Ronnie and Annie Corbett followed him to Hanover Square with their act. Danny's became the 'in' place. There's always an 'in' place. Danny La Rue was one of the most hard working pros I knew. He'd appear in Panto, or his own spectacular in the provinces, for instance, then drive down the motorway to appear in his London club *the same night*. Superbly gowned, he often teased me, "God, Trent, you've got more beads on than I have." I adored Danny. He was the ultimate pro to the end and a very good friend.

Gibraltar

I was invited to fly out to Gibraltar to perform at a concert. 'The Rock' is a limestone lump, one of the Pillars of Hercules. Ceuta in Morocco is the other Pillar. It's just 15 miles across the straits, between the two pillars. The ocean surface current flows east at a walking pace, but 250ft down, a sub current rushes west, into the Atlantic. It's the only way the almost landlocked Med is refreshed and kept alive. I looked across the straits towards Tangier, recalling my lucky escape from probable death in 1960 when that earthquake shook Agadir to pieces. I made friends with the famous apes, the Barbary macaques. Sadly, I saw people teasing the apes, noisy and badly behaved people, whilst the apes remained dignified and correct. Every year, apes are shot for biting tourists. Barbary macaques have a very strong social order and their corpses and skeletons are never found on the Rock. There is said to be a secret mortuary established by the apes, in the recesses of the limestone Rock of Gibraltar.

A Run of Fun

In 1970 Tony and I wrote 'Yoko' as a novelty number. Obviously we were looking at the commercial aspect. Lennon married Yoko Ono in 1969 and we wrote the song in 1970. We pulled in a load of stage school kids to sing along with us on the track. 'Yoko' received lots of airplay in Japan. At the time, Yoko Ono was probably the most unpopular woman in Britain.

Julie Budd

One day this Yiddishi gal from Brooklyn, NY came into my life. We were about to write an album for her. But I'll let Julie tell the tale herself:

It was the early 70's and I was a teenager, in my second year of high school.

Jackie and I both had something in common. We were both 'born in a trunk' as one would say. Two kids at opposite ends of the pond, who started out in show business at a very young age. Jackie in her home, the UK. And I as well, made a name for myself in the USA as a young performer doing all the major TV shows, tours, plays & recordings.

I performed alongside great artists such as Frank Sinatra, Bob Hope and the brilliant Liberace, who I played alongside at The London Palladium when I was just 16 years old. And, just as Jackie was able to sustain in this industry and to perform as a mature artist, I had the great fortune of being able to enjoy my performing career in my adulthood. Even to this present date I am still recording. I am still touring and enjoying what I love to do the most, to sing for my audience.

But it was the recording aspect of my career that brought Jackie Trent and her husband of that time, Tony Hatch, into my life. I was signed to RCA records. They were very powerful, not only domestically here in the USA, but all over the world. I was now recording in other languages and had recordings in South America and releases in Japan. And then RCA decided to pair my musical abilities with the producing and writing team of Tony Hatch & Jackie Trent. I knew who they were of course, because of all the great work they did with Petula Clark. And of course I was aware of the individual abilities that Tony Hatch & Jackie Trent could offer.

The meeting took place at RCA here in New York City and it was then planned that I was to go to London & record at a place called PYE studios. I was thrilled and overjoyed. London!!!! How cool is that!! Most of the plans and conversation took place between my manager and the record company. I was, after all, just a kid trying to figure out how I was going to mail my homework back to NYC each week, on time...

My manager at the time was Herb Bernstein. He was also my musical director and a very famous orchestrator and producer in his own right. He produced and orchestrated hits for Laura Nyro's first album, arranged music for John Denver, Tina Turner, The Four Seasons, The Happenings & Dusty Springfield. Just to name a few...

Phone calls went on for a while, as everyone was deciding on the direction of this recording. Remember, there was no computer, no Skype, no Faxes. Just the phone and packages going across the ocean every other day, so that Jackie & Tony would have lots of material & get a real sense of who I was.

Finally, it was time for me to make my journey. I was so excited, as I was staying in London for about a month, at a little place called The Kensington Palace Hotel. It was sweet, right in the neighborhood I had to be in, and just what we needed. I remember we called Jackie and Tony to say that we had arrived and would meet them at the studio the next day. Tony said, "No, meet us at my office, we are not ready for recording just yet."

Up bright & early the next day, we were ready to begin our English adventure. We took a cab to Tony's office. I was so taken with the English Cabbies, so lovely, they knew everything about the city and were so helpful. I was used to the NYC Taxis, "Hey lady, Where ya going?"

Being Me

I absolutely loved London. I imagined myself staying there and felt at one with that town. Finally we arrived at our destination. Tony's office was large and looked very businesslike, all pulled together and very busy busy. He greeted Herb and I right away. Tony was very nice, but all business. He was nice to me, but a bit stand- offish. I thought, 'Maybe that's just the way they are here??' He had a little sort of dry sense of humor. But like I said, all business. He liked Herb a lot. He seemed to have great respect for him and I know Herb liked Tony too.

Later in the meeting, when we were now seriously picking the material & getting keys, Jackie arrived. She was Completely Different !!!! A totally different energy. I wondered, 'They are married??' If there were two people in the world that seemed absolutely opposite from each other, it was Tony and Jackie. Jackie was open, fun, engaging, welcoming, like a big sister. Right away, she felt responsible for this little kid. We were giggling & were instantly pals. I thought to myself, 'Oh my gosh, I feel like I know her from another life!' Throughout my stay in London and during the recording, I was overjoyed when I could be with Jackie. Unfortunately, that was not to be, as Jackie was writing a lot and each day I had loads of music to learn. More of my time was spent with Tony & Herb, learning the orchestrations, as Tony was writing each night as well.

I was a very serious & disciplined little gal. I was not fooling around and I knew that things were coming to me that only other young artists could dream about. While I was rehearsing with Tony & Jackie for the sessions, I was also studying Tap at Dance Center In London. My teacher was a gifted wonderful gal by the name of Molly Malloy. What a talented and terrific teacher! Molly created the Malloy Technique of Jazz Dance, which she reportedly taught to Arlene Phillips, the dance choreographer and judge on UK's hit dance competition, 'Strictly Come Dancing.'

I was rehearsing like mad in between my recording as Liberace had asked me to join him again on tour. I had to be ready, right after my sessions with Tony and Jackie, to join Liberace back in the States. We were going to do a huge tap number from the Broadway Show, 'No No Nannette.' I had to be prepared. I was burning the candle at both ends and working like mad but... I was loving every minute. London became my dream destination. I felt like I was home.

We were now getting ready for the sessions and It was the night before everything was going to begin. Herb & Tony realized that we were going to be in England a lot longer than we anticipated. It was Jackie who then suggested, "Why don't you stay with us? When the time runs out at the hotel, and you know you'll need to stay someplace, just move into our house."

You see, that was Jackie. Right there. That's the whole thing. That is the warm and wonderful person we grew to love.

I loved Jackie's home. It was beautiful, warm and wonderful. Just like her. She couldn't do enough for you and your comfort was always important to her. I should mention that I think one of the immediate feelings of closeness that I had for Jackie was that we both grew up in show business and were both out there at such a young age. She was a real show biz veteran & I guess I was too. We had a real friendship and Jackie protected me, as I was just a kid. I recall, being one night in the music room of their home. It was before the big sessions were starting. I felt a bit of concern for Tony. He did a lot of writing & hard work on these sessions and was constantly orchestrating, through long hours. It was the first time I thought to myself, 'There is trouble in paradise.'

I noticed a lot of tension and a real lack of communication between Jackie and Tony.

Tony was tired and short- tempered with Jackie, and Jackie was, in her way, a bit childlike and lighthearted about everything. They looked as if they were like oil and water, so completely separate and disconnected, yet in the same home. I was sad to see this, as it was my first look at what was happening behind the scenes.

We were at Jackie's & Tony's house the night before the first session. This was where I really saw the huge differences between who these people were. Tony was tense, going over the music, wondering, 'Will this kid pull this off?' Jackie was organic & understanding to the fact, "This is a rehearsal. Don't worry. She will turn right on when the Orchestra plays the first downbeat." I saw them go at each other. It was really uncomfortable for me. Almost like I should not have been there, seeing something that personal. I wondered, 'What keeps them together?' I thought, 'It's the Music. It has to be the Music.'

They certainly did not represent a love story to me.

First day: Sessions and Band day. I thought I'd died and went to heaven. Pye was a wonderful place to work, with enormously talented people and a terrific engineer who caught every nuance. The musicians were amazing. And, just as our Jackie knew would happen, I sang with my heart in every note. You see, Jackie was not just a wonderful writer, but a great performer as well. She understood that process and knew exactly what was going to happen.

After the first sessions I noticed that Jackie was not around as much. I personally think that Tony preferred working solo and had personal challenges with Jackie's energy. I was very surprised by Tony and Jackie, and I think staying in the house gave me an insight to them that I might not have had otherwise.

Positive thoughts from Julie, which she never spoke of at the time.

Positive Thinking

We were great friends with Eric Morecambe and Ernie Wise and I made regular appearances on their show. On stage, Eric enjoyed using me as his alternative 'straight man', uninvited! I'd be in the middle of a big number, belting it out, as Eric crept on stage, making faces behind my back. The audience would finally give the game away, bursting into laughter.

Once in Biaggi's restaurant on the Edgware Road, just around the corner from Pye studios, Tony and I were sat having dinner. One minute Eric was sat at table across the room, the next minute our tablecloth parted, to reveal Eric's head rearing up between my legs. "I thought I'd just drop in and say hello!" whilst madly rocking his trademark glasses on his face.

"Why don't you use the front door, like everyone else?' Shouted Dick Emery the comedian, sat next to us.

Eric must have crawled under at least 4 tables of diners to end up under our table. He just couldn't resist larking about. Eric and Ernie asked us to write a song for them. "Write us a song about someone full of gloom and doom, someone with no positive outlook on life, something that will lift his spirits. *And I'll have another, thanks, spirit, that is. I thank yoouu!"* That was Eric Morecambe, through and through. "We just want people to be happy"

So we wrote 'Positive Thinking,' with an upbeat feel:

When you feel down, try positive thinking
That's what I thought a man said
Don't wear a frown, try positive thinking
Laugh at your troubles instead

In other words, take everything as it comes. Be positive. It's up to you to change the way you look at life. Eric & Ernie were always great fun to work with. The recording session for 'Positive Thinking' proved a laugh a minute. Eric couldn't be serious about anything; he had the musicians in stitches. Image the brass section trying to concentrate, playing trumpet and laughing at the same time. Impossible! So the song took three times as long to record as normal, but it sure was a very special recording session of which to be part. All good, clean fun.

There were so many special 'fun' times, right then. On one special trip, the fun started the minute we boarded the train from London to Cardiff. Bob Monkhouse, the brilliant raconteur and comedian, was our travelling companion to a gig at a club just outside Cardiff. We never stopped laughing. That is until we arrived at the club in the freezing cold, to be greeted by a stage piano with its front missing. The lavish fare that night amounted to piles of cheese and onion sandwiches, already stacked at each table. We just stared at each other in wonder.

"I'm going to die on my feet here," said Bob, and shot off to the dressing/storeroom with his medicinal bottle of Johnny Walker whisky, which he promptly dropped. The reek of whisky floated everywhere from the smashed bottle.

Then the drummer turned up, "I'm really sorry, but I can't play. I'm still recovering from a bout of flu." We never did figure how that might have affected his drumming but we coped somehow. Bob knocked the audience's socks off with his usual charm. He even wangled a replacement bottle of scotch at 'trade price' and six packets of cheese and onion crisps for our emergency ration journey home. After the show, we were just in time to catch the night milk train back to London. It seemed to stop everywhere, picking up mail. The whisky and crisps just lasted out for our 5am arrival, back

Being Me

in London. Such a relief. All of us swore to have words with our booking agent!

Clubs and Z Cars
Les drove me up to Manchester for a TV Special. We gave Alvin Stardust a lift back to London. On the way south, we called in at Mum's in Stoke.

"Jack, some of your showbiz friends were here yesterday. They ate us out of house and home. Mind, they were a happy lot."

"Who were they, Mum?"

"Gene Vincent and the Blue Jeans. Is that the right name for them? They stayed overnight, so we gave them our bed. Les and I slept downstairs, on the couch."

"Sorry Mum. I gave Gene your address and said they should call in and say 'Hi,' if they were in the area. I never thought they'd stop over. I'll give you some money for their food."

We all had a cup of tea and then we were back on the road to London.

Talk of the North, Eccles, Manchester.
'The Talk' was reckoned to be one of the top nightclubs in the north west of England. I'd go further. To me, what the club offered was equal, probably better, than anything in London at the time. Joe Pullen ran 'The Talk.' He had a strict dress code, men with jacket and tie, ladies were not permitted to wear trousers, of any sort. Lord Snowdon once turned up at the door with a party, all in evening dress. Snowdon was wearing the latest fashion collarless dress shirt and no tie.

"No admittance," declared Joe.

"Do you know who I am?"

"I don't give a fuck who you are. You're not coming in without a tie."

Someone found a tie and Lord Snowdon was finally admitted. There was a rumour running through showbiz circles at the time, 'Did you hear what happened at the Talk? There was a fire, but Joe Pullen wouldn't let the firemen in without a tie.'

The Catholic priest allowed the club to use his church car park just across the road, in exchange for racehorse tips as Joe had a racehorse himself. Joe Pullen spoke in a very direct manner and we got on well together.

"I hear you once banned Dusty Springfield, Joe?"

"Damn right I did, Jackie. She nearly killed someone. Right in the middle of her song, a member of the audience stood up to go somewhere, so she threw a benny and pushed the grand piano almost off the stage. I came out onstage right away. I told her, "Right, you're out of 'ere. You're banned. "

"You can't do that."

"I'm doin' it."

"I'll sue you."

"Go ahead. I've got enough witnesses in this club that you nearly killed somebody."

Dusty certainly had problems. We were friends but she wanted me as a very close friend. One night we were both appearing at the De Montfort Hall in Leicester. We shared a dressing room with the Lana sisters, one of the sisters was Dusty's current girlfriend. There was a big falling out. I ducked down whilst Dusty threw crockery everywhere, screaming.

I tried to steady her, "Calm down. You're onstage soon. You'll have no voice left"

On tour, the Searchers would visit the local market to buy cheap crockery as fresh ammo for Dusty.

In 1970 I was invited to play Ruth Dawson, girlfriend to one of the regular cast of the very popular TV police series, 'Z- Cars.' In its day, 'Z- Cars' was the equivalent of the American hit TV series, 'Hill Street Blues,' without the music and quasi- comedy style. Real policemen told me that Z- Cars was fairly close to real- time policing

Being Me

of the day in UK. Nottingham City Police certainly had their 'Z-cars,' the Mechanised Division, fast, black patrol cars dealing with crime only, no road traffic incidents to clog the system. I appeared in two episodes of 'Z- Cars' as Ruth, a blond bombshell who drove a Triumph TR sports car, supposedly!

"Jackie, for this scene we want you to jump into the car, drive up to camera, stop, then sort of slide out of the car, showing plenty of leg, if you would? You do drive, of course?"

"Oh yes, of course I do."

Of course I did *not* drive, but I wasn't going to admit to it.

'Can't be difficult,' I thought as I climbed aboard. Somehow I managed to fire up the engine and work out the pedal arrangement. I found first gear and started to move off. Suddenly the clutch seemed to have a mind of its own and the car lurched around like a wild thing. Someone finally came to my rescue and gave me a quick lesson on driving.

"OK, let's try again?" said the director, patiently.

Finally my big moment arrived. I drive up to camera, stop just in time, then slide out of car saying "Hello boys" huskily to the gathered policemen. We all had a laugh afterwards.

Real policemen, the Flying Squad, sometimes turned up at our home, Crossroads, and used our pool between spells of duty. I met a few of them when we were invited to a Metropolitan Police function, where I was sat between John Thaw, the actor and Sir Robert Mark, the Metropolitan Police Commissioner. Dennis Waterman sat at another table with the lads, getting pissed. Thaw and Waterman starred in a very popular TV police series, The Sweeney. My feet were killing me, so I slipped off my shoes. Problem is, afterwards I couldn't find them again.

"I'll go down there and have a look for you, if you like, Jackie," said Sir Robert. At last minute, someone across from us found the errant shoes. We invited some of the lads home for a nightcap, afterwards.

In the winter of 1970/71 we were invited over to tour Australia again and once more we took 'Two Of Each' along with us. Byron Davis took over from redhead Jackie on drums. We had Byron mime the singing parts, bless him. We went down well again with the Aussies.

The clubs in Australia were a whole different story. They left the Brit clubs light years behind. The first we played was the St George Leagues Rugby Club, set on the Princes Highway in Kogarah. The club started out in 1963, with just two poker machines, a stage and one long bar. By 1971 it had grown to become known as 'The Taj Mahal,' because there was so much marble used in its very grand construction. The club had every facility you could imagine, including a huge stage with two glitter staircases, one either side of stage, to make the grand entrance, depending on not catching one's heels and going arse- over- tit. It was a matter of 'flashing eyes and teeth,' concentrating hard on the steps down to the stage. The auditorium seated 1500 people, all seated at table. This was some club, set on 3 floors. It was magnificent. We opened on 2nd February 1971 to sell out houses every night, Tuesday to Sunday, over a three week booking. We certainly were popular in Australia!

We filmed a TV Special there and Byron the drummer recorded the tour generally with his cine camera, when he wasn't miming! I still have a copy of the film that Byron gave me.

The RSL clubs were like mini Las Vegas clubs. The slots pulled in millions of dollars that were re- invested in the clubs. Food and booze were cheap and everyone got a great deal.

I loved playing 'Twin Towns' in Northern NSW. The club had gone from strength to strength, buying the land opposite that housed the police station. In its place a hotel was built, with an air bridge across to the club. The auditorium was on the top of the building and perfect to work. Twin Towns is at Tweed Heads, where you only had to walk across the road to be in Queensland, and an extra hour's drinking time. A new police station was built up the road, by the way!

Back in UK, Tony suddenly seemed anxious to sell up and move. It was 1972.

"I've been advised to sell Crossroads, to free up capital."

Free up capital, with all the money we earned each year? I really did not want to move from my lovely home, but he had his way, as usual. The Times ran a feature article and the house sold immediately. Two people viewed, Status Quo's drummer and a Director of Slater Walker.

The house sold in a week. The Slater Walker man acted quicker. We found Kelvin House in Westerham, a house I didn't particularly like, but we bought it. Looking back, I wonder now at the financial advice Tony was given and even at his own common sense. We sold lovely Crossroads for £57,000 and bought Kelvin House for £77,000, with mortgage… *to free capital?* Yes, it put short term monies in the bank, only to pick up a mortgage. Tony handled our cash flow, both his and mine. I started to wonder if Tony really was in control of our finances. It took me a long while to like Kelvin House. The seller's wife had much less time to think of moving out. Her husband only told her on the morning we moved in! At least there was an apartment over the garage for my Madge and Jim, so I could keep Madge to help me.

Football - Stoke City FC (The Potters)

By the early 1970's I was something of a household name in Stoke. But in 1971, Stoke City FC's reputation had steadily grown to eclipse me back home because, in the 1971/2 Football League Cup season, they kept winning matches:

4th Round	27.10.71	Manchester United	1 - 1	Stoke City
Re- play	08.11.71	Stoke City	0 - 0	Manchester United
2nd re- play	15.11.71	"	2 – 1	"

Jackie Trent

Semi- Final
1st leg	08.12.71	Stoke City	1 - 2	West Ham
2nd leg	15.12.71	West Ham	0 - 1	Stoke City
On Aggregate			**2 – 2**	

I took a call at home in Kent from Tony Waddington, Stoke's manager.

"Jackie, we're through to the semi- final of the League Cup against West Ham. We never lose when you're at the match. You have to be there. Can you make it? We'll be playing at Hillsborough."

The players felt that I brought them luck. I was a Potters fan and went to watch the game whenever I was in town. It's true, they didn't seem to lose when I was there! So I turned up for the match at Hillsborough:

Replay   05.01.72   Stoke City   0 – 0   West Ham

So far so good. For the final replay at Trafford Park, Waddo sent a car to collect me from Manchester Ringway airport:

2nd replay   26.01.72   Stoke City   3 - 2   West Ham

'Hey! The Potters were on their way to Wembley for the League Cup Final!'
Afterwards, back home, I 'phoned Tony Waddington, "Tony, we need a football song here. Something the team can sing along with us. How's about we write a song? We can record it at the ground."

Waddo thought that was a good idea so 'my Tony' and I set our heads into football mode.

We'll Be With You - 1972
We came up with a simple, stirring song, 'We'll Be With You', that fans could shout from the terraces on match day. Then we gathered a mass of recording equipment from Pye studios and set off north. The supporters club provided a room for the recording and lusty supporters to add their voices to the proceedings. Word got around and we had to lock ourselves in, all due to a swarm of 'extras' who wanted to gatecrash.

Being Me

At one point I needed the local police to help me out with crowd control!

In the ladies loo I came across some 'extras', Janet Barker, Tina and Mary. "Jackie, we're desperate to join in. Can you help us?" And in the corridor David Pegg with his wife and nephew, Graham. They all wanted 'in' too. I found a side door and led everyone over the stage to join in, past a slightly dumbfounded Tony at piano. We all had a ball, making that recording. Those who couldn't sing were tactfully steered away from the mikes. Janet Barker later told me:

"I think it was Central TV who filmed the recording. And there I was next day on TV, stood in the front row. The girls at Staffordshire Potteries gave me a round of applause afterwards. Thanks, Jackie!"

Meanwhile, excitement was building in the town for the coming Cup Final. John Pye, a probationary constable of Staffordshire Police was on night shift, patrolling Church Street, Newcastle. He watched the scene unfold:

Saturday, February 12th 1972 had been a bitterly cold day. I pulled my cape around my shoulders for a bit more warmth as I trudged my town centre beat on night duty. A group of middle aged men came walking along Church Street towards me, only to see another similar group come into view, heading in the same direction. The quietness was disturbed even further as vans, cars, motorbikes and pushbikes appeared, and more and more people started to emerge from every alleyway and side street. "What the hell's going on?" I said to one group.

They were all on a mission. "League Cup Final, application forms for tickets, on sale this morning." I radioed the situation in. It was the Victoria Ground and the sight was amazing for there were already thousands of people queuing up with two braziers already lit. The crowd had swelled to twenty thousand and every single ticket was spoken for. I finished duty at 10 a.m. that morning, (4 hours overtime), tired, cold and hungry, but happy in the thought that I would get my two tickets. I went down to Wembley with my fiancée, Gladys, on Saturday 4th March that year to watch Stoke.

John Pye 'The Nick of Time' 2008

Meanwhile, Tony and I kept the party spirit going, down in London. On the Wednesday before the Cup Final we invited the team, trainers and management along to our home in Kent for a party. I prepared enough food for an army and the players quietly quaffed Bacardi or whisky in their 'soft drinks.' Our nanny Petra proved a major attraction to the players. She was from Clayton, Staffordshire and had been a Miss England finalist.

The Big Day - Saturday 4 March 1972 - Wembley Stadium
Tony and I went along to Wembley as guests of Stoke City FC. We watched the match, enthralled. 97,850 other spectators also watched the match, 35,000 of them from Stoke. We held our breath as Gordon Banks, Stoke's goalie, saved a penalty kick in spectacular fashion. And Stoke City won: 2 – 1. *'Oh Glory!!'*

The celebratory party afterwards at the Russell Hotel in London ran on into the night. I rose to sing, with what little voice I had left. In the excitement, Gordon Banks, our hero goalie, accidentally trod on the bottom of my gown and nearly ripped it off. Thanks Gordon, but you're still my hero, my No 1!

And the League Cup itself? John Pye again:

'Officials from Stoke FC contacted the police station. Could they leave the League Cup in safe custody? It was placed 'in safe custody', in cell number one. Later that night, the Cup was given temporary police bail and at the 2 a.m. meal break the lads had a brew of tea ceremoniously poured from the League Cup.'
John Pye 'The Nick of Time' 2008

To this day, 'We'll Be With You' is still sung on the Stoke City terracing on match days, although my old mate Tom Jones' 'Delilah' has mostly taken its place on the terraces at Britannia Stadium. That's good. 'Delilah' is a stirring song and Tom loved flirting with me.

Travelling On
We were forever travelling. In October 1972 we were in Mexico for the World Congress of Composers and Authors. I appeared on TV there and helped judge the song festival.

In February and March 1973 we toured Australia, in concert with John Bouchier, 'England's funniest ventriloquist.' We played:

26 Feb - Brisbane Town Hall, then down the coast to Ballarat.
6 March - Ballarat Memorial Hall, then flew on to Melbourne.
7 March - Melbourne Dallas Brooks Hall. More flying – to Tasmania.
9 March - Hobart City Hall.
10 March - Launceston Albert Hall, then back to mainland Australia.
14 March - Adelaide Apollo Stadium.
16 March - Perth Concert Hall.

Chapter 26
Musicals, Bankruptcy and Betrayal

'The Card' - 1973

"Jackie, Cameron wants us to write the music for a new musical production, Arnold Bennett's 'The Card.' Keith Waterhouse and Willis Hall will be the scriptwriters. What do you think?"

"Sounds great. Burslem, Stoke, that's my territory. When do we start?"

The 1952 film of 'The Card' starred Alec Guinness as Denry Machin, with Valerie Hobson and a young Petula Clark. It was shot on location, in Burslem, Stoke-on-Trent. Burslem boasted a grand Town Hall and the terraced houses and cobbled streets of the area were the perfect background for the film. And guess who was also in the background of that very film?' *Me!*

In 1951, age 11, I saw an ad in the *Sentinel,* 'Extras wanted for 'The Card.' Just turn up.' And so I did. They dressed us in period urchin clothing, with basic instructions, "Just play in the street as people walk up and down. And don't look at the cameras!" We urchin extras were paid 5/- a day, plus food. That was my very first sighting of Petula Clark, though she didn't see me of course. Little did I know that some ten years or so down the line, I'd be co-writing Number 1 hit songs for her!

Being Me

Of course, Arnold Bennett's 1911 story was filmed in 1951 Stoke- on- Trent, with its ever growing array of rooftop TV aerials. Therefore each day before filming, the 'H'frame aerials had to be taken down, then put back up each night in time for the four hour BBC TV transmissions. Each household was paid for the inconvenience caused. Yes, four hours TV screening each night is all there was then in the UK, if you were lucky enough to own a telly, that is!

The Plot

After WWII, when I was a child, money was in very short supply. The Provident Company, based in Bradford in the north of England, was one example of organisations providing credit for hard up local people, all paying small weekly amounts into 'the club.' Local shops kept a Provident account paying- in book.

In 'The Card' Denry Machin came up with such an idea. He worked as a humble clerk in the Lord Mayor's office. He was a 'likely lad', an opportunist, and he wanted a better future. So he started a club card savings scheme, where members paid in a few pennies a week in regular savings and were given vouchers to buy goods on credit. 'Our Denry' took a small percentage of the savings monies *and* sales commission from shops accepting the vouchers as payment for goods. He took a commission at both ends, so a nice little earner all round!

The part needed a strong, energetic voice for Denry's character to really shine through, singing 'Nobody Thought Of It But Me.' He was a likely lad with get up and go:

Nobody thought of it but me.
Nobody saw the great potential,
Bright & beautiful ideas somehow suddenly appear.

John Alderton desperately wanted the part. He was hot on TV at the time with 'Please Sir' and 'Upstairs/Downstairs', so he was definitely a contender. John took singing lessons. He and his lovely wife Pauline Collins even stayed with us several times in order for

John to sing and to read the script. Pauline said to me, "He badly wants to do this, Jackie."

We listened to John warm up, in the lounge, "But he can't bloody sing, can he?" said Pauline. Pauline Collins later won fame staring in the wonderful film, 'Shirley Valentine'.

"No he can't. And he never will," I had to admit.

Otherwise John Alderton was a perfect Denry, lanky and tall, a box office name and with a perfect accent. 'The Lad Most Likely' for our Denry would have been Michael Crawford, but Crawford would have played himself, or Frank Spencer. He was already typecast in the public eye, so we passed on Michael. We all finally agreed on Jim Dale as The Likely Lad.' And he could sing. The Mayor was played by John Savident. John later joined Coronation Street and was there for many years.

Tony and I worked on the musical score for 'The Card' over several months, between other commitments. Keith Waterhouse and Willis Hall were the scriptwriters and they both hailed from Leeds. Arnold Bennett and I were 'Stokies, from Stoke- on- Trent, so we all fitted the location. The Card was set in the Potteries and this really was my territory as I'd grown up there: the Potteries, the land of Wedgewood, Royal Doulton, Minton and Spode bone china. At one time, it's believed there were more than 1500 pottery works in the area.

'Bone China – a 'Potted' history

The Chinese invented porcelain ware in the 7th or 8th Century AD, hence the word *'china.'* War and taxation eventually killed off the China trade and transport ships were commandeered for war. A 100% plus import duty finally proved too much for Chinese importations to compete, as the European industry took over. Stoke-on-Trent was sat very nicely on the basic ingredients for earthenware manufacture, coal and clay, but lacked the bone china. Josiah Wedgwood helped solve that by pioneering the Trent and Mersey canal, bringing Cornish china clay right into town, by barge. And 'bone china' was literally that, 50% animal bone ash.

The pottery industry created employment for the men hewing coal and cutting clay. It also gave work to thousands of local women. Leaf gold decorated the finest porcelain and figurines, applied with a steady hand. The artist would be bent for hours over a small turntable, rotating the platform with the little finger of one hand, applying gold and lacquer with her other, using the finest brush, a brush with maybe just a couple of hairs. Those women had constantly raw fingers. My elder sister Sheila did that work. I remember our Sheila coming home from work at Leigh Pottery in Middleport, always with a raw, blistered little finger. At the end of every shift those fine brushes were inspected for gold residue and the work areas were carefully cleaned down into special containers.

I understood this raw environment as I'd grown up with it. I'd lived the risk of death and injury that Dad brought home every day from the pit, I'd breathed the constant fumes that the 1500 plus kilns spewed out every day and I'd entertained those same workers, male and female, on their nights out at the working men's clubs. As I said, this was my territory.

Arnold Bennett/Denry Machin understood that environment too. No wonder Arnold and Denry, both in real life and in fiction, escaped to London as soon as they could. Keith Waterhouse and Willis Hall were born into heavily industrialised Leeds. They too, eventually took themselves to London. But all of them took their heritage along with them, to be recalled later in their written work.

Keith Waterhouse

Keith was born in Leeds in 1929, growing up in poverty on a council estate. He loved books and became an avid reader. He left school, age 14, taking employment where he could. In 1950 he finally found his destiny as a writer, working for The Yorkshire Post as a junior reporter. Two years later he went south to London. In London he persuaded The Mirror features editor to employ him, freelance. His first commission was to find a talking dog. He found one apparently, in Cardiff.

"That's no bloody good," said the editor. "The sales push is in the north west. Find one in Liverpool!"

In his spare time, whilst working with The Mirror, Keith co-wrote his best selling novel 'Billy Liar', which is where Willis Hall came in.

Willis Hall

Hall and Waterhouse were both pupils of Cockburn High School in Leeds. They both attended the same youth clubs and compared notes on the girls. The two lived close by each other. Peter O'Toole's family lived nearby too and their parents sometimes drank with O'Toole's parents. After school, Willis tried journalism, North Sea trawler fishing and finally joined the military, seeing service in the Malaysian jungle. In 1959 he wrote 'The Long and The Short and The Tall.' Hall and Waterhouse wrote 'Billy Liar' as their first joint enterprise. In 1973 they set to, co- writing a musical version of 'The Card.' I once called in at their office, to find them sat facing each other, at identical desks, firing lines of script at each other over their typewriters. We all got on well together. I even gave them some unique Stoke colloquial expressions for their script.

Tony and I found the perfect melody and title to fit the two main characters of the musical, 'Opposite Your Smile.' It worked perfectly in every way. In the show, Denry Machin and Nellie, his secretary, sat opposite each other in the office, as in reality did Willis Hall and Keith Waterhouse. In fact they gave us the idea for the song, which we liked so much that we recorded 'Opposite your Smile' ourselves. Tony Blackburn, BBC Radio One DJ, made it his

'Record of the Week.' We enjoyed lots of airplay with that song. It was a 'fun' song. Cameron Mackintosh's West End production of 'The Card' opened on 24 July 1973 at the Queens Theatre. It ran for 130 performances, so it did 'OK.'

By the early 1970's, and still in our early 30's, our joint output included 30 hit songs, one musical, over 300 TV and radio broadcasts and 3,500 cabaret and theatre appearances. Not bad! One such appearance, on 30 April 1974, was at the Fairfield Halls, Park Lane, Croydon. By coincidence, Keith Goodwin handled the press enquiries for that one. *The* Keith Goodwin of New Musical Express, who I'd duped into carrying my suitcase at Euston station when I first hit London, back in 1956. The innocent man I kidded into thinking I was a French Mademoiselle no less!

Rock Nativity – intro 'Sting'

Tony and I wrote the music for another musical, David Wood's Rock Nativity. It was fun, being involved in a warm Xmas musical. The show was presented by the Tyneside Theatre Company and opened at the University Theatre, Newcastle- on- Tyne over the 1974/75 Xmas season. One Gordon Sumner was the bass player. He'd recently qualified as a teacher. Gordon is better known now as 'Sting.' He married my dresser at the time. The show toured UK during 1975/76, and was even televised.

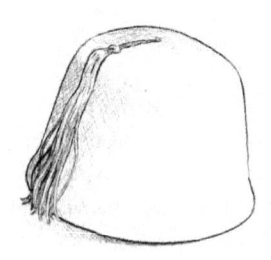

Tommy Cooper - some light relief

Tommy Cooper was ultimate fun. I appeared regularly on his show too. He stood 6' 3" (1.93 metres) tall in his size 16 boots, always wearing a fez onstage. The very sight of him had audiences laughing

Jackie Trent

without him even saying a single word. He played on that, of course. One Sunday, a whole gang of us gathered at Helen Bradley's guest house in Roundhay, Leeds. We were there for a black tie Bar Mitzvah ceremony for the son of Pinky or Perky, I can't remember which, but they were both famous Leeds theatrical booking agents. Helen only accepted top entertainers as lodgers. I suppose that way we could enjoy privacy amongst our own kind. Tommy was there in brown suede shoes, but he needed black dress shoes, "Can anyone find me some black shoes - size 16?"

Well of course nobody could. "How can I go without black shoes?"

"We could find some boot polish to black- up the suede', I suggested"

We left Tommy crashing around the house and went off to the ceremony. I'll let Barry Stevenson, retired Detective Inspector, Leeds City Police, take over the story:

I was at the same Bar Mitzvah ceremony, as it turns out. I was sitting at the same round dining table as you, Tony and Jackie. Tommy was my close friend and he asked me to save him a seat next to me, which I did. But the ceremony started without him. Tommy was nowhere to be seen. The room went silent as the ceremony started. Then people at one table started to giggle, the laughter spread to the next table and the next again. Then I saw the reason for the laughter:

Tommy's head was bobbing up and down between the lines of chairs, looking for me. When he finally found me, he sat at the table as if nothing unusual had happened. He spoke to me in a low voice, 'low' enough to be heard by others around him, "I'm sorry I'm late, but I couldn't find my dress shoes." He nudged me, "I had to put these on." Tommy pushed back his seat and lifted his foot up, almost onto the table, to show the big brown boots he was wearing. Of course, everyone collapsed in laughter.

You remember Jackie, Tom had a great reputation for being tight? Well, after the meal and drinks Tommy said, "Let's go to the bar downstairs and talk magic." Later we were joined by Tommy's wife Dove and his driver, John. Dove asked Tommy if she could borrow two shillings to buy John a drink. Tommy gave her a two shilling piece and said, "I'll stop that out of your housekeeping money next week."

I started to laugh. Dove cut me short: "Don't you think he's joking, Barry. He will stop it out of my housekeeping. He always does if I borrow anything from him."

Thanks for that, Barry.

Another time, working at the Circus Tavern in Dartford, Tommy was collected by car from his hotel and his radio mike was fitted as they drove to the theatre. But the stage door was locked when they arrived and heavy rain was falling. Remember his radio mike was already live. The audience *inside* sat fascinated, listening to Tommy crashing around *outside* in the rain, desperately trying to find a way in, shouting, "Will somebody please let me in!" When he finally walked into the theatre, via the front entrance, he was met with rapturous applause.

The strain of life eventually caught up with Tommy and alcohol slowly took over. Tommy passed away, onstage, in 1984.

In 2008 Sir Anthony Hopkins unveiled the Tommy Cooper memorial in his hometown of Caerphilly, South Wales, wearing the fez, of course.

The Critics

Tony and I were now firmly established as a double act. It did frustrate me at times. We played the Talk of the Town for three weeks from 27 February 1978, immediately following my old mate Vince Hill's season there. We were only the sixth couple to play the 'Talk' in its 20 years of existence. How would we be received? I anxiously read the opening night reviews:

James Green, writing 'First Night' for the London Evening News, was pleasantly critical: *"Nine for presentation. I notice he's shorter than her, hence the Cuban heels. Content? Eight. Too much lovey-dovey talk. Doing your clean washing in public, as they say. She's a belting type of singer who likes to shout 'em home. Star quality? They've already proved they have it as songwriters, and as performers they're not top of the class. They'll get a living in clubs and on TV, I imagine.*

Anthony Shields, for Night Life in 'What's On In London' wrote: *"Tony Hatch joins [her] fairly tentatively, in duets. Jackie is in fine voice and really makes me wonder why she has not achieved even greater success than she has so far. She's a convincing and entertaining singer who understands phrasing and communicates the songs to the audience."*

Nigel Hunter in Music Week: *"Marital togetherness on stage needs to be handled and presented with care to avoid plunging into a cloying quagmire of saccharine sentimentality. [They] made it quite clear frequently that they are in fact married and that they write songs together which might have had us crying into our Talk Of The Town soup. She has a powerful voice which constantly emphasised the fact that Tony's vocal chords are less than powerful. Jackie looks good, moves well and sings intelligible words in tune."*

Fine for me, not so good for Tony.

Starting Over In Southern Ireland 1978
After some serious financial problems, not of my causing, which forced us to sell our beloved home, we started a new life in Southern Ireland. We knew Ireland as we'd appeared on RTE TV shows and at top nightclubs in Dublin. We loved the Irish way of life and Ireland offered low taxation to artists, giving us a chance to pay our bills and to recover financially.

Dennis
We found a place to rent. Working from home we needed privacy, which that meant an ex- directory telephone number, so I went to the telephone company. And that's where I met Dennis, sat in his little office.

I asked him for an ex- directory telephone number. "That's quoite OK, missus. We'll arrange t'hat roight now. As soon as ya muve in, gi' me a call an' oi'l give ya da noo number."

He gave me his direct extension number. We moved in. I 'phoned

Being Me

Dennis from the house, "Good morning Dennis. This is Mrs. Hatch again." I gave him the address. "You changed the 'phone number to a private one for us? Would you tell me the new number?"

"Well oi couldn't exactly be doin' dat. Dis is a privut number, ya know. How do oi know dat ya are who ya say ya are?"

"Well we've met, I gave you my name. And I'm using the 'phone right now."

"Ah! Dat still don't prove who ya are!"

"So how would I have your name and your extension number? Look, ring me. You have the new number to call, and if I answer, you'll know who I am."

"Roight,' I'll do just dat."

I put down the receiver. A few minutes later the 'phone rang. "Hello, is that Dennis? What number are you calling?" I wrote it down. "So that is our new number?"

"Well… it will be from tamorra, when dey cum and put ya a nuw telephone in. Da nuw number will be on da frunt a' the 'phone."

"But there's a perfectly good telephone here now. We don't need a new one." Next day, along they came with the new 'phone, with my new private number printed on the front…

Eventually I found a nice house in Blackrock, and a supportive bank manager to grant us a small mortgage. That was the easy part. A telephone line would prove much more difficult, impossible even. We lived in that house for 5 or 6 months and had to rent a bedsit in Blackrock, just for its 'phone line! I finally found us another house that had a telephone line installed. It seemed to me that in the Dublin area, houses fetched 10,000 Punts more if they had a 'phone line. We spent four happy years in Southern Ireland, working amongst its warm, open hearted people. Off duty Garda even laid paving slabs for me in the back garden. There were three of them, moonlighting for a bit of cash.

"Now look boys. It rained last night and the water ran towards the house, not away. The kitchen floor's all wet. And the slabs have sunk. They're very uneven."

"Dat's alroight missus. We'll sort dat out for ye. Now look, we're all on noights, so it'll haf to be later."

Three weeks later, along they came, happy as you like, and re-laid them.

Nice lads…

In November 1979 we took a trip to Jersey for a special Royal Variety Show, hosted by Sir Billy Butlin and his family at the Fort Regent Gloucester Hall. Remember, my first summer season was at Butlin's Holiday Camp, Skegness, back in the 50's? Since then Sir Billy and his family had become friends of mine. We had a great line up of performers for the show: comedy/magician Paul Daniels, comedian Jim Davidson and the Ray McVay Orchestra. The band had a very quiet start as their 4 singers were held back from the stage by security. Prince Philip was attending the show so security was really tight. Eventually the singers were released to join us all on stage.

What a performance we all put on, and what a mixed bag: Vera Lynn, Arthur Askey (Hello playmates!), Tony and I, Miss UK and Miss World. The 11 Kasatka Cossacks had everyone on the edge of their seats, Morecambe and Wise were called up from their seats to be together, for the first time in 9 months. Eric couldn't resist announcing, "You bring a warm glow to my wallet."

Then the Three Degrees hit the stage like a sledge hammer, closing the bill. To round off the evening, Sir Billy presented Prince Philip with a cheque for £40,000 for the Children of Variety.

On more humble ground, back in Ireland, we borrowed £25,000 from ATV Music in advance of royalties. So in January 1979 we bought the house in Horizonte, Menorca for £15,000, then bought the plot next door for £3,000. In 1980 we built the extension dining room, kitchen, lounge and swimming pool.

In Ireland, we played one big nightclub, but our major work was mostly RTE television. We had two series, one after the other, 'Words and Music,' with Irish guest singers, then a six month break, followed by 'It's A Musical World,' this time with international guest performers, including David Gates, Vince Hill and Elkie Brooks. The programmes were broadcast to Ireland and Scotland. 'Musical World' was briefly screened in UK when the electricians union came out on strike in UK in defiance of Margaret Thatcher.

With homes in Ireland and Menorca, our dreams were realised, or so I thought…

Mum and Dad spent quite a lot of time with us in Ireland. Dad's breathing was suffering badly. I wanted to send him to a specialist, but he wouldn't have it. A few weeks after leaving us, for the last time, as it turned out, Dad was diagnosed with cancer. We took the ferry over to the UK to visit him in hospital. Then Tony and I drove down to Menorca in our Peugot 405 estate. We had to attend to matters at our holiday home there. At the time, Tony and I had serious personal issues so the atmosphere was a little strained in the car, but I put on a happy face.

1980
We arrived in Menorca on the Friday. The following morning, our friend Don Chandler called by with a message, "Would you 'phone home? Your Dad's very ill, Jackie. They said you'd best come home right away."

There were no flights to UK 'til the following Monday. Come Monday, Don was at our door again, "Sorry Jackie, but your Dad's passed away this morning." And we were just preparing to leave the house. Tony and I flew straight home to be with Mum, in Chesterton. At least Dad had realised his final wish, to be back home in Chesterton, sitting with his old pals at the bottom of the Hollows, passing the time of day.

God Bless You, Dad!

Chapter 27
Montreux, 'Michael' and My Country

Duets for Piano And Voice – One of Our Best Creative works

RTE loved our ideas for work. We were asked to come up with a special show, so we created 'Duets For Piano And Voice', a musical history of the piano and its part in life through the ages. RTE loved 'Duets' so much, they entered the show for the Montreux International Television Festival. 'Wow!'

Once we had a green light, the writing took us just one week of solid work. Just a week, that's how fast we worked when motivated! It was so exciting that the words just fell onto the page. We never stopped working. I think we shopped just once when one of us went out for fish and chips. That was it. RTE gave us everything we needed for the production and a great team:

Norman Maen
A man of Ballymena, he'd really made his mark as a choreographer:
- he choreographed the Royal Variety Performances for 12 years;
- Rudolf Nureyev once performed to his choreography with a giant pig, in a '*Swine Lake*' sequence on The Muppet Show;
- The Norman Maen Dancers' featured on the 'This Is Tom Jones' TV show series, with Liza Minnelli and Juliet Prowse.

Norman finally won an EMMY for 'Outstanding Choreography:'1950 - 1975. And about time too!

Judy Moorcroft
Judy was an international costume designer for film and theatre. She was painstaking in detail. For 'Duets,' everything I wore was original, even the leather buttoned shoes. Much of my costume clothing had graced period film sets and stage productions of the past, even my costume for the 'Flicker' black and white silent movies. The very thought still gives me goose pimples. It also gave me the inspiration for my lyric to 'Silent Movies:'

> *I wish I'd been a star in silent movies*
> *Just think of all the roles that I could play*
> *I could do a Sarah Bernhardt to perfection*
> *And I would swoon when Valentino looks my way*
> *The world will not forget those silent movies*
> *The comedy, the drama of each scene*
> *And the piano would play as they flickered away*
> *Up there on the silver screen*

Judy went on to design film costumes for 'The Europeans' (1979); 'Yentl' (1983); 'A Passage to India' and 'The Killing Field' (both 1984).

The Raidio Tellefis Eireann Concert Orchestra.
They were all great characters and musicians. I remember one time, during a camera rehearsal for an episode of '*It's a Musical World,*' the studio was so cold, the muso's all refused to play. The union leader was the contrabass player, "Down instruments, lads. It's too bloody cold ta play."

I countered, "Look boys, my dress is so flimsy that I'm almost falling out of it. And my nipples are standing out like chapel hat pegs. You've nothing to complain about!"

That raised a laugh. They gave in and played on, with Audrey Parkes, our lead violinist, wearing a massive scarf *and* headscarf. Somehow I managed to sing without laughing. Maureen Carter was our make-up genius. Nobody ever realises the importance of make-up under spotlights and camera. Noel D Greene was our producer and director. He wanted the orchestra to have haircuts in the 40's style. They all flatly refused!

'Duets For Piano And Voice' was all about the piano and its part in daily life and in musical history. So we wrote:

- 'Duets For Piano And Voice'
- 'Everyone Loves A Piano'
- 'Silent Movies'
- 'Praise the Lord'
- 'Madigan's Rag' - the male dancer was an ex-bricklayer
- 'Chanson Triste' - some of it sang in French
- 'Jazz'
- 'The '50's Rock Sequence' - my sister Mally led that number
- 'Mussels For Two'(pianos) Our double piano - one of only two in the world, I was told - was loaned by Dublin museum. "You bastard!" the pianists chorused at Tony, reading the intricate score that he wrote for them
- 'Sadie's Saloon' - my favourite piece
- 'Where Do We Go From Here'

We all had fun performing, 'Sadie's.' Two of the male singers decided to do a 'Johnny Cash' imitation. 'Big Jake' made his big entrance through the saloon swing doors, "Big Jake's just ridden into town," bursts out 'the old-timer,' grandly.

"Fer Feck's sake! I give ya one loine and yer makin' an epic oud of it. Ged it roight now, or feck off!" That jibe was aimed at 'old-timer.' "An' yuv all got one take only fer the fight sequence. We've no more furniture ta replace the chairs yu'll all be smashin' uup!"

Noel Greene was a very positive director…

'Where Do We Go From Here' was our closing number. It was

the closing song for 'Duets.' My wistful lyric spoke of the ups and downs in our personal lives together at that moment, Tony and I, with a few regrets:

> *Forget the past and leave it all behind*
> *What are we doing now, where do we go from here?*

Sometimes I look at that lyric. At various times there were three of us in our marriage, and number three certainly wasn't the piano.

We all had fun working on 'Duets.' The show was recorded on 6 November 1979. We had it 'in the can.' Irish viewers saw it first. 'Duets For Piano and Verse' was broadcast on RTE on 11 April 1980. Now we were all ready to do battle in Montreux.

Montreux Music Festival
23 Countries would be competing, in various categories. 'Duets' would be competing in the 'Light Entertainment' category. It would truly be a week to remember. I flew to Geneva, alone. Tony couldn't make it as he had other commitments, back home. Noel Greene would meet me in Montreux at our hotel. Just he and I would be there to support our entry. RTE made all the booking arrangements for us.

I took the train up to Montreux through the mountains, a very pretty place. There was nobody to meet me, so I called a taxi and gave the driver the name of my hotel. To my dismay we drove *out* of town, past all the fine hotels. My heart sank lower as the taxi drove higher and higher up a steep hillside to my hotel, which I immediately christened 'Castel Colditz.'

Jackie Trent

Inside, the hotel was in a time warp. The bedrooms were 19th century style, but with modern baths seemingly installed as a concession to the 20th century. The public areas were massive and very cold, with high, vaulted ceilings. And the staff crept about the place like old retainers of an owner who had long departed this world. Then Noel Greene finally arrived, only to bugger off with a truck driver he met in the lift. He disappeared for three whole days.

I still recall my first evening at the hotel as I was the only guest in the dining room. Dinner was just watery soup and a schnitzel. I had a real feeling of foreboding, *'I was not going to be a happy bunny here.'* It was impossible to change hotels. They were all booked up in town, so I was stuck there, well & truly. When Noel finally turned up three days later, looking rather tired, I gave it to him with both barrels, "I'm going back to the UK."

"Ya carn't do dat. We're in fer a major award."

"How the hell would you know? You disappeared."

I often look back on that week. It reminded me of my early years in Germany, *'You're on your own again, girl. Just get on with it. Vonnie, why me? Why am I alone again?'*

In Montreux itself, I found friendly refuge with the BBC. Their TV producers and directors, even Billy Cotton Jnr, were all in Montreux. Bill was then Controller of BBC 1. He was a wonderful man, television through and through.

Billy Cotton Jnr OBE, CBE. For me - *'Mr. BBC.'*

Billy Cotton Jnr was born into showbiz. His illustrious father Bill Cotton Snr,' was known for his famous 'Wakey Wakey' call to the nation every Sunday morning. It was rumoured to have originated when, early one morning, he roused his 20 strong band from tiredness, after a hard week on the road. That's *real* showbiz!

"My Dad's musical talent amounted to 'waving his arms about,"' said Bill Jnr.

Bill Snr certainly had great versatility in life. He even came 4th in the 1949 British Grand Prix motor race, in an ERA. Racing cars were one of his passions, but he never learned to read music.

Being Me

Bill Jnr's role at the BBC was legendary. He stole Ronnie Barker and Ronnie Corbett from LWT and their initial 13 week 'trial' show ran on for almost 20 years. He signed Eric Morecambe and Ernie Wise from ITV, their BBC TV Special attracted almost 20 million viewers each Xmas. Bill created 'The Parkinson Show.' Like I said: *'Mr. BBC.'*

I sat by this brilliant man as 'Duets For Piano And Voice' was screened, in Montreux. "Now that's real television, Jackie. That's how television used to be," said he. Do you know, his words still ring in my head as one of the highest compliments ever paid me. I spent most of my time with the Beeb lot. Seeing I was alone, they kindly invited me along to all their hospitality do's. I sat next to Billy Cotton Jnr for the awards. He'd been one of the judges.

"You should win the Light Entertainment Award, Jackie. 'Duets' is a proper television production."

From the reaction of his fellow judges, Bill was convinced we'd won. But he failed to mention Denmark, who apparently took exception to our Mission Hall sequence. We missed the 'Golden Rose' by 1 point to Canada, whose all- singing, all- skating extravaganza won. But we were awarded a 'Special Citation' award, an award unheard of at the time. So the result was more than close. Anyway it was a good result for the hard work we all put into the show, but not as good as winning.

The BBC won the comedy honours that year for their production of 'The Plank.' Tony never phoned me whilst I was in Montreux, but after the success of 'Duets,' RTE gave us our 2nd show, 'It's A Musical World'.

Listen and Learn 1981

One day my hairdresser gave me a demo tape, "It's my nephew's group, Jackie. They're really good. Listen to them when you get home and tell me what you think. They just need a chance. You could have their contract for £3,500, a special price to you."

I took the tape home and played it. They *were* good. We had our own music publishing company. Excited, I played the tape to Tony and Les.

"No, no. They're too commercial. We're not interested," said Tony. Les agreed.

"For heaven's sake, what's too commercial? These boys are good."

But they weren't interested. Next visit to my hairdresser, I gave him back the tape, with apologies.

"George will be disappointed, Jackie." *George* was Georgios Kyriacos Panaylotou – *or **George Michael***. I recall there were three tracks on that tape and every one of them became a major hit!

So the Hatchet Man, as he was known, of the ATV talent show 'New Faces' really axed himself there, and me too. Tony really could be very blinkered in his approach to things. That would have been a major coup for us, and a serious little earner.

And yes, in the 1970's Tony had been labelled 'The Hatchet Man' of New Faces. The show was recorded at ATV studios in Birmingham. At the time, some viewers hated Tony's behaviour on that show so much, it wasn't uncommon for people in cars alongside us in traffic queues to wind down their car windows and shout abuse at him. And did some of them lay into him! I would smile sweetly, I had to. Ted Ray, a fellow judge on New Faces, didn't take kindly to Tony's performance either.

The UK winter of 1981/82 saw us back in Australasia, working the clubs and enjoying the Australian way of life. We were slowly becoming part of Australian society. We played Twin Towns Services Club, to capacity audiences.

On 17 February '82, we performed at Mayoress Alderman Halina Hedditch's Charity Concert at Sydney Civic Theatre and on 4 March 1982 our brand new song, 'My Country' was launched on the Don Lane Show.

MY COUNTRY
A poem by Dorothea Mackellar
Set to music by Jackie Trent & Tony Hatch
– the flood and fire and famine, the beauty and the terror of the Australian outback.

Paul Fitzgerald

Reg Robertson gave us the idea. He produced and directed our first two Australian Television Specials in 1969 and 1971 and gave us a book of Australian poems to read, which included Dorothea's poem, 'My Country' written, partly, in the UK when she was reputedly homesick. Dorothea Mackellar was fiercely defensive of her country, at a time when nationalism was not fashionable in Australia. Her strong words inspired me.

"This would make a wonderful song," said I to Tony. And together, we created our song, 'My Country.'

I love a sun- burnt country A land of sweeping plains
Of ragged mountain ranges
Of droughts and flooding rains
I love her far horizons
I love her jewel sea
Her beauty & her terror
The wide brown land for me
Australia for me

We put it all together, made a demo with my voice, and sent it off to the Mackellar Estate, asking for copyright approval. Reg then approached Channel 7 TV in Canberra, who video recorded us performing the song in open air locations around the Canberra countryside which is pretty well sunburnt! I was worried about snakes.

Reg said, "Go and walk through that long grass whilst we film you, singing."

I declined, "No way! I'm not about to walk through tall grass, inviting snakes."

The final video production included shots of the Australian Army, Navy & Air Force - soldiers, battleships and planes, even a film clip, flying over Gallipoli, plus wide sweeping views of Sydney harbour and the bridge. That's patriotism for you! Thereafter Channel 7 closed transmission every night with that video footage. The song was recorded with a 20 piece local orchestra. *'And I was bloody proud of us for coming up with that song for Australia, though I say it myself!'*

This was our 8th trip to Australasia since 1969. We knew that we'd be returning to Australia next European winter, so we found a place on Sydney harbour overlooking the harbour bridge, to rent on a long- term basis. We kitted it out with new furniture, ready for our return, which proved far sooner than ever we expected.

I felt we were guests in Ireland. I wanted to know more of the history of Ireland, so I bought a book - the novel 'Famine' - written by Liam O'Flaherty. It paints the picture of *'an Gorta Mor'*, The Great Famine, suffered by the Irish peasant population. Between 1845 and 1852 at least 1million people died of famine and disease, and more than 1million people emigrated from Ireland. I'll say that again. One million people died of starvation, not so long ago. Yet although food was plentiful in Ireland at the time, most of it was shipped to England. The overpriced surplus was beyond the reach of the Irish peasant, so they starved. Some likened that period in time to a deliberate act of genocide.

Living in Ireland as I did, I sensed the historical crime and tension of the past. So I can understand, in part, what next happened to me when we flew into Dublin airport from the UK. Yes, I was dressed in my finery, fur coat and all, but no way did I like being violently accosted by an armed, inebriated Garda.

I was stood, waiting for Tony to collect our car from the airport car park. A man approached me, swaying slightly. He was in plain clothes. He just took hold of me and shook me violently, with no explanation, no reason. It happened twice. He even had a set- to with Tony when he returned with the car, before we finally escaped the airport. We reported the matter, but decided not to press charges. Instead, next day we turned up smartly at the Australian Embassy in Dublin to apply for emigration to Australia. Why not? We had a home there. Our application seemed to tick all the right boxes and we passed the medical. Six weeks later we were off to 'the Land Down Under.' That fast!

Chapter 28
Neighbours' with Sammy Davis Jnr

Variety International

Tony and I became heavily involved with Variety International, the Children's Charity. We became members of New South Wales Tent 56 and donated a number of appearances to help raise money around the world. But Variety started a long time before, in the 1920's.

On Xmas Eve 1928, a one month old baby was found at the Sheridan Square Movie Theatre in Pittsburgh, Pennsylvania, swathed in blankets. There was a note tucked between the blankets:

'Her name is Catherine. I can no longer cope. I have 8 other children and my husband is out of work. I've heard of the goodness of show business people. I hope you can help look out for her.'

It was signed: 'A heartbroken mother.'

At the first annual dinner of Variety, at the William Penn Hotel in Pittsburg, a circus- style big top was erected in the penthouse ballroom to accommodate all of the guests. Sawdust was laid, to add authenticity. There was a Chief Barker and the helpers were 'the crew,' all circus speak. The 11 founding fathers of Variety International temporarily 'adopted' the baby, christening her Catherine Variety Sheridan. She was later adopted into a new life. The story and the vision spread around the world. Regions of Variety are known as 'tents.' We became members of Tents 56 Australia and Tent 36 UK. Jarvis Astaire, International President at the time, made me an International Ambassador in New Zealand. By year 2000, my Variety pocket directory lists some 80 Variety Club Tents around the world.

I re-found Margo Thatcher, an old friend, through Variety. We'd worked the boards together in the '50's and 60's, entertaining American troops in the UK and Europe. Now she was an 'A'- list photographer in Sydney. Margo gave a lot of her time and her photography to Variety. Yet Tony always tended to be rather rude with her.

Colouring My World with Friends

Through my charity work for Variety International I met and befriended so many people, Dr Christiaan Barnard for one. On 3 December 1967 Barnard, a South African surgeon, achieved fame by performing the first successful heart transplant in the world. I was sat by him at a dinner and couldn't resist asking him, "But how many did you lose, prior to this?" He smiled, but never really answered my question. Christiaan Barnard was born in South Africa. He condemned South African racial policy, but refused to agree that the political system should be turned over to the black majority. He died on 2nd November 2001 on holiday at the Coral Beach Hotel, Paphos, Cyprus, *about 1 mile from where I'm sat, right now, working on my bio.*

Maureen Arthur and Aaron Ruben worked closely with Variety and became my close friends. Maureen was a famed actress and singer. Her most prominent film performance was in 1967, in 'How To Succeed In Business Without Really Trying.' In 1978 she featured in her husband Aaron's TV series, 'C.P.O. Sharkey,' as did Betty Thomas of 'Hill Street Blues' fame.

Michael Jackson, at a Variety function, gave me a fab punch line when he confided, "Jackie, I Lu- uv your music. I should record it."

"Michael, you really should. You own all the copyrights!" Michael really didn't know that he owned 'us,'

And Stevie Wonder. One night backstage, after a busy convention in Australia, Stevie and I got up to sing together. We jammed for a loo- ong time. One of his people said to me, "He might be blind, but he ain't stupid. Stevie can smell out the prettiest women in any room, every time!"

Through Variety I met and befriended the most amazing people: Buzz Aldrin, Harry Belafonte, Billy Butlin, Michael Caine, Goldie Hawn, Edmund Hillary, Robert and Janet Holmes A Court, Henry Kissinger, Burt Lancaster, Ginger Rogers, Margaret Thatcher, and Betty Thomas, the energetic Sgt Lucille Bates star of the iconic US TV cop series 'Hill Street Blues.'

In 1983 Betty Thomas jetted in to NZ to join us for Variety NZ's Telethon '83. There were walkathons, runathons, talkathons, any –'thon' to raise money for the Family Trust. We had brass bands, pipe bands, pop bands and Wellington's Ngati Poneke Maori cultural group. Everyone threw themselves into raising money for the kids. Clothes were auctioned off. Betty Thomas' Hill Street Blues t- shirt raised $600, Murray Mexted's All Black rugby jersey fetched $400. Even a flower, fresh from the Hill Street Blues set, went for $130. In Nelson, NZ the Paraplegic Association raised $1100, pushing two wheelchairs the 55km from Motueka to Nelson. Anzac airmen ran 500km through the Sinai desert, from Sharm- el- Sheik on the Red Sea to El Gorah near the Mediterranean, in sweltering heat, to raise more than $11,000 for Telethon. That was the power and emotion of Telethon. That was why I was so committed to Variety International and Telethon at the time. By the way, in 2009 Betty Thomas would become the most successful woman film director ever, grossing $200 million at the box office for the film, 'Alvin and the Chipmunks - The Squeakquel.'

Tony and I even wrote, 'Make The Sun Shine For The Children' for Variety. We wrote the song in a day. Singers and musicians from Western Australia gathered in Perth to record it. Our brand new song was performed for the first time at the October Sunday Teddy Bears Picnic in Channel 7 TV's grounds, in Perth.

A Trader- style boat came into our lives. We christened it 'Music Maker.' We bought the boat, even before we bought our new home to be in St Ives, in the Sydney suburbs. The Hawkesbury River offered a perfect mooring at Akuna Bay, a short drive from St Ives, so we spent most weekends on the boat when we weren't working. We invited many guests onto the boat, friends, family and international stars. We had a whale of a time on Music Maker on the Hawkesbury. I never caught a whale, but one time I did land a hammerhead shark, a small one, I grant you. I hauled it onboard the transom. It was about 2ft long, thrashing about like mad, with a full set of mashers. I cut the line and put it back into the water, "Tell your mummy I let you go."

We fished a lot off the boat. It was food for the Barbie. We were always lucky fishing, and *Pete's Bite* was a fab spot to moor up for the night, an exclusive water access only restaurant on the Hawkesbury. We spent many happy times on the Hawkesbury with friends.

Neighbours
In the UK we had been good friends with Australian TV producer Reg Watson. Reg played a major part in UK TV history. He helped create the ATV Midlands TV channel. He also created 'Crossroads,' the long running UK TV soap series, starring Noele Gordon.

Reg had returned home to Australia to work with Grundy TV in Sydney, where we now lived. One day he called us, "Could we write a theme song for a new TV series, 'Ramsay Street' – ASAP?" Tony and I were dead good at deadlines and we made a start right away.

We wrote the theme tune in a little over 9 hours. Tony put down the backing track in our recording studio upstairs, whilst I wrote the lyrics in the kitchen as I prepped the veg for dinner. I set my trusty note book on the kitchen sink drainer. My hands were wet, but the damp pages were still readable. We changed the title name to 'Neighbours,' feeling 'Ramsay Street' was too close a title to the UK 'Coronation Street.' Now we needed a vocal for the demo. It never entered our minds that I, or we, should sing it ourselves, and many people have asked why. Instead, we phoned our dear mate and neighbour, Barry Crocker, who has a wonderful voice, to get his arse round to our place. And it all went like clockwork. Barry drove round to us. We all worked through the night to find the right sound and balance for the song. By morning, the finished product was on Reg Watson's desk at the Grundy Organisation. He was amazed how fast we'd worked and loved the suggested title change to 'Neighbours.' The first broadcast went out on 18 March 1985 on the Seven network. And the rest is TV history…

Kylie Minogue & Jason Donovan were Young Talent Time stars in Australia, a Saturday morning TV show for kids. They got their break in the original cast of 'Neighbours.'

Neighbours, everybody needs good Neighbours.
With a little understanding, you can find the perfect blend.
Neighbours should be there for one another.
That's when good Neighbours become good friends.

Carols by Candlelight – Pure Gold

100,000 people and more, all gathered together at Xmas to sing carols under the stars, all holding candles that flickered in the dark. Now, can you imagine the sensation of leading that throng of people up onstage, singing my heart out. Well I did exactly that for many years at Xmas in Australia. It was an absolute privilege to be there.

Someone traced the origin of 'Carols' way back into the 19th Century, to Cornish miners carol singing, with lighted candles stuck in their helmet headbands. Cornish they might have been, miners certainly they *would* be. Why? Gold fever had hit South East Australia. On 12 February 1851, one Edward Hargreaves found his 'Ophir,' fields of gold, some of it not 75 miles from Melbourne Post Office, would you believe? Melbourne itself became a ghost port, full of rotting hulks with the streets so abandoned, one could sink up to the knee in mud. All because almost every able bodied man was in

Being Me

the goldfields, seeking his fortune. By 1852 an average of 20,000 plus ounces of gold were being shipped to England *every week*.

Sammy Davis Jnr – a very Special Person
It was my good fortune to meet and befriend Sammy Davis Jnr, probably *the* highlight of my whole life. Not everyone gets to meet and befriend the most accomplished entertainer the world has ever known. It happened this way...

We were booked for a short tour of the Australian east coast with three weeks each in Sydney, Adelaide and Melbourne, with Sammy Davis Jnr as headliner, then us, two shows a night, dinner and supper. All seats were sold out, well before opening night. 'Wow!'

We opened in Sydney but Sammy didn't seem to notice us. By week three Sammy was more relaxed. I saw him hobbling around, leaning on a stick. The world's No 1 dance entertainer didn't look so slick, right then. He'd recently undergone a hip scrape. Next stop Adelaide. On the 'plane to Adelaide, Sammy sat just behind us. He stood up, tapped me on the shoulder and said, "What are you doing tonight?"

"Why?"

"Nobody's ever asked me *whyyy!*" in his very best Noel Coward English accent.

"I wanted to invite you to my suite for dinner, that's *whyyy!*"(Noel voice again.)

"Well why didn't you say that in the first place? We'd love to. By the way, your special sidekick with the heels is improving with each performance, 'cause I watch it!" That brought a big smile to his face. From then on we were firm friends, Sammy and I. Sammy laid on dinner for us in his suite at the Adelaide Hilton, silver service, the works! We sang together whilst Tony sat and watched. Then Sammy hit me with, "Hey girl! In Sydney, you made up the words on your last number. You forgot the line!"

"The cheek of you. So you watch me on stage too? Only you would know that. Well, at least the lines all rhymed."

One morning in Adelaide, I escaped the confines of our hotel. There was a very good book shop, just around the corner from the Hilton. I love travel books, so I popped in and browsed the rows of bookshelves, but I kept hearing this voice saying, "Jackie!" in whispered tones.

"Who the hell's that?"

A stack of books in front of me slid to one side, to reveal 'Inspector Clouseau' himself staring right at me, Peter Sellers' character from the famous Pink Panther film series. But it was Sammy in drag: hat, dark glasses and wrap- around mackintosh, the works!

"I've escaped."

"Sammy it's you!"

"Sssssh. Let's not draw attention to ourselves."

"How can anybody miss a small, black, one eyed Jew dressed like Inspector Clouseau?"

He roared with laughter.

"There you go again, Trent. Nobody's ever said that to me before, either."

We paid for the books we'd chosen and left, together.

"Let's go back to the hotel '*and take tea.*"(Noel Coward again)

We sat in the hotel foyer, in full view of everyone, taking tea and sandwiches. We drew lots of attention, believe me! Word must have got around, because Sammy's security people suddenly turned up. Boy, had they been panicking, trying to track him down. He loved all of that.

On tour, Sammy carried a full kitchen, along with his professional gear. He liked his Cajun cooking, "Don't eat tonight, Trent. I'll cook

Being Me

for you." I was about the only person his bodyguards would let past the door. Sammy always booked a whole penthouse floor, lining one room out in plastic sheeting, for him to cook expressively.

"Why aren't you eating, Sam?"

"I've been *tasting* all day, that's *why!* And it's a distraction for me Jack, a refuge. I can hide from the world here, just doin' my cookin'."

We sat and talked for a long time.

"Hell, it's been a long, hard road for a black Jew, ya' know?"

"Difficult times, Sam?"

"Jack, when I'm cookin', I think of the old days on tour with Dad and Will. Dad, heatin' cans of beans on the engine of our old touring car we used, to get us around. The 'Will Mastin Trio'. That was us. Life can be shit!"

Sam's dresser, Bernard Wilson, stood patiently in the background. He'd been with Sam for years, laying out his stage suits, his shirts, ties and incredible jewellery, for Sam to decide what he was going to wear that night.

"Poppa, that was me. Hey, Dad always called me 'Poppa.' I never knew why."

I told him of my struggles in life and all of the letdowns along the way.

"Hey, that's nuthin! Wyoming! You ain't black. Try it sometime! I was 17, couldn't even read. I went through shit at infantry basic training centre in Cheyenne, Wyoming. Then Sgt. Williams loaned me some books. He made me want to read. I bought a pocket dictionary from the PX and sat in private, learnin' to read. That's how I found education, girl! After so much crap, I decided, Ain't nobody gonna put me down no more!"

We got onto the subject of our mutual friend, Sinatra.

"Hey, that man gave me my chance. He made everything possible, or I'd still be part of the Will Mastin Trio. He took me for dinner whenever he could."

I told Sammy how I'd met Frank in London, in his apartment, "He seemed a nice guy, Sam. I was blown away by him."

Sammy replied, "Well he became my friend for life. He said that to me himself, and he meant it. So it really cut me up one time, when

I saw him, just walkin' down Broadway, no hat, his collar up, totally alone. Nobody recognised him, absolutely no one. That was a really bad time for him."

"We all have bad times, Sammy. I've had some of those"

"Jackie, that's true. I had bad times, ya'know? See this glass eye? Lost the real one in a car crash. Ended up with the damn thing hanging out in that crash."

I knew Sammy had been friends with Elvis, so I mentioned singing with 'the King' in Germany.

"Sure, we used to hang out, Elvis and me, ya' know?" said Sammy. "We both used ta cruise on motor cycles. I had a cut down Harley. Did ya know he really wanted to be a straight film actor?"

"Yes, I did. He told me so."

Sammy said, "There was a film, The Defiant Ones, we would have co- starred together. But the Colonel vetoed him doing it with me. Elvis wept when he had to admit that to me."

The following year, 1989, Sammy was invited along to Sydney to receive the annual Humanitarian Award from Variety International. He brought his wife Altovise along with him. "So you're the Jackie he's always talking about?" We were sat together, watching his show.

"Well we do talk a lot. I think we have a lot in common. And boy, can he cook!"

We all got on great together. After his show, Sammy persuaded Tony to get on the piano whilst he and I sang together. We had quite a session at the Darling Harbour Convention Centre, 1500 people, all walls lined with Sammy posters. I recall we all went to dinner the following night. Sammy booked the table.

My lovely Sammy Davis Jnr died within a year of that meeting, completely destitute. But he gave me something to remember him by, something very precious, a signed copy of his autobiography, 'Why Me?' It's dated May 18 1989. I still have it. And something else, a tiny red rose, pressed between pages 49 and 50. It's still there…

Chapter 29
Clones and Golden Girls

Dear Diary
We led a busy and eventful life down under, during the European winters. I looked through my 1988 diary:

14 January - spent the day in the rain on boat, fishing. Caught a 1m shark and ate it. Wonderful fishing.
30 January - Jupiter's Club - to Wed 3 February. Flew back to Sydney.
4 February - 10am Ladies of Variety meeting. A 'good meeting' I was totally committed to Variety International in those days, the children's charity. I was a Celebrity Ambassador for Variety, until I was shoe horned out.
17 Feb - Twin Towns, Coolangatta. Appearing for 5 days.
22 April - St George League's Club, Kogarah, with Barry Crocker.

Being Me

24 April - to UK.

27 April - Menorca. We now have a home on this Mediterranean holiday island.

5 May - To UK. 7 May - In New York, auditioning for Jerry's Girls for Larry Alford. I got the part. Larry wanted my strong voice for one of the lead players.

11 May - NY to Nashville direct, AA 471.

14 May - Nashville to Chicago, AA 234.

20 May - Chicago to NY, AA 226.

24 May - LA to Sydney.

30 May - Diet! Tony 11st 7lb; JT 11st 12lb. Must lose 11/2 stone before UK. I have eight weeks!

1 June - Ricky May died.

4 June - Ricky's funeral.

5 June - Cleaned boat. Lovely day.

9 June - To Ayers Rock. 8am 'plane.

13 June - Back to Sydney.

14 June - Got the flu.

30 June - Tone's birthday.

17 July - Ricky May tribute dinner.

21 July - Get everything packed.

23 July - To London.

24 July - Arrive UK 9.10am.

18 Aug - Our Wedding Anniversary.

28 Aug - Boating! On Music Maker II.

6 Sept - JT Birthday. Went to El Cid. Nice dinner.

9 Sept - Back to UK.

19 Sept - Mandy, Bernard and kids arrive. House in absolute mess for a week, wet towels everywhere. 'Patience,' but Tone should look after his own kids, not me. But then, he doesn't really like kids. He should never have had kids.

Sept 26 - Mandy and Bernard finally leave. JT to Australia. Took off from Heathrow

Sept 27 - Dubai 3.45am. On to Kuala Lumpur 6hrs 30mins. S/over in K/L 3hrs. Left K/L 10pm. Flew through massive electrical storm and torrential rain.

Sept 28 - Arrived Melbourne 6.35am. Transit flight to Sydney, arrived 8.20am. Tony met me late, but with a rose. How romantic. Flowers on the doorstep. Back to Oz life. Pauline had a lot of problems. Tony has been marvellous and helped out.

Oct 1 - Discussing 'Albatross,' Pauline suggested I played Dorothy. It all ended in a row. My fault again! God I'm jet lagged. Don't like this buddy- buddy thing between T & P.

Oct 22 - Worked on invitations for picnic. The 3 of us, yet again

Oct 24 - Sponsors luncheon, Sheraton. All went very well. As usual, the 3 of us.

Year of the Clone

Oct 31 - Regent AGM. Felt really off and quiet this evening. Think I'm getting an attack of the Pauline's. It's all getting a bit too chummy. The terrible threesome, or is it?

Nov 1 - Melbourne Cup - Hilton. All went well.

Nov 2 - South Australia AGM. Tony and Pauline overnight in Adelaide. Why do I feel I'm beginning to lose. I've got one of those funny feelings again about this. Or is my imagination running amok?

Nov 8 - Tone and Pauline in Melbourne.

Nov 10 - Tone bought me a beautiful coat and hat. I wish Pauline wasn't so pushy. Sometimes I feel as if I'm intruding on Pauline and Tone's lives. I wonder...

Being Me

Nov 12 - Dinner party for 9. 'How to host a murder'.
We made love and it was so wonderful.
Nov 13 - Today was the worst day of my life. My husband is in love with Pauline McFetridge. I spoke to Pauline. Nothing resolved there. The two of us went out on the boat. We're both in bits.
I made a long diary entry, 'All is calm at the moment. I'm trying to maintain a good mood. The atmosphere is fraught. I've got to try and take the pressure off the situation by remaining as calm and communicative as possible. It's my only chance of keeping him. There's no good asking myself how this happened. It's all too obvious. In a way it had to happen. I'm glad I'm here with him. At least it gives us a fighting chance.'
Nov 14 - This morning is the start of the beginning of my life, or the end as I know it. Pauline picked up Tony at 10.30am. I now know what it's like to bleed to death. He came back to me, he's suffering so. I can't bear to see him like this. I love him so much. Will things ever be the same? Maybe they'll be much better and we can get some of that spark we had years ago. God, I'll try so hard. Pauline is in a mess. The whole thing is a mess. God help us all.
Nov 15 - Well today looks so much better. I do believe he loves me and the crisis is over. We have to be very reassuring to each other. It's still going to be difficult. The next few days will be a test to all our characters and I want to come out with flying colours.
Nov 16 - Pauline and I have a long chat. Tone's said some pretty shitty things about me, really hurtful. Cocktails at the Gazebo Hotel. We had a terrible row.
Nov 17 - Variety National AGM, Boulevard Hotel. A very good evening. Everything seems to have calmed down.
Nov 18 - Fainted in the morning. Tony very concerned.
Nov 21 - We now seem to have everything smoothed. Pauline is now back to normal relations. I just hope I'm not put on the spot again. Time will tell.

Nov 22 - We made incredible love.
Nov 23 - Tony and Pauline went to Bash and Convention meeting. As I said, it's all back to normal. I think Tony really loves me.
Nov 25 - What is wrong with Tony? Sometimes I think he gets a kick out of making up things then making me out to be paranoiac. Maybe I'm sometimes right. Things do get a little close for comfort.
Nov 28 - I am still not crazy about it, this situation. Still, it's something I've got to live with, for the time being. Guess it was one of those days I was unsure of what I wanted to do. Once again a late- night dinner and a discussion about the usual things. I have certainly got everything under control re myself, but I know Tone can't handle any pressure unless the balls in his court.
Nov 30 - It's amazing you know, no matter how I try, I can't win. I ask for a little time and I'm bloody whinging and heavy. Maybe one of these days, when I'm too busy to bother, he'll understand just how I feel. Maybe one of these days I'll have the guts to not bother either.

I said, 'Couldn't you spend a little more time downstairs?' According to Tony, I'm getting heavy again. Do you know something? I just can't win.
Dec 4 - Tony and I sat on the boat, chatting under the stars. Last night it was really lovely. Then made love, a bit cramped, but great. Caught more fish, what a feast!
Dec 7 - I spoke to Pauline. She said they had discussed things. I asked Tone at dinner. He said he loves me very much. Maybe I won't have to suffer that one again. Really, I can never be sure, can I? It's a dreadful load to live under, really. Why does he do this to me?
Dec 14 - Went to Dr Stone. Had ECG. He wants to make me an appointment with a cardiologist. I'm obviously a little worried. I'm sure everything will be OK.
Dec 15 - I'm getting a little overpowered by the friendship situation. Things are still not right at home. I don't want to feel she will come in on Tony once I've gone to London. I love him so much.

Dec 17 - Carols in the Domain. 'Carols' went great.
Dec 18 - Tony and I sat by the pool. In the evening, had bottle of French 'Champoo.' It was really lovely. He loves me very much.
Dec 24 - We fly UK at 1.30, seats 4A and 4 C.
Dec 25 - We arrive UK.

In London we took a flat in Weymouth Street, near the BBC. After my audition in New York, I knew I had a part in the musical, 'Jerry's Girls.' Jerry Herman wanted my strong voice for one of the principal characters in the musical. The UK audition would be a formal run through.

'Jerry's Girls' would be a combination of three Jerry Herman shows, including 'Mack and Mabel.' His problem was Louis Benjamin. Louis, no longer with Pye records, had become head of all the London theatres. He didn't like 'Mack & Mabel.' Herman said, "I want to include Mack and Mabel." So Louis wouldn't let him have a theatre.

Tony stayed with me in London for a while, then decided to return to Australia. I remained, waiting to sign my contract. The show was ready to run, just as soon as a theatre became available. I spent three months waiting. Then a distressed phone call from a female friend in Sydney had me on a Singapore Airways flight to sort my life out, back in Australia, where Tony and I had a serious confrontation.

I also applied a little self- therapy, I bought a copy of Judy Hogg's book, 'Splitting Up.' I wrote in the flyleaf:

1989 'Should do this. Fact, fact.
JT, have the guts to get rid. No love, no future.
JT you need better than this!!
One day!!! "Love."
It will happen to you. You will find the love of your life.'

The Iron Lady
Like her or not, Margaret Thatcher had strong convictions. She held office as UK Prime Minister from 1979 to 1990. Tony and I met her at the Waldorf Astoria NY Lifeline Dinner, a Variety International fund

raising dinner, the proceeds split with Thatcher's own nominated charity as well. Tony wrote the musical background setting for the dinner. There were blue drapes on stage, with a Union Jack one side and the Stars & Stripes on the other side. Mrs. T liked the lectern to be set front centre-stage, with the lighting focused on her. There was a short run through of the proceedings in the afternoon. Mrs. Thatcher complimented us, "Best lighting I've ever had. And I love your music, you two."

She certainly came over as a very positive, forthright person. Henry Kissinger stood nearby, surrounded by security. I knew I was in the company of some very powerful people: Thatcher, Kissinger, plus Anthony Quinn, the film star. In the early 80's Mrs. Thatcher unknowingly brought our RTE shows 'Words and Music' and 'It's A Musical World' to UK television viewers, after a union strike in UK was called, preventing normal TV transmissions. So they had to 'import' programmes like ours into the UK.

East Meets West
I was briefly 'exported' to Germany. The BBC decided to hold a gala concert in East Berlin, 'East Meets West', to be recorded and broadcast from the Berlin Concert Hall. The Alyn Ainsworth and Robert Farnon orchestras would provide the music. Robert was a friend of mine and was both a fine arranger and conductor. He lived in Guernsey at the time. The BBC asked him to choose a performer as his guest and he chose me, God bless him! Tony Christie and Lena Zavaroni were there too. My Tony came along for the ride. We all boarded a chartered Boeing 737 at Luton airport. The front seats were removed to accommodate the musicians instruments, all stowed under a big net. We were sat on the first row of seating, with Dorothy Solomon, Lena's manager. Robert Farnum sat with Alyn Ainsworth in the row behind and Tony Christie sat alone. After take-off, the stewardess came around with drinks, and a bottle of champagne for me.

"Compliments of the Captain, Miss Trent."

Christie tapped me on the shoulder, "Eh up. Who's got preferential treatment then?"

Stewardess: "And another bottle for you on the way back, Miss Trent. The captain is a fan of yours."

Being Me

Christie ordered scotch & beer. It was a pleasant flight, until we reached the Berlin Corridor, an enforced 10,000ft ceiling, and in bad weather too. It proved a very bumpy ride.

In East Berlin, coaches took us from the airport to our hotel. We saw no visible war damage to buildings along the route. In fact everything looked immaculate with no war damage at all. In a spare moment, we took a walk around Berlin with Tony Christie. We ended up in a Bierstube for lunch, leaving Christie stood on the top of a table, singing his head off, pissed. At our hotel, he was in the next room to us. I loved Tony Christie!

We had two days of orchestra rehearsals, then the Gala Concert. All went fine. And yes, I did enjoy the second bottle of champagne, on the flight back, shared, of course!

Enter the Cloughs

We first met Paul and Margaret Clough at someone's party in Menorca, sometime around 1980. After that they seemed to make a point of befriending us and at parties and functions they always seemed to be there. Then we shared holidays in Thailand and Ibiza. It rained so much in Ibiza that we sat playing cards most of the time, out of the rain! Paul was my partner at cards. We always thrashed Tony and Maggie.

Show business is a hard road to travel, crisscrossing the country to the next theatre, concert hall or nightclub, so we grabbed relaxation whenever we could. Our passion was boating. We had Music Maker I in Australia in Akuna Bay and Music Maker II in Menorca in Mahon harbour. The boat was shipped over from the USA to UK and Tony and Paul Clough brought it down to Menorca from there. In Menorca, we were part of a regular crowd, often partying by boat on the Isla Colom, off Es Grau, near Mahon. The Burns family of Guernsey and Angela and Geoffrey Foley of Harleyford became my lifelong friends. Beryl Burns had been a beautiful, courageous young spy for the British on German occupied Guernsey during WWII. Beryl had style...

Sometimes the 'party scene' was tiring. Yes, I'd known for long enough that being a celebrity was like drawing bees to honey. I'd learned to hate being a show pony all the time, constantly entertaining people, some of whom I really didn't like, forever being invited out to a party, no doubt as a showpiece. But there was always the humorous side. One world famous English film star, at a function, once muttered to me, *"Get rid of the midget!*

"Now that's really propositioning a gal!"

Party life was hectic, perhaps too hectic. Often, fresh off the boat, we'd go for a meal ashore on Mahon harbour where we moored Music Maker. I realised the Clough's couldn't match our spending power, but Maggie Clough always wanted to join in, of course. Paul, her husband, tried his best to keep up.

"Hang on Maggie. We're not rich like the Hatch's. We don't have that sort of money."

She would whine until Paul gave in. I really saw the Cloughs as good friends at the time so, to help out, I often bought Maggie's clothes. I did that for people. Penny Docherty, a member of Variety International in Sydney, hit hard times so I helped her out financially. I bought a lot of her weekly provisions. I was pleased to help out. It gave me pleasure to share what I had. I've always done that.

We had lots of invited guests at our lovely home in Australia, on Lynbara Avenue, St Ives, a lush and leafy suburb of Sydney. All day long the trees were full of noisy, rainbow coloured parrots, the air filled with their day long chattering and screaming. It was a piece of heaven. Our home once featured in the August 1990 edition of Australian 'Home Beautiful'. For one of the photos, I posed, curled up on the stool in front of our Steinway ex- BBC concert stage piano.

Paul and Maggie came over to Australia twice and stayed with us in St Ives. We rented a big boat at Hamilton Island, Queensland, the 'Phoenix." She came complete with a captain and a cook and the boat had a Jacuzzi on the upper deck. One day, at sea, we all four relaxed in the Jacuzzi as it bubbled away, until tempers bubbled over from an 'in your face' incident.

And Margaret Clough had problems handling alcohol. At her 40th birthday party, she suddenly fell forward, headfirst into her prawn cocktail and stayed there. Everyone carried on eating. This was not the first time that this had happened, by a long way. She did a similar thing at our house in Horizonte, Menorca. She collapsed in the toilet, wedging the door firmly shut with her body. We finally had to take the toilet door off at the hinges to get her out. But they were friends. Hey Ho!

This Is Your Life

This world famous TV series originated in the USA, featuring the lives of (mainly) celebrities. In 1955, This Is Your Life came to Britain, initially hosted by Eamonn Andrews, with his famous Irish brogue. It was an instant hit and ran for some 43 years, on and off. Surprise was always an essential ingredient. The first smell of prior awareness by an intended 'victim' and the show was immediately pulled.

TIYL came to Tony and I in 1991, in the form of Michael Aspel, armed with microphone and the Famous Red Book, at the Belvedere restaurant, Holland Park, London. Michael became host after Eamonn's death in 1987. We entered the restaurant, completely innocent. Suddenly Michael Aspel walked up to us.

Aspel: "Well what a surprise, eh? Hello folks, how are you? I can't shake hands because I've got the microphone here. This isn't the menu. In fact it's the Big Red Book that says tonight, Tony Hatch and Jackie Trent, 'This Is Your Life'."

"Oh my God!" said I. All words verbatim, from the TV script. We were whisked off to the TV studio post haste, straight onto the prepared Thames TV stage set, with invited family and guests already seated in front of the cameras.

In Studio

Petula Clark was shown on screen, singing a medley of our songs, then walks onstage in person, having flow in specially from New York.

Aspel: "It's obvious these two made an impact on your life."

Petula: "Well yes, really they changed my life. They changed the whole course of my career. They're still great songs. They haven't aged at all. We have, but the songs haven't.

Aspel to us: "After 28 years together you rank among the most successful songwriting and performing partnerships in the history of popular music. Little wonder that you are known as Mr & Mrs Music."

Various celeb's appeared to greet us and to tell their tale:
- The Searchers
- Max Bygraves on video, from Surfers Paradise in Queensland, Australia
- Marti Webb
- Danny La Rue
- Sacha Distel from Paris, on video.

They played an excerpt from 'Duets for Piano And Voice,' Tony and I singing, 'What Are we Doing Now, Where Do We Go From Here?' Rather apt I thought sadly, considering our lives at the time. I still have 'The Big Red Book;' its gold lettering is rather faded now.

'Hollywood'

At every pool you'll find a new Garbo waiting patiently for fame
She's been around for so many years but still she can't recall her name
A celluloid producer winks an eye; his chauffeur driven wheels are standing by
If he says goodbye, she'll just die

Trent/Hatch

I viewed Hollywood at first hand from the Polo Lounge at the Beverley Hills Hotel. 'People watching' is one of my favourite pastimes. They called the hotel the Pink Palace, where anyone who worked there, from room service to maid or waiter, was all out to catch the eye of a so called producer. And a casting couch was always nearby. Hollywood: a place to see and be seen. In Hollywood you're nothing unless you are on the 'A'- list. Bea Arthur, of Golden Girls fame, was an 'A'- list lady. She was also my friend.

Bea Arthur - Golden Girls

Bea was an actress, comedienne and singer and her career spanned seven decades. Born Bernice Frankel, she retained her first husband's surname - Arthur - throughout her life.

Bea and I first met at a Variety International convention cocktail party in Vancouver, British Columbia. We were introduced, got talking and hit it off right away. Bea was a great fan of Gracie Fields. For a laugh, we would break into song together, with 'Sally, Sally, Pride of Our Alley'.

"Bea, I suppose you know that Gracie had a bad press at the beginning of WWII, for living in America? She had a home in Italy, so during the war, she tried to redeem herself, leaving her place on the Isle of Capri, to descend on unsuspecting British soldiers at the Royal Place NAFFI in Rome. The troops came to dread her popular greetings, 'Ow do lads' and 'Sall - eee' and 'Ee ba gum lads, 'ave a cup o' tea!' That's not all. Spike Milligan and Harry Secombe, the famous Goon Show comedians, were once trapped into performing with her at the finale of the Festival of Arts show in Rome. Secombe was in charge of lighting. Accidentally, he turned Gracie a nice shade of green, when the lights should have been red for her 'Red Sails in the Sunset' finale!"

Bea burst out laughing when I told her all that. I could hardly control her. At that very moment we were stood together at the convention, watching an exhibition of lumberjacks chopping down trees. Bea called for two large gins and ice, announcing to one and all very dryly, "Have you ever seen anything so fucking boring in your life!"

That was Bea. We've been lifelong friends ever since.

I remember when Bea Arthur came over to London with a friend for Tony and my 25th Wedding Anniversary. She complained to me, "Oh God! Have I to wear shoes?

I said, "Darlin,' if you've decided to wear a few sequins, then shoes are in order."

She complied, but the shoes didn't stay on for long. We got up to sing. I have a wonderful picture of us together, singing away. I looked down, guess what? Bea was barefoot.

This tall, beautiful woman considered herself part of my family and that was great by me. Bea played a major part in the Gay Rights Society in Los Angeles. She never discussed the matter with me, even when I stayed at her home. She had this huge bed that she bought after her last divorce. It was her greatest pleasure, to just lie there, reading the New York Times every morning. Bea would pick me up from LA airport in her black Mercedes open top sports car. She was always barefooted. And she had a routine of 'cocktails at 6pm.' I absolutely adored the woman, she was intellectual and very talented. At the time she was working in her One Woman Show. The studio would pack for her. Shoes were another matter. She really hated shoes. She always complimented me on *my* packing. My lovely quarters at her home were across the courtyard, by the pool. "Come over, the puppy's shit again!" She had two Doberman Pinschers, a mummy and puppy. I would go over and lay on her massive bed and she would read to me of all the problems around the world. They were very special moments for me.

Bea Arthur had the biggest soft centre of anyone that I had ever met. When asked to be involved with children, her 'front' was, "Don't make me do this. It does my head in and I'll always cry." So will I, every time I think of my dear, dear Bea. She passed away on 25 April 2009. I posted a tribute to her on my web site at the time.

Leaving Australia
We loved our boat on the Hawkesbury with so many happy times shared with friends we'd invited on board. So it surprised me when Tony said, "Jackie, we should sell the boat. We're hardly using it. Let's sell." It sold at a small profit. That was at the end of 1994. Then Tony decided he didn't want to do 'Carols at Xmas' any more. "I need to be back in London, to be back into musicals, Jackie. We have to sell up here." Personally, the last thing I wanted to do was to abandon Australia.

So why the slow push to get back to the UK? I didn't want to leave Oz. I'd just secured our Australian citizenship, through a fan of mine in the immigration department. At the time, we didn't really qualify for citizenship. "I looked at all the angles, Jackie. You've just not clocked up enough time in Australia to qualify. Tell you what, if you sign one of your portrait photos for us, the department will make a concession for you, and for Tony."

The Department of Immigration even laid on a formal Citizenship ceremony for us, at Observatory Hill Park, The Rocks, Sydney, near the harbour bridge. It was a very emotional moment for me, knowing I was about to leave my beloved Australia behind. My pal

Margo Thatcher was the official photographer, so I guess we were 'A'- list people! We appeared on the front page of 'Post Migration, June 1995 edition 99, the Department of Immigration and Ethnic Affairs official magazine. On 13 July '95 the Australian Immigration Department celebrated its own 50th Anniversary.

I loved Australia and its people, but Tony was my husband, despite the hiccups, so I went along with him. I let him sell our home. It sold within 6 to 8 weeks. Selling by auction is normal in Australia. I went along to the sale but Tony didn't bother. In May 1995 we finally said goodbye to Australia and flew back to Europe and to our home in Menorca. Our furniture and possessions followed behind in crates. In June 1995, Lyric Productions was incorporated, with 50% shares each for Tony and I.

Chapter 30
Birthdays, Betrothals and Bust- ups

Back in Menorca, we slipped back into our Spanish social life. The Cloughs lived and worked on Menorca so we were all together quite a lot. Tony said he needed to get fit so he disappeared each morning to the gym, for a work out.

But something was wrong, life at home between Tony and I became far too remote. I loved my husband and it concerned me that he no longer wanted to make love to me. So I challenged him on it.

"Jackie, I'm having treatment for prostate cancer. I'm so sorry, I can't make love."

I was worried, and confused, I suppose.

All Change! Birthdays, Betrothals and Bust Ups!

Maggie Clough's birthday came first, on 2 September 1995, with a party held at their house. Mum and I were aghast when my daughter, Michelle's boyfriend Guy proposed marriage to her, in front of everyone. Why would we be shocked at such warm news? Because it was obvious that Mum and I were the only two people in the whole gathering who didn't know it was planned. We both felt ignored.

Being Me

Mum had words with Michelle, "Have you said anything to your Mum about this?"

"Well I assumed that Mum would know," admitted Michelle.

Sad, I felt my daughter had let me down and ignored my feelings. But we had to take it all with a pinch of salt. There was no option. "It would have been nice if you'd spoken with me about this"

"Well we both assumed you would know that we would be getting engaged."

Not really, not at all, in fact.

Four days later my birthday came around, on 6 September. For my party I booked the Picadero restaurant on the Sant Lluis road, where Terry was mine host. All of my family and our friends were invited. I let Maggie Clough order the cake as I'd seen a cake she'd organised for someone previously. Paul had set her up in a small manicure treatment business and she gave my nails a clean and polish on the morning of the 6th. That night we filled the Picadero with our crowd. There was music and dancing, but Tony was clearly avoiding me. I pulled him onto the dance floor.

"What the hell's going on between you and Maggie?"

"I don't know what you mean," said he lamely.

I insisted, "You know exactly what I mean."

"Well, you might as well know, I've been in love with her since I first saw her. She's the love of my life and I want to spend the rest of my life with her."

"And haven't I heard all that before from you, Tony?!"

"Don't make a scene," was all the manly statement he could come up with.

I just stood there on the dance floor, like a piece of stone, whilst he walked away.

The UK media pestered me for days to give interviews to spill the beans. Like a fool, I thought of my family and their privacy, and my pride. I wrote it all down -the sad saga of manipulation by so many people – but I refused to speak publicly: more fool me!

I went through a really rough patch for quite a while: my body froze and Mum had to spoon-feed me for a while. I shed masses of bodyweight, but slowly recovered.

It was time to keep better company.

High Society

I was invited to play the part of Margaret Lord in Cole Porter's 'High Society,' directed by Simon Phillips. The production originated in Australia and was devised for the state theatre of South Australia, with Tony Tripp's sumptuous set. Tony was with the Melbourne Theatre Company. I accepted the part, mostly to front up and prove I could still go out there and wow the audience. The show opened at the Sheffield Lyceum at the end of April 1996 and toured nationwide. I was very keen to read the reviews after each show, to see how I was doing:

22.5.96 Sunderland Empire *'electrifying solo spot;'*

03.9.96 Belfast Grand Opera House *'full house, clamouring for more Margaret Lord;'*

16.10.96 Cliff Pavilion, Southend *'Jackie Trent stole the show;'*

31.10.96 The Orchard, Dartmouth *'Jackie Trent dominates the stage;'*

28.11.96 Llandudno, North Wales Theatre. I reminisced that my last visit to Llandudno was as a child in the 1940's, arriving on a coach trip with Mum and Dad...

I took a break from High Society for my daughter Michelle's wedding on 7 July 1996. My daughter wanted a society wedding herself, so I had to cough up for the Waldorf Astoria hotel, in London. That set me back some £27,000. Yes, money I didn't really have; a damn lot of money. At first, Tony wouldn't contribute. He finally stumped up about a third of the £27,000. At the reception afterwards,

I went to my room. Someone persuaded me to come down, to have the customary dance with Tony. Always just the one dance eh, Tony? At the reception, there's a formal photograph of Tony, Michelle and I together. He's stood on the step behind me, so that his head was more or less at level height with mine. Such vanity still!

After the family 'high life,' I was back on the road with High Society again. We were still pulling in the crowds who were clamouring for more. It was great to be back up there, fronting up at something I'd done for all of my life. Maybe I should have stayed solo. I might have made it good in America, like Dusty Springfield. After 'High Society' I went back on the road for a while, with Les driving me places, appearing at City and provincial theatres and clubs.

Chicago

'Chicago' the musical came to London. It would open on 18 November 1997 at the Adelphi theatre in the West End. I applied for the part of Mama Morton. Suzanne Smith Casting wrote to me, "Please find enclosed the music for 'Mama Morton' as well as the sides. We would be grateful if you could learn, 'When You're Good To Mama' before we see you on Thursday 15th May at 10.15am at Pineapple Studios."

I really, really wanted that part. I turned up for the audition. Everyone liked me except the choreographer. I was wrong build, wrong weight for the part. My recent personal disasters had cost me dearly. I was like a scarecrow, I'd lost half my body weight since 1995 so sadly no 'Mama Morton' for me.

By November 2000, after me being steered into financial disadvantage, Tony and I reached a point of severe financial disagreement. So finally I took the case to the High Court in London.

For the court, I wrote:

"I cannot express the trials and tribulations of a man I deeply love. I stood there and accepted everything that was thrown at me.
I look at everything, good, bad and indifferent. I had great admiration for his talent as an orchestrator. He really was wonderful. I now know my 'loving' husband didn't see me in the same light. I believe he cannot accept that anyone is better than he is. I was a challenge to his talent.'

Judge Kenworthy-Browne heard the evidence. She finally had to impress on both parties "to settle, otherwise costs were going to be astronomic." In November 2001 we settled, the very minimal amount I found acceptable.

So there it was, 7 November 2001 and a free woman at last. What next? Well that's a story for another day…

Being Me

Jackie passed away on March 21st 2015 in Menorca, Spain, surrounded by her loving husband, Colin and her two children, Darren and Michelle.

She found love again (and this time, enduring love) whilst awaiting the departure of her flight to Spain at "Luton Airport" in January 2005. She always told this story with great humour, adopting her best "Lorraine Chase" voice when recalling how they met!

Colin came from a non- showbiz background and together they enjoyed a very happy ten years until her death. Semi- retired, she now had the opportunity to truly enjoy life at leisure.

She has indeed left a lasting and worthy contribution to the world of popular music and her legacy will be eternal.

A Final Tribute

Julie Budd, once more…

Many, many years had passed and I don't know what it was; I think I was recording again. I saw something online regarding Jackie and saw that she was still performing. I thought that I just had to call Jackie and reconnect. Somehow I got her number… and I called.

A lovely man answered and said he was Colin. I introduced myself and in my heart of hearts, I knew right there and then, why they were together. He was warm and wonderful and I knew just in those few moments that he loved his Jackie.

"Let me put her on, I know she will want to speak to you."

She took the phone and we picked up, just as we left off. I was then reminded instantly why I loved her so much, years ago. We made plans to get together again; our careers and lives moved us around. Then Jackie told me that she had moved to Spain. I was going to meet them in Europe!

Before I knew it, Our Jackie had become ill, and just like the passing of a season, this beautiful spirit was gone. I'll never forget how in this period of time, I felt so close to Colin, as if I had known him forever and wanted so to comfort him in his deep grief. It was as if Jackie had put us all together for a greater reason.

You see…There are some people that come into your life who are special, unique souls. They are kissed by the Almighty above, as

Jackie Trent

if they are angels. And, not only do they leave behind a body of work for generations to love and enjoy, but they leave a piece of themselves too, in everyone that they touch.

That was my pal, Jackie…

Being Me

Just *a few* of 'Mr & Mrs Music' JACKIE TRENT/TONY HATCH songs...
AMERICAN BOYS
BEAUTIFUL IN THE RAIN
CLOSE TO YOU
COLOUR MY WORLD
COME HOME MY LOVE
CRANES FLYING SOUTH
DIDN'T I SAY I LOVE YOU
DON'T GIVE UP
DON'T SEND ME AWAY
DON'T SLEEP IN THE SUBWAY
DON'T STAND IN MY WAY
FACES
GOODBYE MR CHIPS
HAVE ANOTHER DREAM ON ME
HEROES (Jackie Trent)
HOT TO TROT (Jackie Trent)
HOLLYWOOD
I AM YOUR SONG
I COULDN'T LIVE WITHOUT YOUR LOVE
I LOVE YOUR KIND OF LOVIN'
I WANT TO SING WITH YOUR BAND
I'LL BE THERE
I'LL BE WITH YOU
IF YOU EVER LEAVE ME
JOANNA
LET'S DO IT AGAIN
LIFE AND SOUL OF THE PARTY
LOOK AT MINE
LOOK AT THE RAIN
LOVE IS ME LOVE IS YOU
MARIE DE VERE
MOVING ON
MR AND MRS
MY COUNTRY (Australia)

Jackie Trent

MY LOVE
NEIGHBOURS
NOW IT'S COME TO THAT (Jackie Trent)
OPEN YOUR HEART
POSITIVE THINKING
SEND HER AWAY
SIGN OF THE TIMES
TAKE ME AWAY
THANK YOU FOR LOVING ME
THE ONLY ONE TO LOVE ME
THE OTHER MANS GRASS
THERE GOES MY LOVE
THIS TIME
WE'LL BE WITH YOU
WHEN SUMMERTIME IS OVER
WHO AM I
WALKING ON AIR
WHAT WOULD I BE
WITH EVERY LITTLE TEAR
YOUR LOVE IS EVERYTHING

Jackie left behind a hand- written message on her piano music stand: *'Being Me,'* a very powerful, almost unearthly lyric - *about herself.* Jackie's lyrics very often painted pictures of her own life. In time, 'Being Me' will be set to music and recorded…

'BEING ME'

Does anyone out there know how I feel
When the nights are so strong and the mornings unreal
When the wounds you inflict on yourself never heal
When you look in the mirror it can never reveal
What is buried deep down in your heart

Being Me.
There's an out side and in side that so few ever know
No one sees the real me that I found long ago
It's all part of an image that I put on for show
When the bad days have torn me apart

And they say 'God she's strong – you're a joy – you belong
And your part of the 'A- set' at last'
But you know deep inside, with yourself you can't hide
When you're living with ghosts of the past

Being Me.
You don't know who I am, but my life is no sham
With each day I survive – no façade
I'm no pup - no beginner - always end up a winner
But believe me, I'm always on guard

So don't ever (you) wonder, no one steals this girl's thunder
There were times that decisions were hard
When they close that big book, they'll take one final look
Being Me was one hell of a card…

Join the active world- wide discussion fan group at
www.jackietrent.com

Lightning Source UK Ltd.
Milton Keynes UK
UKHW02f2153211117
313124UK00013B/612/P